Korea Yearbook

Korea Yearbook

Volume 1
Politics, Economy and Society
2007

Edited by

Rüdiger Frank
James E. Hoare
Patrick Köllner
Susan Pares

BRILL

LEIDEN • BOSTON
2008

This work was supported by the Academy of Korean Studies (publication grant AKS-2006-P-04).

This book is printed on acid-free paper.

A Cataloging-in-Publication record for this book is available from the Library of Congress.

ISSN 1875-0273
ISBN 978 90 04 16440 6

© Copyright 2008 by Koninklijke Brill NV, Leiden, The Netherlands.
Koninklijke Brill NV incorporates the imprints Brill, Hotei Publishing, IDC Publishers, Martinus Nijhoff Publishers and VSP.

All rights reserved. No part of this publication may be reproduced, translated, stored in a retrieval system, or transmitted in any form or by any means, electronic, mechanical, photocopying, recording or otherwise, without prior written permission from the publisher.

Authorization to photocopy items for internal or personal use is granted by Koninklijke Brill NV provided that the appropriate fees are paid directly to The Copyright Clearance Center, 222 Rosewood Drive, Suite 910, Danvers, MA 01923, USA.
Fees are subject to change.

PRINTED IN THE NETHERLANDS

CONTENTS

Preface xi

Chronology of Events in the Korean Peninsula 2006 1
    South Korea 1
    North Korea and inter-Korean relations 5

South Korea: Domestic Politics and Economy 2006-2007 9
    Patrick Köllner
    1   Domestic politics 9
    1.1 Electoral defeat for the governing party 9
    1.2 Changes in political personnel and the constitutional court
          nomination controversy 11
    1.3 Dealing with the past: court rulings, amnesties and the
          collaborator issue 12
    1.4 Hot issues: gambling and the (partial) relocation of
          the capital 14
    1.5 President Roh Moo-hyun and the splintering of the
          Uri party 15
    2   The economy 17
    2.1 Of sandwiches and nutcrackers: Korea's economy between
          China and Japan 18
    2.2 Growing inequality and rising housing prices 23

North Korea: Domestic Politics and Economy 2006-2007 25
    Rüdiger Frank
    1   The 2006 parliamentary session 25
    2   The 2007 New Year joint editorial 29
    3   The missile launch and the nuclear test 30
    4   Other domestic developments 32
    4.1 Projects and campaigns with social overhead capital 32
    4.2 Exhibitions and conferences 33
    4.3 Administrative and personnel changes 34
    4.4 Natural disasters 34
    5   Other reports 35

Relations Between the Two Koreas 2006-2007 37
James E. Hoare
1 Aftermath of the September 2005 agreement 37
2 North Korean missile tests 39
3 North Korea's nuclear test 41
4 Return to the Six Party Talks 44

Foreign Relations of the Two Koreas 2006-2007 47
James E. Hoare
Introduction 47
1 Republic of Korea 47
1.1 Relations with the United States 47
1.2 Relations with the People's Republic of China 51
1.3 Relations with Japan 51
1.4 Other international issues 53
2 Democratic People's Republic of Korea 54
2.1 Six Party Talks and relations with the US 54
2.2 Relations with the PRC 57
2.3 Relations with Japan 58
2.4 Relations with Russia 58
2.5 Other relations 59

Online Grassroots Journalism and Participatory Democracy
in South Korea 61
Ronda Hauben
1 The public sphere and South Korea 61
1.1 The global Internet and the netizen experience in Korea 62
2 Participatory democracy in the Korean context 63
3 OhmyNews 64
4 2002 candlelight demonstrations for two dead girls 67
5 Roh Moo-hyun's election campaign 69
5.1 Role of netizens in the election campaign 71
5.2 Nosamo: a new online institutional political form 72
6 Stem cell fraud and the netizens: a case study 75
7 Conclusion 79

CONTENTS

The Lone Star Scandal: Was it Corruption? 83
James C. Schopf
1. Examining the problem 83
2. Defining and measuring corruption 85
2.1 Definitions 85
2.2 Measuring corruption 85
3. The Lone Star takeover of Korea Exchange Bank: was it corruption? 87
3.1 Assessing the evidence against Korean financial authorities 88
4. Rent to Lone Star? 95
5. Bribes from Lone Star? 99
6. Comparison with the Chun industrial rationalisation 100
7. A political explanation 106
8. Conclusion 108

Changing Perceptions of Inward Foreign Direct Investment in Post-Crisis Korea (1998-2006) 113
Judith Cherry
1. Inward foreign direct investment in pre-crisis Korea (1962-97) 114
2. Inward foreign direct investment in post-crisis Korea (1998-2006) 118
3. Case study: European investors in Korea 130
4. Conclusions 134

Emergence of China and the Economy of South Korea 139
Joon-Kyung Kim and Chung H. Lee
1. Introduction 139
2. Convergence in export structure 141
3. Expanding bilateral trade 145
4. Trade in parts and cross-border production networks 146
5. Korea's investment in China and Korea-China bilateral trade 150
6. Effects on Korea's manufacturing industries 153
7. Concluding remarks 161

Korean Modernism, Modern Korean Cityscapes, and Mass Housing
Development: Charting the Rise of *Ap'at'ŭ tanji* since the 1960s ... 165
   Valérie Gelézeau
   1   Introduction 165
   2   The model of the *apat'ŭ tanji*: hybrid modernism at the
       source of modern Korean urban neighbourhoods 168
   2.1 The *ap'at'ŭ tanji*: standard of modern urban
       neighbourhoods 168
   2.2 The *ap'at'ŭ tanji*: a hybrid product of modernist urban
       theories 171
   2.3 Trajectories of modernism: reconsidering the Japanese
       mediation 174
   3   The *ap'at'ŭ tanji* at the core of the modern Korean
       cityscape and urban society: trajectories and outcomes
       of a modernist product 175
   3.1 The backdrop: hectic urban growth and drastic housing
       problems of the 1970s and 1980s 175
   3.2 A mass housing policy changing the Seoul cityscape 176
   3.3 The *ap'at'ŭ tanji*: an 'urban middle-class production
       factory'? 179
   4   From a modernist ideology to a genuine Korean
       modernity? 182
   4.1 *Ap'at'ŭ tanji*, modernist ideology and control of the
       population 182
   4.2 Beyond the housing problem and land pressure:
       ap'at'ŭ tanji as products, vectors and symbols of Korean
       modernity 184
   5   Conclusion: re-thinking Korean and Western in modern
       Korean cityscapes 186

New Ancestral Shrines in South Korea 193
   Heonik Kwon
   1   Introduction 193
   2   Beyond left and right 196
   3   Lamentations of the tragic dead 198
   3.1 Form of the ritual 198
   3.2 Aesthetic dimensions 199
   3.3 Rehabilitative initiatives 201
   4   New ancestral shrines 203

| 4.1 | Example of Hagui village | 204 |
| 5 | Democratic kinship | 208 |

The Political Economy of Patriotism: the case of *Hanbando*............215
Mark Morris
1	The film: story, style, stars	216
2	The company and the critics	224
3	Politics of the flashback	227
4	Screen wars	229
5	A kind of conclusion	231

Negotiating with North Korea: Lessons Learned and Forgotten......235
Robert Carlin
1	Themes and topics	236
1.1	You can't deal with them	236
1.2	Empty words	237
1.3	Overall pace	238
2	Role of the Agreed Framework	238
3	Implementation	240
3.1	Falling short	240
3.2	Missile talks	241
3.3	Mechanics	242
3.4	Getting to the talks	243
3.5	At the talks	244
3.6	Multilateral aspects	245
4	Problems	245
4.1	Obsession with 'cheating'	246
5	Looking to the future	249

List of Major Negotiations 1993-2000 251

Perilous Journeys: The Plight of North Koreans in China................253
Peter Beck, Gail Kim and Donald Macintyre
1	Introduction	253
2	Leaving the 'workers' paradise'	256
2.1	The border region	257
2.2	Crossing over	259
3	Going underground	261
3.1	Crackdowns	261
3.2	Changes in the Chinese border area	261

3.3 Changing push-pull factors 263
4 New patterns, new networks 265
4.1 Temporary border crossers 266
4.2 Traffickers and rural brides 269
4.3 The underground railway..271
5 Forced repatriation...274
6 Recommendations 276
6.1 Seeking asylum..277
7 Conclusion...278

A Brief History of the Sino-Korean Border from the
18th to the 20th Century 283
Larisa Zabrovskaya
1 The early frontier...283
2 Transformation of the neutral zone into Jiandao 286
3 The border issue and Korean migrants 290
4 Sino-Korean border line after the Second World War 291
5 Territorial compromise by China...293
6 Conclusion...295

About the Authors and Editors 299
Map of the Korean Peninsula 305

PREFACE

We welcome readers to the 2007 edition of the *Korea Yearbook—Politics, Economy, Society*. The *Korea Yearbook* is, in a sense, both an established and a brand-new publication. It is an established publication because it builds on its German-language predecessor, *Korea—Politik, Wirtschaft, Gesellschaft*, which was published annually from 1996 to 2006 by the Hamburg-based Institute of Asian Affairs (since 2006, the Institute of Asian Studies, GIGA German Institute of Global and Area Studies). The *Korea Yearbook* continues all the central features which characterised *Korea—Politik, Wirtschaft, Gesellschaft*. The yearbook is essentially a hybrid publication which combines refereed scholarly articles on political, economic and social affairs on the Korean peninsula and concise overviews of developments in South and North Korean domestic affairs, the external relations of both Koreas plus inter-Korean relations. A chronology of developments on the Korean peninsula in the year preceding publication supplements the 'year-in-review'-type articles. In order to be as up to date as possible, overview articles cover the twelve months from April of the year preceding publication to March of the current year. The *Korea Yearbook* is, however, also a brand-new publication. Its new English-language format permits us not only to reach many more readers than before, but it also broadens the scope of the yearbook in terms of new authors and topics covered. Moreover, while the former yearbook was edited by a single person, the *Korea Yearbook* brings together a team of British and German editors who individually contribute their respective expertise, skills and contacts. The editors are supported by two overseas editors, Charles Armstrong in the United States and Sung-hoon Park in the Republic of Korea. Finally, the *Korea Yearbook* gives us the opportunity to aim for new professional standards by co-operating with the Leiden- and Boston-based international academic publisher Brill.

We are happy to be able to present in the refereed articles section of the *Korea Yearbook 2007* a wide range of stimulating papers on political, economic and social affairs on the Korean peninsula. The articles have been written by both well-known and younger scholars based in France, Great Britain, Russia, South Korea and the United States. South Korea-related articles in the yearbook deal with online grassroots journalism and participatory democracy (Ronda Hauben), the politics and economics of the Lone Star scandal (James C. Schopf), changing perceptions of inward direct investment (Judith Cherry), the impact of China's economic ascendancy on South Korea's economy (Chung H. Lee and Joon-Kyung Kim), modern cityscape and the rise of mass housing production (Valérie Gelézeau), new ancestral shrines and the legacy of the past (Hoenik Kwon), and the political economy of patriotism as reflected in recent films (Mark Morris). Additional articles highlight lessons of negotiations with North Korea (Robert Carlin), the plight of North Koreans in China (Peter Beck, Gail Kim and Donald Macintyre), and the historical evolution of Korean-Chinese border issues (Larisa Zabrovskaya). We hope that the articles will find the attention they deserve. We will strive to present in *Korea Yearbook 2008* a similar range of interesting papers on domestic and external affairs of the two Koreas plus inter-Korean relations. The editors are particularly interested in papers dealing with North Korea and inter-Korean affairs plus papers which analyse Korean affairs from a comparative perspective. We encourage interested scholars to contact the editors for more information on how to contribute to the *Korea Yearbook*.

The editors would like to express their gratitude to the Academy of Korean Studies for making the publication of the *Korea Yearbook 2007* possible by providing encouragement and financial support. We also would like to thank the dedicated staff at Brill, in particular Albert Hoffstädt and Patricia Radder, who accompanied this publication with enthusiasm from its inception to the final printing process. We are grateful to Emeritus Professor Keith Pratt and the Design and Imaging Unit at Durham University for making available the map reproduced in the yearbook. Special thanks go to Siegrid Woelk who did a fine job (again) by making the yearbook look the way it does.

A final word on transcription and the rendering of Korean names: in the *Korea Yearbook* we basically follow the conventions of the McCune-Reischauer system. The only exceptions regard international renderings of well-known geographical units and Korean words (Pyongyang, Seoul, won) but also individuals (e.g. Syngman Rhee, Park Chung-hee, Kim Dae-jung, Kim Il Sung, Kim Jong Il). Moreover we respect the way Korean persons, including authors, have transcribed their personal names—as long as these transcriptions are known to us.

Patrick Köllner, Rüdiger Frank, James E. Hoare, Susan Pares

Hamburg, Vienna, London, August 2007

CHRONOLOGY OF EVENTS IN THE KOREAN PENINSULA 2006

SOUTH KOREA

10.01.06 Seoul National University investigation into claims by Professor Hwang Woo-suk that he had cloned human stem cells announces he falsified data.

19.01.06 ROK-US foreign ministers agree to permit American 'strategic flexibility' in using troops stationed on the Korean peninsula as a rapid deployment force to deal with possible conflicts in northeast Asia.

29.01.06 Artist Paik Nam-june dies.

20.02.06 Deputy Foreign Minister Chun Young-woo appointed ROK chief delegate to Six Party Talks.

23.02.06 French-ROK agreement in principle to jointly digitalise Korean texts looted by French troops in 1866 from Kanghwa island, for publication in CD-ROM form.

25.02.06 First human cases of bird flu confirmed in ROK.

01.03.06 President Roh Moo-hyun criticises repeated visits by Japanese leaders to Yasukuni shrine.

06-13.03.06 President Roh visits Egypt, Nigeria and Algeria.

14.03.06 Prime Minister Lee Hae-chan resigns.

15.03.06 KBS journalist Yong Tae-young freed by Palestinian militants one day after being kidnapped in Gaza.

23.03.06 Lee Seong-tae named governor of ROK central bank.

24.03.06 Nicholas Cheong Jin-suk, archbishop of Seoul, among fifteen new cardinals installed.

25.03.06 Han Myeong-sook nominated as prime minister, the first woman to hold that office.

29.03.06 ROK-Uzbek agreement on bilateral co-operation in energy, trade and investment.

29.03.06 ROK and US agree to study ways for ROK to regain operational control of its armed forces during wartime.

03.04.06	President Roh attends Cheju memorial ceremony for those killed in 1948-49 uprising.
17.04.06	ROK and PRC defence ministers discuss setting up of naval hotline to prevent accidental armed clashes in West Sea.
22.04.06	Japan cancels plans, announced on 14.04., to carry out maritime survey in waters around Tokdo island. In return, ROK agrees not to seek to register Korean names for topographical features in East Sea seabed at forthcoming international hydrographic conference.
28.04.06	Chung Mong-koo, Hyundai Automotive Group chairman, arrested on charges of creating illicit slush funds and misappropriating corporate funds.
07-14.05.06	President Roh visits Mongolia, Azerbaijan and United Arab Emirates.
09.05.06	ROK elected as member of new UN Human Rights Council.
13.05.06	Professor Hwang Woo-suk indicted on charges of fraud, embezzlement and violation of bioethics law.
16.05.06	ROK signs free trade agreement with 9 out of 10 member countries of ASEAN.
18.05.06	President Roh attends ceremony marking 26th anniversary of Kwangju uprising.
20.05.06	Park Geun-hye, chairwoman of Grand National Party (GNP), slashed in face while campaigning in Seoul mayoral elections.
31.05.06	Local government elections end in defeat for governing Uri Party.
05-09.06.06	1st session of ROK-US negotiations on bilateral free trade agreement.
06-16.06.06	Prime Minister Han visits France, Portugal, Bulgaria and Germany.
09.06.06	Five South Koreans working in the Niger Delta region of Nigeria released after two days' captivity at the hands of an unidentified armed group.
12-13.06.06	5th round of ROK-Japan talks on delimiting their exclusive economic zones in East Sea.
19.06.06	Lim Chae-jung (Uri Party) elected speaker of National Assembly.
02-05.07.06	ROK conducts survey in waters around Tokdo island.

11.07.06	GNP elects Kang Jae-sup as its new chairman.
10-14.07.06	2nd round of ROK-US negotiations on bilateral free trade agreement curtailed amid differences.
16.07.06	Nationwide flood warning after heavy rains.
18.07.06	Government decision to construct dams in Imjin, South Han and Nam rivers to tackle flood control.
16.08.06	ROK official protest against Japanese prime minister's visit to Yasukuni shrine.
03-08.09.06	President Roh visits Greece, Romania and Finland.
06-09.09.06	3rd round of ROK-US negotiations on bilateral free trade agreement.
12-15.09.06	President Roh visits US, meets President Bush, 14.09, in Washington DC.
18-27.09.06	Prime Minister Han visits United Arab Emirates, Libya, Kazakhstan and Uzbekistan.
28.09.06	ROK establishes Northeast Asia History Foundation to counteract alleged historical distortions, primarily by China and Japan.
09.10.06	ROK-Japan summit ends without a joint statement.
13.10.06	President Roh discusses ROK-PRC relations with President Hu Jintao in China. Both states express support for UN Security Council resolutions on the DPRK's missile and nuclear tests between July and October 2006.
14.10.06	UN General Assembly elects ROK Foreign Minister Ban Ki-moon to succeed Kofi Annan as UN Secretary-General.
20.10.06	38th ROK-US Security Consultative Meeting agrees on transition period of between 15.10.09 and 15.03.12 for transfer of wartime operational command of ROK troops from the US.
25.10.06	ROK says it has developed cruise missile with range of 1000 km.
07-09.11.06	At inaugural session of Korea-Africa Forum in Seoul, ROK pledges to triple its development aid to Africa by 2008.
19-22.11.06	President Roh visits Cambodia.
22.11.06	Demonstrations against negotiations on free trade agreement with US.
26.11.06	Confirmation of outbreak of avian flu in southwest of country leads to slaughter of poultry.

03-10.12.06	President Roh visits Indonesia, Australia and New Zealand.
04-08.12.06	5th round of ROK-US negotiations on free trade agreement make limited progress.
06.12.06	ROK-US agreement on 6.6% increase for 2007 and 2008 in ROK's share of costs of maintaining US forces in Korea.
14.12.06	Ban Ki-moon inaugurated UN Secretary-General.
22.12.06	National Assembly approves extension of ROK troop deployments to Iraq for another year.

North Korea and inter-Korean relations

03.01.06.	Kim Jong Il visits the electronic library at Kim Chaek University of Technology.
08.01.06	57 staff members withdrawn from the Kŭmho light-water reactor site.
10-18.01.06	Unofficial visit by Kim Jong Il to the People's Republic of China (PRC) as guest of President Hu Jintao.
04-08.02.06	13th DPRK-Japan talks on normalisation of relations held in Beijing, the first for over 3 years, end inconclusively.
09.02.06	DPRK announces its intention to observe domestic and foreign financial norms.
10.02.06	ROK and DPRK teams participate as one team in opening ceremony of Winter Olympics in Turin, Italy.
13.02.06	ROK National Assembly representatives submit bill aimed at establishing inter-Korean special economic zone near DMZ.
16.02.06	Kim Jong Il's 64th birthday celebrated.
21-23.02.06	7th inter-Korean Red Cross talks at Mt Kŭmgang agree on confirmation of fate of those missing during and after the Korean War.
27-28.02.06	4th video reunion for separated families.
01.03.06	US State Department's 23rd annual report on the international production and movement of drugs finds no clear links to the DPRK government.
04.03.06	Talks between ROK and DPRK military leaders on preventing naval clashes in west coast waters end without agreement.
07.03.06	Unofficial US-DPRK meeting at UN on US financial sanctions against DPRK.
08.03.06	DPRK test-fires two short-range missiles within its borders.
20-25.03.06	13th reunion of separated family members at Mt Kŭmgang.
22.03.06	DPRK business official and his family defect in Budapest.
23.03.06	DPRK condemns annual ROK-US joint military exercises in the South.

28.03.06	ROK Ministry of Unification signs agreement with World Health Organisation on improving health of babies and children in DPRK.
28.03.06	Ground-breaking ceremony for joint ROK-DPRK water treatment plant at Kaesŏng.
11.04.06	Shin Sang-ok, ROK film director who was reportedly abducted to the DPRK, where he and his wife lived from 1978 to 1986, dies in Seoul.
12.04.06	4th session of 11th Supreme People's Assembly.
15.04.06	94th anniversary of birth of Kim Il Sung celebrated.
21-24.04.06	18th inter-Korean ministerial meeting in Pyongyang agrees to co-operate on issue of persons missing during and after Korean War.
05.05.06	UNHCR's 2006 work plan includes efforts to support DPRK defectors in the PRC and Mongolia.
06.05.06	For the first time since the passing of the North Korean Human Rights Act in 2004, the US government accords official refugee status to six North Koreans.
08.05.06	2nd meeting of DPRK-PRC co-operation committee on economic, trade and scientific and technological issues.
09.05.06	ROK Minister of Unification visits Kaesŏng joint industrial complex.
10.05.06	World Food Programme reaches agreement with DPRK on resumption of food aid, but on smaller scale and with fewer WFP staff.
18-19.05.06	Meeting of inter-Korean economic co-operation promotion committee discusses trial runs of trains, set for 25.05.
20.05.06	Joint statement from the pro-ROK Mindan and the pro-DPRK Ch'ongnyŏn (Chōsen sōren) organisations of Korean residents in Japan on increasing co-operation in the future.
22.05.06	Associated Press Television News opens resident office in Pyongyang.
23.05.06	DPRK cancels test runs for North-South trial rail operations on grounds of security issues.
03-06.06.06	12th inter-Korean economic co-operation talks. ROK agrees to provide DPRK with materials for its light industries if DPRK moves to open the cross-border railways.

14.06.06	ROK and DPRK jointly mark 6th anniversary of 15 June 2000 inter-Korean summit.
05.07.06	DPRK test launch of seven missiles over East Sea (Sea of Japan).
10.07.06	DPRK-PRC agreement on economic and technological co-operation.
12-13.07.06	19th inter-Korean ministerial talks end in ROK rejection of North's request for economic aid, citing provocation of DPRK's test launch of missiles.
14-16.07.06	Heavy rains cause damage to farmland, infrastructure and property in DPRK and render many homeless.
15.07.06	UN Security Council (UNSC) resolution 1695 condemns North Korean missile tests and calls for compliance with measures to limit DPRK's access to missile-related technology.
15-16.09.06	Kim Young Nam, chair of SPA presidium, attends 14th summit of Non-Aligned Movement in Havana.
09.10.06	DPRK conducts underground nuclear test.
11.10.06	Japan bans North Korean imports and prohibits North Korean ships from entering Japanese ports.
14.10.06	UNSC resolution 1718 calls for measures against DPRK, including a ban on the supply of conventional arms, nuclear-related materials and luxury goods to the DPRK, inspection of North Korean cargoes, freezing of financial assets related to weapons of mass destruction and a travel ban on persons connected with the North Korean nuclear arms programme.
18.10.06	ROK government announces that tourism to Mt Kŭmgang and projects at the Kaesŏng industrial complex will continue, despite the DPRK's nuclear test.
31.10.06	DPRK decides to return to Six Party Talks on the understanding that lifting of financial sanctions would be discussed.
01.11.06	UNSC lists items banned to DPRK that could be used in various types of weapons.
13.11.06	ROK announces it will not participate in the Proliferation Security Initiative to stop and search DPRK ships.

16.11.06	ROK votes in favour of UN General Assembly resolution calling on DPRK to respect human rights, after years of abstaining on the issue.
25.11.06	International Red Cross signs agreement with DPRK on water supplies, disaster prevention and provision of medicines.
25-28.11.06	Visit by members of EU parliament to DPRK.
07.12.06	Five members of an alleged pro-DPRK group indicted on spying charges in ROK.
08.12.06	KEDO and KEPCO agree on liquidation of reactor project.
14.12.06	DPRK-Syrian agreement on mutual co-operation in security matters.
14.12.06	Delegation from North Korean Ministry of Finance visits Russia.
17-22.12.06	Russia and DPRK negotiate on dismantling of North Korean debt to Russia.
18-22.12.06	5th round of Six Party Talks resume in Beijing.

Chronology prepared by Susan Pares from the following sources: Cankor (Canada-Korea Electronic Information Service), *Korea Focus*, *Korea Policy Review*, *North Korea Weekly Report*, *Vantage Point*.

SOUTH KOREA:
DOMESTIC POLITICS AND ECONOMY 2006-2007

Patrick Köllner

1 DOMESTIC POLITICS

Politics in South Korea were in turmoil in early 2007. The governing Uri party (Yŏllin Uri-dang), which had not only done badly in the local elections of May 2006 but had also lost every single by-election since its landslide win in the 2004 general election, was on the verge of break-up. As a consequence of the defection of a number of National Assembly members, the Uri party lost its status as the biggest parliamentary party in January 2007. President Roh Moo-hyun, whose popularity had hit rock-bottom in 2006, announced that he would leave the party. This step was widely interpreted as an attempt to revive flagging support for the Uri party. With less than nine months to go until the presidential election of December 2007, it remained unclear whether the governing party would be able to field a viable candidate or, indeed, whether or in what form the party would continue to exist at all. In the following overview, we will highlight domestic political and economic developments in the twelve months up to the end of March 2007.

1.1 *Electoral defeat for the governing party*

In the nationwide local elections taking place on 31 May 2006, nine governors of provinces, seven mayors of metropolitan cities, 230 heads of local administration, 733 provincial and metropolitan assembly members and 2,888 members of city, county and ward assemblies were chosen. Election turnout stood at 51.3 percent, i.e. 2.7 percentage points higher than in the preceding local elections. A particular nasty incident took place during the election campaign when the then chairwoman of the Grand National Party (GNP, Hannara-dang), Park

Geun-hye, was knifed by a ex-convict who claimed that he had been falsely imprisoned for 14 years. Park had to be hospitalised and her assailant was later sentenced to (another) 11 years of imprisonment.

The May 2006 nationwide local elections resulted in a major triumph for the GNP. While the governing Uri party managed to win only one of the 16 major posts up for grabs (the governorship of North Chŏlla province), the GNP prevailed in twelve gubernatorial and mayoral races. The GNP was not only victorious in the mayoral contest in the capital city of Seoul (where Oh Se-hoon succeeded Lee Myung-bak) but triumphed in the greater Seoul region as a whole. The GNP, aided by the majority-favouring electoral system, won all directly elected 96 seats in the Seoul city council and captured the governorship of Kyŏnggi province and the post of mayor in Inch'ŏn, the transport hub in the vicinity of the capital. Even the small oppositional Democratic party (from which the Uri party had originally emerged) was more successful than the governing party, gaining governorships in two provinces. The final governorship fell to a nominally independent candidate. Of all available posts and seats, 13.6 percent went to women (in 2002, 3.2 percent had done so); this significant rise was, however, mainly due to new quota rules pertaining to party lists.

Even though a defeat of the governing party had been widely expected in the face of plummeting support for both the Uri party and President Roh Moo-hyun, the sheer scale of the Uri party's election debacle stunned observers of South Korean politics. The election made it clear that sizeable shares of voters who had contributed to the landslide win of the Uri party in the 2004 general election had deserted the governing party in the directions of both the GNP and the opposition progressive Democratic Labour party. While the latter group felt that the government had not made good on its reform promises, the first group were clearly unhappy about the haphazard policies of the government and the ideological bent of parts of the Uri party's elite cadre. Chung Dong-young, chairman of the Uri party, stepped down on 1 June 2006 to take responsibility for the party's crushing electoral defeat. His successor Kim Geun-tae became the Uri party's eighth chairman in two-and-a-half years. Voter dissatisfaction with the Uri party did not subside after the local elections: in nine parliamentary and local by-elections taking place in late October 2006, the governing party failed to pick up a single seat. The two National Assembly seats at stake went to candidates from the GNP and the Democratic Party.

1.2 Changes in political personnel and the constitutional court nomination controversy

After the GNP's landslide win in the May 2006 local elections, Park Geun-hye resigned from her post as party chairwoman in order to concentrate on her bid to compete in the presidential election of December 2007. In July 2006, South Korea's main opposition party elected the 58-year-old Kang Jae-sup, a five-time legislator and former prosecutor, as new party chairman. The post of GNP secretary-general was given to National Assemblyman Hwang Woo-yea. The year 2006 also saw a number of changes in political personnel in the governing camp. In early August, Kim Sung-ho, until then deputy head of the presidential Korea Independent Commission against Corruption, succeeded Chun Jun-bae as justice minister after the Uri party had objected to President Roh's first choice, a former presidential aide. A much more unpleasant episode for the government was the scandal that led to the resignation of education minister Kim Byong-joon on 2 August 2006. Kim, who had assumed office only 12 days prior to his resignation, was accused of plagiarism and engaging in other unethical behaviour at the time when he served as professor at Kookmin university in Seoul. Though Kim vehemently denied the allegations, he was seen as too much of a liability for the government. Kim was replaced on 1 September 2006 by Kim Shin-il, a professor emeritus of Seoul National university.

In the wake of North Korea's nuclear test on 9 October 2006, the government undertook a full-scale reshuffle of its top personnel in charge of security and unification affairs. Unification minister Lee Jong-seok, defence minister Yoon Kwang-ung and the head of the National Intelligence Service (NIS) all resigned from their posts. In early November 2006, Lee Jae-joung, a former Uri party lawmaker and head of a presidential advisory council on North Korea, and Kim Jang-soo, former head of the army's general staff, assumed the posts of unification and defence minister respectively. The reshuffle in late 2006 was completed by Song Min-soon's taking over of the foreign affairs portfolio. Song, an advocate of engagement with North Korea, replaced Ban Ki-moon, who was to become new UN Secretary-General in December 2006. At the beginning of the new year, career bureaucrat Kim Young-joo, until then head of the Office for Government Policy Coordination, took over the commerce, industry and energy portfolio from Chung Se-kyun, who rejoined his duties as Uri party lawmaker. Finally, in March 2007, President Roh Moo-hyun named former finance minister Han Duck-soo as new prime minister. The 57-year-old Han had also served as trade minister and as ambassador to the Organisation of Economic Cooperation and Development (OECD). Han succeeded Korea's first female prime minister Han Myeong-sook, who had served in this post since March 2006. Mrs Han, a native of Pyongyang and two-term lawmaker, resumed her duties as National Assemblywoman amid speculation that she might run on the Uri party ticket as candidate in the 2007 presidential election.

The appointment of a new head for South Korea's constitutional court developed into a protracted process that left the court's top job vacant for four months. In mid-August 2006, President Roh Moo-hyun had nominated Chon Hyo-suk, constitutional court justice and former supreme court justice, to become the first woman to serve as president of the constitutional court. The nomination came after a string of corruption scandals involving several judges had led to a decline in the public's trust in the judiciary. Chon was persuaded by the presidential office Chŏngwadae to resign as constitutional court justice in order to be able to serve a full six-year period as head of the court. Technically she was thus a civilian when she underwent National Assembly confirmation hearings. This, however, represented a breach of the constitution, which states that the head of the constitutional court has to be selected from its incumbent members. The opposition GNP protested against Chon's nomination on legal grounds and forced President Roh to withdraw his nomination and to go instead for former supreme court justice Lee Kang-kuk. Lee was eventually confirmed by the National Assembly.

1.3 Dealing with the past: court rulings, amnesties and the collaborator issue

In July 2006, a wiretapping scandal which had rocked Korea in the summer of 2005 led to the conviction of two former heads of the NIS. Lim Dong-won and Shin Gunn, who had presided over the country's spy agency between December 1999 and April 2003, were found to have been formally responsible for the NIS's monitoring of cell-phone conversations of about 1,800 leading figures in Korea. As the two former NIS heads were only indirectly involved in the wiretappings, the sentences of four years of imprisonment were suspended. The scandal had surfaced when a 1997 telephone conversation between a former publisher of the daily *JoongAng Ilbo*, Lee Hak-soo, and a top executive of the Samsung group, Hong Seok-hyun, was leaked to the public. In their conversation the two men discussed the provision of illicit campaign funds to candidates in the 1997 presidential race. The emerging scandal led to the resignation of Hong, a brother-in-law of Samsung chairman Lee Kun-hee, from his post as ambassador to the United States. Both Hong and Lee were, however, cleared in December 2005 by the prosecution from charges of involvement in illegal campaign financing.

In an appeal trial, former Daewoo chairman Kim Woo-choong, who had been sentenced in May 2006 to ten years in prison on charges of embezzlement and accounting fraud, had his sentence reduced by the Seoul high court to eight-and-a-half years. He was also ordered to forfeit 18 trillion won (US$19.2 billion) and to pay a fine of ten trillion won. Kim had fled to France in 1998 after the Daewoo conglomerate, then the third largest in Korea, had collapsed under debts of US$82 billion of debt in the wake of the 1997-8 Asian financial and economic crisis. The former Daewoo chairman returned to Korea in June 2005 to face charges. In the meantime, parts of Daewoo had been broken up and sold, with General Motors acquiring a major stake in Daewoo Motors, which became GM Daewoo in 2002. In reducing the sentence to eight-and-a-half years, the Seoul high court acknowledged Kim's role in building the Korean economy.

Under a special presidential amnesty aimed at creating 'a favourable atmosphere to focus on economic recovery and achieving national unity', 434 convicted business leaders and politicians received pardons in early February 2007. Most of the businessmen who benefited from the amnesty had been jailed for embezzlement, tax evasion fraud or donating illegal political funds. Among the amnesties was former Doosan chairman Park Yong-song, who had been given a suspended sentence of three years and a fine of eight billion won for embezzling from Korea's oldest conglomerate. Also pardoned were Park Jie-won and Kwon Ro-kap, respectively chief of staff and key aide of former president Kim Dae-jung, Kim Hong-il, an ex-lawmaker and eldest son of Kim Dae-jung, and Kim Hyun-chul, the second son of former president Kim Young-sam (1993-8). The four men had been convicted on charges of bribery and/or abusing their power.

For the first time since the Korean peninsula's liberation from Japanese colonial rule in 1945, the South Korean government has embarked on taking legal action against collaborators. In 1948, a task force had been set up by the then government of the Republic of Korea (ROK) to investigate pro-Japanese collaborators, but its probes were foiled by opposition from the ROK's first president, Syngman Rhee. More than 50 years later, in 2004, the South Korean National Assembly passed a law enabling investigations into so-called 'antinational activities' of people who had served above the rank of second lieutenant in Japan's military or who had worked as policemen or members of the military police during the Japanese colonial era. A civilian panel in 2005 accused the late president Park Chung-hee of collaboration—Park had served as a junior officer in Japan's imperial army. The South Korean main opposition party, the GNP, then led by Park's daughter Park Geun-hye, argued that probes into history were politically motivated. Undeterred, the ROK government in July 2006 set up a commission tasked with preparing the confiscation of assets gained as a consequence of collaboration with the Japanese colonial government. A special law to seize such assets was passed in December of the same year. Finally, in February 2007 the government announced a list of about 40 descendants of alleged collaborators whose land is to be seized. The proceeds from the sale of the land, estimated to be worth US$74 million, are to be distributed to pro-independence activists and their offspring. A flood of lawsuits is expected to be launched by persons threatened with confiscations. In all likelihood, it will prove very difficult to verify that the possession of land indeed resulted from collaboration.

1.4 *Hot issues: gambling and the (partial) relocation of the capital*

Gambling is largely prohibited in South Korea. Only one out of 17 officially licensed casinos is allowed to cater for ROK citizens (the remainder are restricted to foreigners). Lax ministerial supervision or worse has, however, enabled game developers and video arcade owners to bypass existing laws. Starting in 2002, the culture ministry allowed game arcades to issue 'cultural gift certificates' to successful gamers. The measure was originally intended to boost the local culture and tourism industry. Unnoticed or maybe even willingly ignored by culture ministry officials, these gift certificates could later be exchanged at a discount into cash. Lured by possible gains, gamblers were pulled to video game arcades, which have mushroomed in Korea in the past few years. According to estimates, the revenues of the arcade market in the ROK rose to 26 trillion won (well over US$27 billion) in 2006. After being harshly criticised for permitting the market release of speculative slot machines and for allowing the use of gift certificates, the government apologised in late August 2006 for its negligent handling of rampant video gambling across the nation. Prosecutors and state auditors were ordered to investigate the scandal. Fifty persons were placed under a travel ban. At the same time, a total of 126 religious leaders declared 'war' on gambling. They argued that Korea had become a 'republic of gambling' and accused the government of having lured low-income citizens into gambling.

In September 2006, the Ministry of Government Administration and Home Affairs (MOGAHA) announced a three-stage schedule for the relocation of government institutions from Seoul to the Yŏngi-Kongju area in South Chungch'ŏng province, about 160 km south of Seoul. According to the schedule, the government will first finish relocating 19 entities, including the Ministry of Finance and Economy, by the end of 2012. The education, culture and labour ministries plus 15 other agencies will follow in 2013, and the twelve remaining entities will be relocated in 2014. The construction work for the new government complex was to start in 2007. Roh Moo-hyun had first voiced his idea to move the South Korean capital in order to diminish regional imbalances when he campaigned for the presidency in 2002. In May 2004, he restated these plans but immediately ran into opposition from both citizens and political parties. Five months later the constitutional court declared the plans to move the capital unconstitutional. Unwilling to give up its plans *in toto*, the government then opted for an administrative town consisting of 12 out of 18 ministries plus a number of agencies. According to the 'light' version of the relocation plan, the Office of the President, the National Assembly, the supreme court and important ministries (*inter alia* the MOGAHA, the Ministry of Justice and the Ministry of Foreign Affairs and Trade) were to remain in Seoul. In late November 2005, the constitutional court affirmed the constitutionality of this plan.

1.5 *President Roh Moo-hyun and the splintering of the Uri party*

In the past five years, the political career of Roh Moo-hyun, the son of a poor farmer and a graduate of a vocational school, who became a self-taught human rights lawyer, has seen many ups and downs. Only a few months after having been propelled into presidential office by South Korea's younger generations and a support network that emerged on the Internet (see also the article by Hauben in this yearbook), Roh stunned the nation during his first year in office when he declared that he felt not up to the job. Roh then became the first president of the ROK to be impeached by parliament. Yet Roh was not just reinstated, but popular disgust about the political motivations underlying the impeachment drive helped his party to gain a landslide win in the 2004 general election and a majority in the National Assembly. Ever since, however, Roh's popularity ratings have been plummeting, reaching single digits at times. Roh has been blamed, *inter alia*, for soaring housing prices, a lacklustre economy, and increasing gaps between the haves and have-nots in South Korean society (see below, 2.2). While some of Roh's most steadfast supporters still find the president's characteristically blunt statements and 'surprising' policy initiatives refreshing, many Koreans look forward to the day when Roh will leave office in February 2008.

In late 2006 and early 2007 it became clear that the president was not willing to let his remaining days in office simply peter out. Instead Roh tried to push two new policy initiatives. In December, ostensibly out of concern for young Koreans 'rotting in barracks', Roh raised the possibility of reducing the duration of mandatory military service, now ranging from 24 to 27 months depending on the service arm. The opposition cried foul against what it perceived as blatant populism in the face of the 2007 presidential election. Former top military brass and defence ministers accused the president of disparaging the military. In January 2007, Roh then revived the idea of a constitutional revision that would allow future heads of state to run for a second term. Roh suggested cutting the length of a presidential term to four years, with the possibility of one more term after a successful re-election bid by the incumbent. Roh even offered to leave his party if the opposition supported his proposal. Though the one-term limit stipulated in the 1987 constitution might indeed no longer be as relevant as it was after decades of authoritarian rule (opinion polls also suggested support for constitutional change in this respect), the opposition parties were loathe to give Roh the opportunity for a last political triumph. They accused him of raising divisive proposals that stood little chance of passing parliament in an attempt to avoid the image of a 'lame duck'.

In late February 2007, Roh declared that he would leave the Uri party anyway, thus paving the way for a political shake-up ahead of the December presidential election. The announcement came after 23 lawmakers departed from the Uri party, which in turn lost its status as majority party. Eight other lawmakers left the party individually. With support ratings for the governing party having fallen to around 10 percent (as opposed to around 50 percent for the GNP), the Uri party was on the verge of break-up in early spring 2007. Party chairman Kim Guen-tae quit his post to make way for the creation of a new party. New party leader Chung Sye-kyun was tasked with sounding out members of the Democratic party and the People First party about the creation of a new party. The Uri party, which had been founded in November 2003, was thus destined to follow the fate of other short-lived parties in South Korea. Since 1963, when laws governing political parties were first established, the country has seen 103 parties formed and dissolved. According to the National Election Commission, a party lasts on average about three years in the Republic of Korea, the maximum life span having been 17 years and the shortest less than 20 days.

Whether the Uri party would be able to regroup under different colours and whether the party or its successor would be able to present a viable candidate for the upcoming presidential election still remained unclear in late April 2007. After former prime minister Goh Kun had aborted in early 2007 his bid to become Korea's next president, all eyes became fixed on the two conservative frontrunners in the polls, ex-Hyundai CEO and former Seoul mayor Lee Myung-bak on the one hand, and former GNP chairwoman Park Geun-hye on the other hand.

2 THE ECONOMY

According to provisional figures released by the Bank of Korea (BOK), Korea's economy grew by 5.0 percent in 2006. This was not only one of the best results in more recent years but was even above the 4.7 percent 'potential growth rate' calculated by the Samsung Economic Research Institute. As in the year before, the economy started strong but lost momentum in the second half of the year. And again as in 2005, exports served as the main growth engine, increasing by some 14.4 percent on a year-on-year basis (2005: +12 percent). In

December 2006, Korea's exports passed a new record mark, registering over US$300 billion since the beginning of the year. Roughly speaking, the ROK now exports as much merchandise in a single day as North Korea does in a whole year. Measured in US dollars, the value of annual South Korean exports has more than doubled since 2001. Substantial trade surpluses have resulted from the strong growth of exports over the past few years. Somewhat masked by these impressive figures is the fact that the ROK still registers a substantial and, more recently, growing bilateral trade deficit *vis-à-vis* Japan (see below, 2.1). Moreover, it is noteworthy that South Korea's balance-of-payments surplus has declined since 2004, reflecting not only the country's traditional deficit in terms of trade in services but also the increasing sums of money spent by Korean individuals and corporations overseas (cf. Table 1).

The increase in the ROK's gross domestic product (GDP) in 2006 was also fuelled by improved capital spending, estimated at +7.6 percent (2005: +5.1 percent), and a growing private consumption (+4.2 percent as against +3.6 percent in 2005). As a consequence of the positive economic development, the number of unemployed decreased by 60,000 in 2006 and the average unemployment rate fell to 3.5 percent. Despite rising oil prices, inflation remained relatively low at slightly over 2 percent (cf. Table 1). Still, the BOK decided to raise the base rate to 4.5 percent in August 2006 in order to ward off any overheating tendencies. With the steady growth of South Korea's economy in the past couple of years, per capita income has also increased substantially. Measured in US dollars, it might well reach US$20,000 in 2008, which would put average South Koreans roughly on a par with Greeks or New Zealanders.

2.1 *Of sandwiches and nutcrackers: Korea's economy between China and Japan*

Popular sentiment in 2006 and early 2007 was clearly not in tune with the generally positive picture painted by macro-economic data. To start with, critics of Roh Moo-hyun argued that with slightly over 4 percent average growth in the first four years of his presidency, the South Korean economy had fallen below standard expectations and

Table 1 ROK basic economic data

	2001	2002	2003	2004	2005	2006
GDP (billion won)	622.1	684.3	724.7	779.4	810.5	847.9
GDP (billion US$)	482	547	608	681	788	912
GDP growth (%)	3.8	7.0	3.1	4.7	4.2	5.0
Per capita income (GDP base, in US$)	10.178	11.485	12.707	14.161	16.306	18.372
Exports (billion US$)	150.4	162.5	193.8	253.8	284.4	325.5
Imports (billion US$)	141.1	152.1	178.8	224.5	261.2	309.4
Trade balance (billion US$)	+9.3	+10.3	+14.5	+29.4	+23.2	+16.3
Balance of payments (billion US$)	+8.0	+5.4	+12.0	+28.2	+15.0	+6.1
Gross external debt (billion US$)	128.7	141.5	157.6	172.3	187.9	263.4
International reserves (billion US$)	102.8	121.4	155.3	199.1	210.4	239.0
Inward foreign direct investment (billion US$)	11.9	9.1	6.5	12.8	11.6	11.2
Consumer prices (%)	+4.1	+2.7	+3.5	+3.6	+2.8	+2.2
Producer prices (%)	+1.9	-0.3	+2.2	+6.1	+2.1	+2.3
Unemployed (in thousands)	899	752	818	860	887	827
Unemployment rate (%)	4.0	3.3	3.6	3.7	3.7	3.5

Note: Data for 2006 provisional.

Sources: Bank of Korea, *Monthly Statistical Bulletin*, 2/2007 (and earlier editions); Bank of Korea statistics webpage, online: http://ecos.bok.or.kr (accessed 25 April 2007); Invest Korea 2007; *Republic of Korea Economic Bulletin*, April 2007.

that the current government was to blame for this. Setting aside the question of what the government could have done differently, such criticism seemed somewhat overblown in view of the general maturation of the South Korean economy. It remains to be seen though, whether the rise of the won (8.6 percent *vis-à-vis* the US dollar in 2006), a dip in capital investment in the first few months of the year and attempts by the government to contain soaring housing prices (see 2.2 below), will lead to a deceleration of the economy in 2007. The continuing high degree of household debts also provides reason for concern.

Discontent concerning the ROK's economic development in recent years could also be traced to more structural causes. Business leaders and a number of analysts maintained that the economy had increasingly lost the dynamism which had characterised it at the end of the last millennium. Back then, both corporations and the government had engaged in massive restructuring and liberalisation in order to overcome the effects of the financial and economic crisis which had befallen South Korea in 1997-8. As a result of this perceived loss of dynamism, the economy was in danger of being squeezed, on the one hand by a rapidly catching-up Chinese economy and on the other hand by a technologically superior Japanese economy—or so it is frequently argued. While talk of the ROK's 'sandwich position' between its two big neighbours is not new, the tone of the debate has become shriller in recent times. Certainly, the rise of the Chinese economy constitutes a double-edged sword for South Korea as a nation. While China's growing import needs have helped to propel Korean exports in the last couple of years, the rise of foreign direct investment in China by South Korean companies exploring new business opportunities, also means that at least some capital investment is diverted from South Korea to China. The much noted decrease in the share of capital investment in the ROK's GDP from 40 percent in 1996 to 28 percent in 2006 reflects this diversification of investment, but of course also South Korea's shift to a more mature stage of economic development, in which domestic consumption and the service sector play ever more important roles. The much talked-about 'hollowing out' of the South Korean industry has to be viewed in this perspective.

Still, the perception that 'Chinese companies threaten not just to complement but entirely consume Korea's industries' (*Financial Times*, 19 March 2007: 9) is strong and will not go away easily. Chinese manufacturing workers earn as little as 10 percent of what their

South Korean counterparts take home, while Chinese companies continue to move up the value chain. The structure of Chinese exports, where the share of electronics and other 'high-technology' products has now grown to nearly 40 percent, bears resemblance to that of the ROK's export structure of ten years ago. This should come as no surprise, as 'Korea's old economic model of imitation and manufacturing-led growth is now China's model' (ibid.). Chinese companies might well produce soon the kind of semiconductors and flat-screen televisions for which South Korean corporations are known today. According to the Korea Electronics Association, the ROK's current four-year lead over Chinese manufacturers of flat-screen televisions is likely to narrow to only one year by 2010 (ibid.). The picture is very much the same with regard to products such as mobile phones and high-end steel. Whole industries feel the heat from China. In early 2007, Chinese shipyards for the first time recorded more orders (in terms of tonnage) than South Korean ones—though the types of ships that are predominantly produced in the two countries still differ significantly (bulk vessels as against large container ships and liquefied natural gas carriers).

While the question of whether the Chinese economy constitutes more of a boon or a bane for Korea (see also the article by Kim and Lee in this yearbook) is present as a main concern in the ROK, the Japanese economy is never off the radar screen either. As even South Korean industrialists will grudgingly admit, the ROK's 'economic miracle' was only possible because Korea's export industries relied heavily on Japanese inputs in the form of machinery, components and intermediary products. In order to become and stay competitive in global markets, South Korean manufacturing conglomerates procured such inputs on a massive scale from Japanese suppliers—and still do. Despite repeated attempts by both the government and large corporations in Korea to promote import substitution in relevant areas, to beef up spending on research and development (R&D) and to foster local suppliers, import dependence on Japan has not gone away. In more recent years, the resulting trade deficit *vis-à-vis* Japan has actually risen again. As Table 2 shows, South Korea's bilateral trade deficit with Japan rose from slightly over US$10 billion in 2001 to around US$25 billion in 2006. (The rise of the won *vis-à-vis* the Japanese yen certainly did not help to reverse the trend.)

Table 2   ROK's bilateral trade deficit with Japan (in billion US$)

2001	2002	2003	2004	2005	2006
10.1	14.7	19	24.4	24.3	25.3

Source: Ministry of Commerce, Industry and Energy, quoted by Bernhard Seliger (2007), 'Korea im Jahr 2006 – Politische und Wirtschaftliche Lage', Seoul: Hanns Seidel Stiftung, p. 25.

Still, there is hardly anything inevitable about South Korea's economy being crushed by the combined Chinese-Japanese 'nutcracker'. Much depends on how corporate and governmental actors in the ROK respond to the challenge posed by the two big neighbouring economies. Among others, the OECD recommends that more resources be invested into R&D, education and training, to make the labour market more flexible and to further open the domestic capital markets. If South Korea does not want to lose ground, there is indeed no alternative to fostering the (hard and soft) infrastructure necessary for innovation—just as everyone else will try to do. Attracting more inward foreign direct investment (IFDI) will be part of the task. However, despite increased attempts to do just that since 1997, IFDI still contributes only a relatively low 7 percent to the ROK's GNP (see also the article by Cherry in this yearbook). Moreover, doubts persist whether the climate for overseas investors is as hospitable as claimed by the government. The investigations launched in 2006 against the US-based Lone Star fund, which had wanted to sell its shares in the Korean Exchange Bank to the local Kookmin Bank at a tax-free profit of around US$4.5 billion, serve as a reminder of remaining economic nationalism (see also the article by Schopf in this yearbook). As for domestic corporations, the globally oriented *chaeböl* will have fewer problems in adjusting to the challenges and indeed chances provided by the Chinese and the Japanese economies. Though it certainly will not be smooth sailing for South Korea's large conglomerates, they are in an infinitely better position than many of the small and medium-sized enterprises (SMEs) in the ROK, many of which are simply not competitive internationally and/or struggle under huge amounts of debt (only to be kept afloat by generous debt guarantees provided by the government). The dual character of South Korea's corporate sector—well-known, globally oriented conglomerates on the one hand and often underdeveloped SMEs on the other hand—has been a direct consequence of the ROK's 'condensed' and chaebŏl-oriented industrialisation process. It will remain problematic for many years to come.

2.2 *Growing inequality and rising housing prices*

Discontent about South Korea's economic development in recent years also emanates from a different direction. There are indications that the fruits of progress are no longer shared as equally as they once were. The ROK's rapid industrialisation from the mid-1960s onwards was linked to a fairly equitable distribution of income. The extraordinary growth trajectory of South Korea came to a halt when the financial crisis that struck the country in 1997 developed into an economic crisis. Even though it was possible to overcome the immediate difficulties quickly, job security has declined conspicuously ever since. In 2005, 37 percent of the workforce was employed on a temporary basis; 34 percent had been with their employer for less than a year. The average income of temporary employees averages only 60 percent of that of 'permanent' employees. What is more, the South Korean informal sector is said to be the largest among OECD countries. According to the International Confederation of Free Trade Unions, of the more than two million workers in the country's construction industry, 80 percent are irregular workers. It may also be noted that the unionisation rate in Korea has declined in recent years: in 2004 it stood at 10.4 percent. Most unionised employees belong to company unions, and more broad-based unions exist only in some sectors (e.g. metal workers). Unions figure most prominently in big conglomerates. The Hyundai Motor Co., which was affected by a costly one-month strike in the summer of 2006, for example, has over 41,000 union members, who form part of South Korea's 'labour bourgeoisie'. Though income disparities in the ROK are still lower than in many other developing and newly-developed countries, their recent rise—the Gini coefficient on household income rose from 0.296 in 1996 to 0.344 in 2004— threatens the equitable development pattern that has been a hallmark of South Korea's economic 'miracle'. Also, and in spite of many government actions in recent years, Korean women still face discrimination in the workplace and elsewhere. As a consequence, the ROK only ranked 26th in the 2006 Gender-related Development Index of the United Nations Development Programme.

The emotionally sensitive issue of growing disparities in South Korean society is also reflected in the problem of rising housing costs, which is especially acute in the greater Seoul area. Although Roh Moo-hyun promised in his presidential campaign in 2002 to do everything to make housing affordable, prices for houses and apartments have risen significantly since 2003. According to government data, real estate prices in South Korea rose by 5.6 percent in 2006 alone. However, prices in Seoul rose at nearly double that rate. In the most popular districts of the capital, apartment prices have tripled since the start of 2003. According to Real Estate Bank, an online real estate information provider, urban households with an average monthly income of 3.4 million won (around US$3,600) have to save their entire salaries for an average of 11 years to buy a mid-sized apartment in Seoul (*Straits Times Interactive*, 20 January 2007).

Whether the rise in housing prices is indeed (at least partially) a consequence of large-scale speculation, or whether it simply reflects the laws of supply and demand, is a controversial subject of discussion in Korea. In any case, resentment is fuelled by allegations that speculators are making huge gains while ordinary families are priced out of the market. Government statistics show that that out of 18 million households in the ROK, 45 percent do not own real estate, while one in 10 owns more than two properties. Construction minister Choo Byung-jik, who had been calling on Koreans to buy no new apartments, had to resign in late 2006 when it became known that he himself owned two apartments in Kangnam, one of Seoul's smartest districts. Government attempts to rein in prices have proved by and large fruitless so far. In August 2005, the government raised capital-gains taxes, which will reach 50 percent in 2007 for owners of multiple apartments. The government has also loosened restrictions on buying real estate overseas and property taxes were increased sharply in 2007. In November 2006, the government also promised to build an additional 125,000 homes in and around Seoul within five years, bringing the total of new units to 867,000. Whether such measures will be more effective than in the past remains to be seen. Most analysts at least expect real estate prices to increase until 2009 or 2010, when increased supply will hit the market. The issue of housing prices is thus likely to remain on the front burner for some time to come.

NORTH KOREA: DOMESTIC POLITICS AND ECONOMY 2006-2007

Rüdiger Frank

Information about domestic developments in the Democratic People's Republic of Korea (DPRK) is not easy to obtain. In addition to occasional news available through various official North Korean sources as well as from foreign media, two regular events of a highly programmatic nature stand out, deserving particular attention. The political tone and strategy are set by the New Year joint editorial, usually appearing in early January. The annual plenary session of the People's Assembly that usually takes place in spring in turn provides some impression of the official view on the status of the national economy. Since the overview section of this yearbook covers events from April 2006 to March 2007, the examination of the parliamentary reports comes first, followed by the major points of the New Year editorial, then a third section covering especially important events, and a fourth section in which other major and minor domestic developments are summarised.

1 THE 2006 PARLIAMENTARY SESSION

The 2006 session of the North Korean parliament, the fourth session of the 11th Supreme People's Assembly (SPA) (*ch'oego inminhoeŭi*), took place on 11 April in Pyongyang. It discussed standard issues, including the work of the cabinet in the preceding year, the report on the implementation of the 2005 state budget and the new budget for 2006.

In line with the general policy of fostering the development and application of information technology, there was special emphasis on the importance of this field for the development of the DPRK's economy and military, and a decision was passed 'On stepping up the development of science and technology to give strong impetus to the building of a great prosperous powerful nation' (see below for more details). Premier Pak Pong Ju emphasised in accordance with the 2006 New Year joint editorial that the main economic task of the coming year was a significant increase in agricultural production. He also mentioned that the Cabinet would focus on 'external economic work as required by the changing circumstances and realistic demand' and the desire to expand exports, actively explore new markets, diversify foreign trade, and collaborate with overseas Koreans and foreigners including joint ventures. (The establishment of the Pyongyang Law Office in January 2007 was a significant development in this connection, since its main purpose is the provision of legal services related to economic co-operation with foreign countries.) A major goal of all these activities was the introduction of advanced technology.

In lieu of standard macroeconomic data, the yearly numbers for the development of budgetary revenue and expenditures are an almost unrivalled indicator for the growth of North Korea's national economy. They are, however, rarely complete and the emphasis on specific issues tends to differ from year to year. Since 2002, no absolute numbers have been reported; rather, the vice-premier usually reports relative increase rates. Their analytical value lies mostly in a comparison with the data of preceding years.

The April 2006 session of the SPA heard that the state budgetary revenue (*kukga yesan suip*) had increased by 16.1 percent over the preceding year, while the state's expenditure (*kukga yesan chichŭl*) reached 104.4 percent of the planned figure (in 2005, an expenditure increase of 11.4 percent was planned; since it actually grew by 4.4 percent more than planned, the increase rate would have been 15.8 percent). While the profits from state enterprises, the major source of state revenue, rose by 14.2 percent, the profits of cooperative organisations (*hyŏpdong tanch'e*) grew by a large 24.3 percent; revenue from social insurance grew by about 5.7 percent.

The DPRK spent 15.9 percent of its budget on national defence and 41.3 percent on various economic projects. Expenditure on agriculture, designated the key front of economic construction, increased by 32.5 percent over the previous year.

For the fiscal year 2006-07, the SPA was told, a growth rate of state budgetary revenue of 7.1 percent was expected. Income generated by cooperative organisations was expected to continue its high growth at 23.2 percent, while revenue from state enterprises would only increase by about 7.2 percent. A cautious comparison can perhaps be made with the development of the Chinese economy after 1979, when the rural economy generated the most impressive growth rates. Revenue from 'utility fees on real estate' (*pudongsan sayongnyo*) was to grow by 12%. The most significant percental increase was expected in revenue from social insurance fees (*sahoepohŏmnyo*), set to rise by as much as 141 percent. (Interestingly, many of the figures in this paragraph are available only in Korean language media such as the *Rodong Shinmun*, not in the English-language report carried on the Korean Central News Agency website).

The report to the SPA on the budget for the 2006-07 fiscal year indicated that expenditure was to grow by only 3.5 percent, i.e. half of the expected increase in revenue. This low figure hints at a previously accumulated deficit that is to be reduced in the long run. Expenditure on the military would remain stable at 15.9 percent, while a 'big portion' of the budget would be spent on the economy. Expenditure on agriculture was planned to increase by 12.2 percent, and by 9.6 percent on the power, coal and metal industries and railway transport. Science and technology and the implementation of social policies received modest increases of about 3 percent. As usual, an unspecified amount was set aside for the support of pro-North Korean residents in Japan. Significantly, the SPA session was told of plans to introduce a new social insurance system for enterprises; and indeed, in the following month, May 2006, each organisation and enterprise in North Korea was reportedly asked to pay 7 percent of total profits from that year for the operation of the social insurance system. The separate insurance premiums are one step towards a more transparent economic structure of the state and businesses on the way to a further normalisation of North Korean institutions.

The premier confirmed that the preceding year (2005) had been economically more successful than its predecessors. The country had been able to increase production of energy by 11 percent, while coal production rose by 10 percent. No specific growth figures were given for other sectors or products. However, the intention to 'fully solve the food problem' hints at a still unsatisfactory situation in agricultural production. A recurring term is 'improvement' (*kaesŏnhwa*), part of the politically acceptable terminology to describe economic changes, reforms and new approaches. (Premier Pak Pong Ju has been identified with a progressive economic policy in North Korea, but stepped down or was replaced in April 2007.)

Choe Thae Bok, secretary of the Central Committee of the Korean Worker's Party, addressed the SPA in a speech that reflected the session's major thematic issue: the need to step up development in science and technology in the interests of building a 'great, prosperous and powerful nation' (*kwahak kisul palchŏnŭl tagŭch'yŏ kangsŏngtaeguk konsŏrŭl himittge ch'udonghalde daehayŏ*). Choe specifically mentioned the fields of semiconductor design technology, a domestically developed operating system for computers and nanotechnology. In terms of application, he highlighted prospecting of underground resources, hinting at increased efforts to tap the country's rich and so far under-utilised natural resources. The current five-year plan for the development of science and technology ends in 2007 and will be succeeded by the 2007-12 plan. Remarkably, Choe made more long-term projections into the future, reaching as far as 2022, with the goal of turning the nation into a 'scientific and technological power' (*kwahak kisul kangguk*). He spoke of the construction of a nationwide information network and of efforts in the field of programming technology that are expected to turn North Korea into 'a power in software development' (*p'ŭrogŭraem palchŏn kangguk*)]; and spread the latest buzzwords, such as nanotechnology and bio-engineering, space technology and oceanography.

Choe identified agriculture and energy as the two major problems that need to be resolved first. Food production is to be increased by a combination of high-yield seeds, double-cropping and mechanisation (an already familiar formula). He urged that the chronic power shortage should be tackled by developing the country's natural resources, modernising existing power stations, utilising renewable energy sources such as wind power and bio-energy, and introducing energy-saving technologies. With regard to the development of natural resources, he specifically mentioned the production of iron, coal gasification for fertiliser production, and oil exploration, as well as lead, zinc, magnesite, graphite, silica and building stone.

To reach all these goals, Choe stressed the need for improvement in education and for 'bold and wide-ranging scientific and technological exchange and cooperation' with foreign partners, including joint research projects.

2 THE 2007 NEW YEAR JOINT EDITORIAL

The year 2007 started with the usual New Year editorial, published jointly by the country's major print media *Rodong Shinmun* (party), *Chosŏn Inmingun* (military) and *Ch'ŏngnyŏn Chŏnwi* (youth league), entitled: 'Let us march forward, opening the golden age of Sŏngun Korea with high confidence in victory'. In lieu of other means of learning about the North Korean government's strategic visions, these annual editorials are widely regarded as programmatic statements.

The 2007 editorial stressed the new situation that was created by the nuclear test of October 2006 (see section 3 below), declaring the latter a major victory and a source of pride for the Korean people. This is not surprising if contrasted with the previously announced goal of building a strong and powerful nation (*kangsŏng taeguk*), a slogan that echoes the Meiji-era Japanese motto of national reconstruction: *fukoku kyōhei* (a rich country and a strong army). The emphasis on the 'Korean nation first' (*chosŏnminjok cheilchuŭi*) is a recurring theme in this and other statements. The major target group has, however, shifted since the 1990s from the pro-North Korean minority in Japan to South Koreans. The editorial's message is twofold; it emphasises that, by joining forces, Korea will be able to advance and achieve its due status as a major power in the region and the world, and furthermore, it urges fellow countrymen to withstand any outside attempts at disrupting the inter-Korean process of reconciliation and reunification, hinting at the important role that military strength plays in this struggle for independence. In the same spirit, it tells North Koreans that the future of their country is closely connected to the Military First Policy (*sŏngun chŏngch'i*). The rise to nuclear power status has demonstrated that all the sacrifices for the development of their military, including the 'arduous march' (referring to the famine of the mid-1990s) were worthwhile. The editorial repeatedly emphasizes the strictly defensive nature of the country's nuclear arsenal, stressing its function as a war deterrence (*chŏnchaeng ŏkcheryŏk*) in East Asia.

The editorial implies that the regime will in future focus on the economic part of *kangsŏng taeguk* now that the military part has been successfully achieved by becoming a nuclear state. While power, coal-mining, steel and rail transportation are still promoted as the pioneer sectors (*sŏnghaeng pumun*) of the economy, they are mentioned only after extensive elaboration on improving the people's standard of living through technological updating of the economy, farming as the foundation of the country, improved health services, and a 'revolution in light industry' to raise output, variety and quality in consumer goods. In particular, the editorial stresses the party line of actively tackling the requirements of the IT era (*chŏngbosanŏp sidae*), highlighting the hope that investment in the knowledge- and labour-intensive, but less capital-hungry IT sector will help bring about a major turn in economic development.

The editorial's renewed emphasis on the cabinet as one of the main administrative units responsible for the economy is noteworthy. The role of officials in 'economic institutions' is to be enhanced, while the 'important position' of the cabinet is stressed. This hints at a continuation of the process of professionalisation of economic management. Other topics are the renewal of the pledge to reunify the country 'in our generation' and to drive US troops out of South Korea, and staunch opposition to conservatives in the South, especially Hannaradang (Grand National Party). The latter has been identified as the main ideological foe, after the ongoing process of nationalist reconciliation and the summit between Kim Jong Il and Kim Dae-jung in June 2000 made the previous undifferentiated criticism of South Korea more difficult.

3 THE MISSILE LAUNCH AND THE NUCLEAR TEST

The two most outstanding single events in North Korea in the period under review were both security related. On 5 July, (4 July American time), the DPRK test-fired at least seven missiles of various types and ranges. The official statement of a spokesman of the North Korean Ministry of Foreign Affairs, published on 6 July, opened by pointing out that the missile launch was part of a routine military exercise. It then stressed the legitimate right of the DPRK to conduct such a test, and pointed at the absence of legal agreements and commitments that would prevent the country from doing so. Referring to the US financial sanctions of autumn 2005, the statement explained that there was no reason for 'self-restraint' in the wake of Washington's uncooperative behaviour. The latter argument, together with the continued listing of North Korea as part of the axis of evil and a terror-sponsoring state, would appear to be the main reasons for the missile test. The spokesman concluded by again reiterating the intention of the DPRK to achieve a peaceful denuclearisation of the Korean peninsula and to continue the Six Party Talks. Unlike the nuclear test (see below), the missile test did not result in excessive displays of national pride in the North Korean media and hence can be considered as having had primarily a military or foreign policy background. The latter appears more likely, given the choice of US Independence Day for the test.

On 9 October, one day before the annual celebrations to commemorate the foundation of the Korean Labour Party and seven days before the 80th anniversary of the 'down-with-imperialism union', the country's first nuclear test was conducted. In preparation for the test, a number of reports had appeared, stressing the reluctance of the country to give up its nuclear deterrence capabilities. Official announcements on the test in the North Korean media, in addition to exhibiting great national pride and contentment, repeatedly stressed the strictly defensive nature of the country's nuclear arsenal and argued that the DPRK's now proven nuclear status would contribute to peace and stability in northeast Asia. On 11 October, an official statement by a Foreign Ministry spokesman, stressed that the test was conducted '100 percent' by the domestic efforts of the DPRK and under secure conditions. It was 'entirely attributable to the US nuclear threat, sanctions and pressure' and was the final effort after the country had utilised dialogue and negotiations with no tangible result. Blame hence attached to the US. Much more effort than in July was put on emphasising the readiness of the DPRK to negotiate and to reach a peaceful solution. To prove this, the most powerful argument possible—a direct reference to Kim Il Sung—was used: 'The denuclearization of the entire peninsula was President Kim Il Sung's last instruction and an ultimate goal of the DPRK.'

The nuclear test was accompanied by a number of public displays of satisfaction and national pride. While the implications for security and international relations have been discussed in other chapters of this yearbook, some very powerful domestic motives may have involved. Most importantly, Kim Jong Il desperately needed a big, visible success. Ever since the death of his father, the country had been hit by a series of disasters and failures. The famine of 1995-7, termed the 'arduous march' in North Korea, in a subtle reference to the earlier Chinese experience, was triggered by a number of natural disasters but in fact reflected the desolate state of the country's economy and especially its agriculture. No regime and ideology can, in the long run, retain its legitimacy if it is unable to feed the population. South Korea, in the meanwhile, was enjoying economic success and international recognition despite the Asian financial crisis of 1997-8. The normalisation talks with Japan collapsed in 2002 and did not bring the hoped-for economic benefits. The long-prepared economic modernisation, having entered its 'hot phase' in July 2002 after prolonged ideological preparation, also created results that were far from satisfactory, including hyper-inflation (perhaps about 200 percent annually) and a disruption of society.

Since public opinion plays only a minor role under an autocratic political system such as the one in North Korea, it is most plausible that among domestic forces, it was the elite that had to be impressed. If this is true, it would not only shed some light on the otherwise rather opaque inner power structure of the DPRK. We could also expect a new wave of economic reforms and diplomatic offers after the more conservative thinkers in the leadership had been either pleased or silenced by the prestigious event of having displayed technological progress and political will by conducting the first ever nuclear test on the Korean peninsula.

4 OTHER DOMESTIC DEVELOPMENTS

4.1 *Projects and campaigns with social overhead capital*

Concentrated efforts to prevent avian influenza were made in a countrywide campaign in early 2006. In line with the policy of improving the irrigation system to ensure more stable harvests, another major waterway project in addition to the Kaech'ŏn-Taesŏngho waterway and the Paengma-Chŏlsan waterway was started in April 2006 after a prolonged preparation period. The goal is to irrigate the Miru plain, a main area for grain production in North Hamgyŏng province on the northeastern coast. The country continued its efforts to construct about 30 middle- and small-sized power plants. The construction of a large-scale hydroelectric power plant, originally started in 1988, resumed after guidance by Kim Jong Il in August 2000 and was reported as almost completed in June 2006.

Rehabilitation of the country's transportation network remains an important issue for economic modernisation. In light of this, the talks with Russia on the reconstruction of railway tracks between both countries are significant. Russia has a strong strategic interest in seeing the railway link from South Korea (and in the future, probably even from Japan via an undersea tunnel) to Europe passing through its territory, thereby connecting a trans-Korean route with the Trans-Siberian railway, rather than through China. Hence it has shown great readiness to make attractive offers to the North Korean side. First summit talks to that effect were held between North Korea and Russia in 2000 and 2001, followed by a number of working-level meetings. In August 2006, another protocol related to the project was signed. It has to be noted, however, that there is the yet distant possibility of linking Japan with Europe via the island of Sakhalin—thereby bypassing not only China, but also both Koreas. As a reflection of attempts to improve the country's capability to conduct foreign economic exchange, the North Korean media reported at the end of 2006 on the completion of two main quays at Namp'o harbour and the near completion of a container quay.

In early January 2007, the media reported the establishment of a cyber education centre at Kim Chaek University of Technology. While ordinary North Koreans have no regular access to the Internet, for many years efforts have been underway to establish a countrywide domestic network. This Intranet can now be used by private, administrative and business users to gain access to lectures by professors of this leading technical university in the DPRK. Some organisations, including the ministries of Foreign Affairs and Foreign Trade, appear to have some limited Internet access.

4.2 *Exhibitions and conferences*

Three exhibitions held in 2006 at the Three Revolution Exhibition Hall in Pyongyang continued efforts at increasing international economic co-operation. The Ninth Pyongyang International Goods Expo, held from 15 to 18 May, attracted a total of about 200 companies from ten countries including China, the Republic of Korea, Syria, Thailand, Spain, Sweden, and France. Participants displayed ferrous, electrical and electronic products, petrochemical products, medicines and food. In September 2006, the Ninth National Invention and New Technology Exhibition took place and later that same month the Second Pyongyang International Commodity Fair, in which about 80 companies from ten nations participated. Also in late September, the Third Nanoscience and Technology Exhibition was held at Kim Chaek University of Technology.

4.3 Administrative and personnel changes

North Korean media reported on 14 June 2006 that Kang Neung Su had been appointed Minister of Culture. He had already served in that capacity from September 1999 to September 2003, and holds the concurrent positions of vice-chairman of the SPA and chairman of the Kimilsungia and Kimjongilia Association (dedicated to the flowers named after the two North Korean leaders).

In late October 2006, the SPA announced that it would split the Ministry of Power and Coal Industries into the Ministry of Electric Power Industry and the Ministry of Coal Industry, hinting at efforts to streamline administration in these fields. Two months later, new regulations for the development and operation of small- and medium-sized coal mines were announced, with the goal of increasing production of coal and solving the fuel problem. In January 2007, Park Nam Chil, the former Vice-Minister of the Power and Coal Industries, was appointed Minister of the Electric Power Industry. The DPRK's Foreign Minister Paek Nam Sun died on 3 January 2007, aged 77, after having been in office since 1998. He was succeeded in May 2007 by 75-year-old Pak Ui Chun, who had formerly served as ambassador to Russia. Sim Giyeop was appointed Minister of Fisheries. On 17 March 2007, Pak Yong Sok, member of the Central Committee of the Workers' Party of Korea, chairman of the Central Committee's Control Commission and deputy to the SPA, died at the age of 80.

4.4 Natural disasters

In mid-July 2006, the country was hit by heavy rainfall and flooding. Severe human and physical damage was reported from the provinces of South P'yŏng'an (6200 houses and 490 public buildings), Kangwŏn (6000 houses and 200 public buildings) and South Hwanghae. The latter suffered a particularly heavy loss in arable land, in addition to the destruction of transportation, communication and energy infrastructure. The UN World Food Programme estimated the loss of arable land to be around 30,000 ha and the number of refugees to total about 60,000. International organisations such as the International Federation of Red Cross and Red Crescent Societies appealed for assistance and carried out relief activities in some areas where they were granted access. As a consequence of the flooding, the planned Arirang mass games was cancelled.

5 OTHER REPORTS

In addition to the major issues noted above, a number of occasional events were reported in the media. These included visits by Kim Jong Il to military units and 'on-the-spot guidances' (*hyŏnchi kyosi*) in farms, factories, educational, administrative and other institutions. Although there is little point in listing them, such visits sometimes provide interesting clues on the overall activity level of the leader (and on his health) as well as a possible emphasis on specific sectors. As of June 2006, Kim Jong Il had conducted 57 such public activities, including 45 visits to military units and five economy-related visits.

One dominating topic between April 2006 and March 2007 was the debate about allegations of illicit activities against North Korea. These found broad reflection in the media and were all denied. After about four years of negotiations, AP Television News, a company that provides international video contents to broadcasters and the Internet, opened its resident office in Pyongyang on 22 May 2006. The organisation is a division of AP news in the US but is London based and is registered as a British company. It will be the first Western news group to provide full-time coverage on North Korea. Other foreign news organisations stationed in Pyongyang include the Chinese Xinhua News Agency and *People's Daily* and the Russian Itar-Tass News Agency.

In September 2006, the North Korean team won the FIFA U-20 Women's World Soccer Championship in Moscow, and on 13 September the opening ceremony of the Tenth Pyongyang International Film Festival was held at the People's Palace of Culture.

RELATIONS BETWEEN THE TWO KOREAS 2006-2007

James E. Hoare

Four distinct phases emerged during 2006-07 in relations between the two Koreas. The first followed on from the aftermath of the September 2005 Six Party Talks agreement.[1] In May-June 2006, the relatively positive atmosphere of the earlier period gave way to growing tensions in the Democratic People's Republic of Korea (DPRK)'s relationship with the outside world, including the Republic of Korea (ROK), as US pressure appeared to increase and as it be came clear that the DPRK was about to abandon its self-imposed moratorium on missile tests. Tension did not abate after the missile tests as it became more and more obvious that the DPRK was also on the point of testing a nuclear device. From the test in October until February 2007, relations remained strained as the ROK struggled to preserve its policy of engagement. A new positive phase then began with a further Six Party agreement reached in Beijing in mid-February.

1 Aftermath of the September 2005 agreement

The September 2005 agreement quickly fell apart in the face of DPRK demands for a light water reactor, United States insistence that the DPRK should have no nuclear facilities and, most important of all, the announcement of a US Treasury investigation into claims of counterfeiting and money laundering by the DPRK, claims that were accompanied by a freeze on DPRK overseas bank accounts.

This development was unwelcome to the ROK government under President Roh Moo-hyun and the Uri party. While there is concern in ROK government circles and among the wider public about the DPRK nuclear programme, that programme is not seen as directed at the

---

[1] The six parties are the two Koreas, China, Russia, Japan and the US. The talks began in 2003 following the DPRK's withdrawal from the Non-Proliferation Treaty (NPT) and announcement that it had a nuclear deterrent.

ROK. The ROK still faces a conventional military threat from the North, but the ROK attitude towards the DPRK has shifted since the mid-1990s. The conventional threat is seen as more manageable; the engagement policies pursued since 1997 have de-demonised the North, whose people are now seen as human beings and compatriots, while the evidence of the DPRK's overall economic decline indicates that while vigilance is still required, the ROK would be the likely victor in any conflict. Many also believe that US and ROK interests are diverging, and fear that the US approach to the DPRK ignores the possible negative consequences for the ROK of a hard line negotiating position. Not surprisingly, therefore, ROK officials indicated that they did not believe that the DPRK was currently engaged in counterfeiting or money laundering, whatever might have happened in the past. The failure of the US Treasury to provide any public evidence to back up the charges added to this scepticism.

The ROK thus continued to develop links across the Demilitarized Zone (DMZ). From the president downwards, ROK officials stressed the need to improve North-South relations. Food and fertiliser aid flowed north, and work continued in the Kaesŏng economic zone; ROK officials, who hoped to have goods produced there counted as ROK goods in the ROK-US Free Trade Agreement under negotiation, were pleased that a delegation of US Congressional aides visited the zone in April. In May, the then ROK Minister for Unification Lee Jong-seok visited Kaesŏng. Red Cross talks, covering people missing from the Korean War, took place in Mount Kŭmgang in February; the issue was taken up at the eighteenth North-South ministerial meeting in Pyongyang in April. The fourth video reunion for separated families and the thirteenth and fourteenth family reunion took place in February. There was another family reunion in May. To facilitate cross-DMZ movement, two checkpoints, one in the east and one in the west began to function in March 2006. Talks began aimed at facilitating the testing of the cross-border railway. May saw the opening of the first ever exhibition of historical and artistic objects ranging from the Bronze Age to the Chosŏn dynasty (1392-1910) from DPRK collections to be held in the ROK. The exhibition opened at the new National Museum in Seoul and was scheduled to move to Taegu from August to October. Former President Kim Dae-jung made it known that he would consider going north, possibly by train.

As usual, even when relations seemed good, not all went smoothly. A DPRK attempt to censor ROK reporting from the Red Cross talks led ROK journalists across the political spectrum to withdraw from Mount Kŭmgang in March. May saw the first references in international commentaries to DPRK preparatory moves for missile tests, and there were signs of strains in North-South relations. The DPRK was not pleased when the ROK was officially represented for the first time at a conference on DPRK human rights held in Norway in early May. One of those attending the family reunion meeting at the end of May was Kim Young Nam, a South Korean who, it was claimed, had been abducted in the 1970s and who later became the husband of a Japanese abductee, Megumi Yokota. Kim maintained that he had not been abducted and repeated the claim that Yokota had committed suicide in 1994. He also said that their daughter did not wish to go to Japan. This aroused much hostility in both the ROK and Japan. North-South military talks held at the end of May to discuss a proposed test run of the cross-DMZ railway ended without agreement. The DPRK military issued a statement blaming the ROK for the failure, arguing that the southern side had refused to discuss issues such as the maritime boundary, and had insisted on concentrating on the western crossing, ignoring the DPRK wish to discuss the eastern crossing. There were references to 'some people' suggesting that they might travel on the train—presumably Kim Dae-jung[2], complaints that Kaesŏng was not completed and a warning that 'Our army will keep a sharp eye on the activities that the south side will adopt in future' (Korean Central News Agency, 27 May 2006).

2 NORTH KOREAN MISSILE TESTS

During June 2006, preparations for a DPRK missile launch became steadily more obvious. The ROK condemned these moves, as did many other countries, and warned that a missile launch would adversely affect North-South relations, including the delivery of food and fertilisers. Despite the concerns over a missile launch, the two sides continued to discuss economic co-operation and there were joint ceremonies on 15 June to mark the sixth anniversary of the summit meeting between Kim Dae-jung and the DPRK's Kim Jong Il.

---

[2] In the event, Kim Dae-jung abandoned his plan to visit the North because of the possible effect on ROK local elections.

On 5 July, the DPRK fired a series of missiles, apparently with mixed results. The ROK joined in the international condemnation that followed, and announced that humanitarian aid to the DPRK would stop. A DPRK proposal for talks on 7 July was rejected. The DPRK retaliated, halting work on a building dedicated to family reunion meetings in Mount Kŭmgang and cancelling planned reunions, while the DPRK side walked out of cabinet-level talks with the ROK. At the same time, neither side wished to break off all contact. Private humanitarian aid and what were described as private commercial contacts were not affected, thus allowing both the tourist visits to Mount Kŭmgang and work at Kaesŏng to continue. Various reports indicated, however, that visitors to Mount Kŭmgang were well down on previous years, an indication that ordinary South Koreans were concerned for their safety and the possible international action against the DPRK.

But the ROK was clearly ambivalent on the issue. The DPRK's actions were not illegal, even though they had been condemned by United Nations Security Council Resolution 1695 on 15 July 2006, since it had not signed up to any of the conventions restricting missile testing. The ROK government made it clear that it did not like the way in which the Japanese government led demands for tough sanctions at the UN; President Roh indicated that 'excessive responses' would not help to solve the problem, while Unification Minister Lee Jong-seok noted that the resolution did not prevent ordinary trading contacts, and therefore the government had no reason to intervene. Engagement would still continue, even if such an attitude was not welcomed by the US and Japan.

In August, the DPRK reported that parts of the country had been hit by heavy floods, which had killed over 500 people, left many missing, and had caused widespread devastation. The Arirang Mass Games were cancelled, as were the proposed joint North-South events marking independence day on 15 August, and the DPRK appealed for assistance. (See also the section on domestic developments in North Korea, 4.4.) The ROK responded, making US$10.5 million available to NGOs and also contributing official aid supplies via the ROK Red Cross. While other countries increased their sanctions on the DPRK, for the ROK it looked increasingly like business as usual.

3 NORTH KOREA'S NUCLEAR TEST

Before long, however, there was another issue. Press reports in August indicated that the DPRK was engaged in unusual activity around a military site which was widely interpreted as preparatory to a nuclear test; hitherto, although the DPRK had claimed since 2003 to have a nuclear deterrent, no nuclear test had ever been detected. Once again, there was widespread international condemnation of the DPRK, in which the ROK joined, warning that such a move would have serious adverse effects on North-South relations. As the crisis deepened, the two sides held military talks at colonel level on 2 October, the first since May. During the talks, the DPRK officers demanded a halt to what was described as an anti-DPRK propaganda campaign by conservative groups in the south. The talks broke up without agreement and without setting a date for their resumption.

Meanwhile, the DPRK rejected all criticism, blaming the US for instigating a crisis as it had done in July, and then on 3 October announced that it would carry out a test on an unspecified date, in conditions in which safety would be 'firmly guaranteed'. This development worried the ROK, but even now, President Roh urged that there should be no hasty reaction to the DPRK threat. On 9 October, despite a strongly worded statement UN Security Council issued three days earlier that 'deplored' the DPRK's move, some form of test was carried out. On 14 October, the UN Security Council unanimously passed Resolution 1718. The resolution condemned the DPRK's action, and called for a ban on the supply of conventional arms, nuclear-related materials, and luxury goods to the DPRK, inspection of DPRK ships, freezing of financial assets relating to weapons of mass destruction, and a travel ban on DPRK officials connected with the nuclear programme.

The ROK joined in the condemnation of the DPRK, describing the nuclear test as 'outright defiance' of the earlier Resolution 1695 after the missile tests, and noting that the tests meant that the DPRK had failed to meet its obligations under the 19 September 2005 agreement and the 1992 North-South Agreement on the Denuclearisation of the peninsula. The ROK also pledged to fully support Resolution 1718 and announced that bilateral co-operation would stop. The aid promised in August was halted.

Once again, however, the ROK made it clear that neither the Mount Kŭmgang tours nor the Kaesŏng project[3] would be halted, despite US calls for such a move, and that ordinary trade would be allowed. The work of ROK NGOs in the DPRK, some of it supported by the government would go on. The chair of the ROK National Assembly Unification Committee, the Uri party's Kim Won-wang also indicated that the ROK would not take part in the 'Proliferation Security Initiative' (PSI)[4], which required the searching of DPRK ships. (China adopted a similar position, and Russia too was ambivalent.) Later, the government argued that attempts to enforce the PSI near Korean waters might lead to armed clashes between the two countries. The most that the ROK government was prepared to do was to send observers to PSI-related meetings. Even that provoked DPRK condemnation.

Like the ROK, China, while expressing concern at the DPRK's action, maintained that the best way to resolve the problem would be to resume the stalled Six Party Talks, and worked hard to bring this about. On 31 October, the DPRK agreed to return to the talks, to the relief of the ROK government. The ROK government was also pleased with an apparent modification in US policy, following the Republicans' loss of control of Congress and the departure of Secretary of Defence Donald Rumsfield. The US also found the members, including the ROK, of the Asia-Pacific Economic Co-operation Pact unwilling to contemplate tougher measures against the DPRK at their summit meeting in mid-November. It was hoped that a new US willingness to engage might lead to progress.

Although the ROK welcomed the resumption of the Six Party Talks, there was no immediate return to the status quo. Some saw a harder ROK line emerging. Figures released by Hyundai Asan, the company that runs the tours, showed that travellers to Mount Kŭmgang fell back from a peak of 300,000 in 2005 to under 250,000

---

[3] In the midst of the lead-in to the crisis over the nuclear test, it was announced that the first goods manufactured in the Kaesŏng zone, some 40,000 pieces of underwear, had been shipped to the ROK on 29 September, in fact, some goods had been shipped earlier, but these were from the main complex. By the end of 2006, there were some 10,000 DPRK workers at Kaesŏng, employed by 15 ROK small and medium enterprises.

[4] The PSI developed from the US government's 'National Strategy to Combat Weapons of Mass Destruction' launched in 2002, and was formally announced in May 2003. It was always heavily targeted at the DPRK—see Mark J Valencia, *The Proliferation Security Initiative: Making Waves in Asia*, (London and New York: Routledge for the International Institute for Strategic Studies, 2005), pp. 25-6. PSI is disliked by a number of countries, including China and Russia.

in 2006—even the 2005 figure was well short of the target of 400,000. In the light of the continued nuclear stand-off, a recovery seemed unlikely. The Ministry of Unification and the Uri party announced on 14 November that the budget for inter-Korean co-operation for 2007 would be cut by 26 percent to US$1.95 billion. On closer examination, much of the 'cut' resulted from the demise of the Korean Peninsula Energy Organisation (KEDO)[5], which had finally closed down at the end of May 2006. When KEDO-related items were stripped out, the remaining budget was only 3.5% percent lower than the previous year. If this was a slap on the DPRK's wrist, it was a very minor one, and the DPRK seems to have ignored it. A more telling figure was that inter-Korean trade, despite all the problems, reached US$1.5 billion (or US$1.3 billion according to another source) in 2006, almost 30 percent up on the previous year. A higher proportion of this, some US$92.8 million, was real trade rather than aid disguised as trade as in the past.

But the ROK decision to support for the first time a UN General Assembly Resolution proposed by the European Union which condemned North Korea's human rights' record did indicate annoyance with the DPRK. And at the end of the year, the biennial defence White Paper raised the Ministry of Defence's assessment of the threat from the North from the 'direct military threat' of 2004, to a 'grave (or serious) threat'.[6] That, plus an unconfirmed report in the *JoongAng Ilbo* that the ROK was developing a 500km-range cruise missile, indicated that the ROK military had not lost their suspicions of the DPRK. There were perhaps similar suspicions in the National Intelligence Service, which led to spying charges against five members, including the vice secretary-general, of the small Democratic Labour Party in December. The charges, which alleged that the group were members of a secret pro-DPRK organisation, were reminiscent of those brought in the past against those a regime did not like.

There was another set of signals, however, pointing in the opposite direction. At the end of the year, President Roh had to find a new for-

---

[5] KEDO was established following the signing of the 1994 'Agreed Framework', which had ended the first DPRK nuclear crisis, in order to finance and set up the two light water reactors promised to the DPRK in the agreement. The agreement had never been popular with US neo-conservatives and the Bush administration worked hard to end it after 2001.

[6] Before 2004, the DPRK had been described as the 'main enemy' of the ROK, so that even the new formula was seen as marginally less hostile than in the past.

eign minister when the incumbent, Ban Ki-moon, was elected UN secretary-general. The new minister, Song Min-soon, a career diplomat who had been vice-minister of foreign affairs, was seen as committed to continued engagement. So too was the new unification minister, Lee Jong-seok, the third unification minister in the year, and a somewhat surprising choice in that he had held no other government post. An ordained Anglican priest turned politician, he had been jailed in 2002 for raising what were deemed to be illegal funds for Roh's presidential campaign. But he was sound on engagement. So too was the new head of the National Intelligence Service, appointed in December. All these appointments were heavily criticised by the opposition and the conservative press, both of which continued to attack engagement, although without offering any real alternative policy.

4 RETURN TO THE SIX PARTY TALKS

The Six Party Talks reconvened in December, but broke up without agreement. However, the new US approach included a willingness to talk directly to the DPRK in certain circumstances and there were early signs that some form of a deal was likely. At first, the ROK was cautious. On 8 January 2007, the unification minister said that there would only be a resumption of humanitarian aid to the DPRK if there was a breakthrough in the Six Party Talks. That same month, the Unification Ministry announced that it would receive new applications from companies that wished to open in Kaesŏng, which was perhaps a sign that it expected relations to improve.

There was however, little movement and much sniping in the North-South relationship until it became clear that there was an apparent breakthrough in the Six Party Talks as a result of direct US-DPRK contacts. This was formally signalled in the agreement of 13 February 2007, under which the DPRK would close down its nuclear plant at Yŏnbyŏn and allow International Atomic Energy Authority (IAEA) inspectors back in to monitor and verify this process. In return, the US would take measure to free DPRK funds blocked since September 2005, five working groups would be established to examine US-DPRK relations, Japan-DPRK relations, energy and economic aid, armistice and security issues, and denuclearisation of the Korean peninsula. In addition, 50,000 tonnes of heavy fuel oil would be supplied within sixty days as emergency energy assistance. The North had already signalled its willingness to resume North-South contacts, but there had been no ROK response. In February however, the situation changed. There were inconclusive talks on a joint Olympic team, but the atmosphere was much improved from earlier meetings.

More substantive talks began at the twentieth cabinet-level meeting between the two sides held in Pyongyang from 27 February. The ROK, while indicating that it would be willing to resume aid, made it clear that such resumption would be tied in with the DPRK's adherence to the 13 February agreement. However, there was early consensus that discussions on family reunions and the cross-border railways should resume, and eventually it was agreed to move forward on a number of points, including joint celebrations to mark a number of anniversaries. Despite DPRK complaints about delays in releasing its blocked funds, and over regular US-ROK military exercises at the end of March, on the grounds that 'dialogue and sabre rattling cannot go together', by April 2007, the North-South atmosphere was definitely better than it had been for most of the previous year.

FOREIGN RELATIONS OF THE TWO KOREAS 2006-2007

James E. Hoare

INTRODUCTION

Inevitably, issues relating to the decisions by the Democratic People's Republic of Korea (DPRK, North Korea) to test a series of missiles in July 2006, and then to conduct a nuclear test in October 2006[1] dominated the international activities of both the DPRK and the Republic of Korea (ROK, South Korea) during the period under review. The DPRK's ability to escape from isolation and tap into foreign assistance was severely handicapped by these two decisions, while the ROK struggled hard to maintain its policy of engagement in the face of widespread international condemnation of the DPRK's actions. An apparent breakthrough in February 2007 on the nuclear issue raised expectations in both countries of a more favourable international environment in 2007-08.

1 REPUBLIC OF KOREA

1.1 *Relations with the United States*

The DPRK apart, relations with the US have been at the heart of the ROK's foreign policy since independence in 1948. The two countries have a mutual defence treaty dating from 1954, there is a large US military presence in the ROK, and there is close integration between the armed forces. Economic ties are strong, and many South Koreans have been educated in the US. The ROK has provided the third largest contingent of forces to Iraq, after the US and the United Kingdom. The relationship has not been without tensions, even when at its best, and in recent years, these tensions have been somewhat more promi-

---

[1] See the survey article by Rüdiger Frank in this volume.

nent. Although the US has generally declined contact with the DPRK, arguing that it was for the two Koreas to sort out their problems, both the George Bush Snr and Bill Clinton administrations did have direct contact with the DPRK, a development that worried some in the ROK since it seemed to exclude the latter from issues that mattered to it. At the same time, however, the Clinton administration supported former ROK President Kim Dae-jung's engagement policy towards the DPRK. The elections of George W. Bush as US president in 2000 and of Roh Moo-hyun in the ROK in 2002 have seen the relationship become more polarised. The Bush administration disliked the 1994 Agreed Framework that had capped the DPRK's nuclear facilities at Yŏngbyŏn, and was sceptical about the ROK's engagement policy. The ROK, for its part, had no wish to see a nuclear North Korea, but also believed that as the country most likely to suffer if there was a conflict on the Korean peninsula, its interests would be better served by continuing engagement with the DPRK rather than increasing the latter's isolation and hostility. This divergence of views has affected many areas of US-ROK relations, even when those did not at first sight bear directly on ROK-DPRK matters. Some continued to detect a basic anti-American attitude in Roh and his advisers; in particular, Song Min-soon, who was chief presidential adviser for security before becoming minister for foreign affairs and trade at the end of 2006, made some sharp comments about the US being warlike at a seminar that led to opposition outcry and claims that he was damaging the ROK's most important relationship.

Formally, ROK-US relations are good, as emphasised by President Roh's visit to Washington in September 2006. The two presidents reaffirmed the strength of the alliance, and their commitment to the Six Party Talks' process on the DPRK's nuclear programme. President Roh pledged continued ROK support for the 'war on terror', while President Bush thanked Roh for the ROK's continued support in Iraq. Both promised to work together to solve two issues under negotiation: the ROK's desire to resume wartime control of its armed forces, and the conclusion of a joint free trade agreement (FTA). But it was clear that there were differences between the two sides, especially on the issue of the DPRK. The US wanted the ROK to go further in support of sanctions against the DPRK in the wake of the 5 July missile tests, but this was a step too far for the ROK. By the end of 2006, it was also clear that while the ROK would continue to support the US on Iraq issues, ROK forces were likely to be withdrawn during 2007.

Some dissatisfaction lingered over what was seen as the US's continued failure to acknowledge properly the ROK's contribution to Iraq, compared with the profuse thanks to Japan and other countries that had sent fewer troops.

The issue of the wartime control of ROK forces came into sharp focus in 2006. The ROK had first passed control over its forces to the US side during the Korean War (1950-53). The position had been further consolidated in the 1978 Combined Forces Command, a move that had aroused domestic and international concerns at the time. Attempts to end what was seen as derogation from sovereignty began in 1990 under President Roh Tae-woo, and peacetime command was restored to ROK forces in 1994 under President Kim Young-sam. The next logical step was the restoration of wartime control, a policy advocated by the both the Roh Tae-woo and the Kim Young-sam governments, and this the Roh administration has pursued despite much domestic opposition. Although this opposition by conservative politicians and former generals was very vocal, the US government was also keen on such a move. It would reduce hostility to the continued presence of US forces in the ROK, and it also fitted in with developments in military thinking.

Negotiations centred on the timing of the proposed move. The ROK argued for 2012, on the grounds that by then ROK forces would be fully prepared (the opposition suggested 2015 or 2020 would be better), while in August 2006, then US Defence Secretary Donald Rumsfeld sent a letter to his ROK counterpart suggesting that control should pass to the ROK in 2009. Some in the ROK saw the Rumsfeld proposal as 'punishing' the ROK for pressing the issue, but it may also have reflected US military assessments of the readiness of the ROK forces. In the event, Rumsfeld's departure from office in the wake of the US autumn 2006 Congressional elections may have modified the US position, and in late February 2007, the two sides signed an agreement in Washington under which wartime control of ROK forces would be gradually transferred from the US commander-in-chief, with the process ending on 17 April 2012. The Combined Forces Command would be dissolved at the same time.

The redeployment of US forces from the Yongsan base in central Seoul to the town of P'yŏngt'aek, south of the capital, which is already a major centre for the US military, also caused problems during the year. The move, planned to be completed in 2008, would free up much-needed space in Seoul, and would also allow a more rapid redeployment of US forces elsewhere if required. To provide for the proposed expansion at P'yŏngt'aek, the ROK government compulsorily acquired large amounts of farmland. This led to violent protests in May 2006 that delayed implementation of the planned move, which now may not take place until 2013. US forces in Korea have expressed concern at the delay, and insisted that the move should go ahead. A somewhat unfortunate remark by General Burwell W. Bell, the US commander-in-chief, to the effect that he would fight any attempt at postponement, also helped fuel the protests, and the ROK government conceded that a move by 2008 would be difficult. On a more positive note, the two sides reached agreement in December 2006 for a 6.6 percent increase in the ROK contribution for the following two years towards the cost of keeping US forces in the ROK. At the working level, relations between the two military structures also remained good, and a number of joint exercises were conducted as usual, despite the also usual objections from the DPRK.

Trade relations also caused tensions. Scrapping continued over market access. The Lone Star case returned to the ROK courts, reviving expatriate concerns about anti-foreign discrimination.[2] Following an agreement signed in January 2006, imports of US-produced beef resumed in early September after a three-year gap, only to be partially suspended again in November, when pieces of bone were found in one shipment. Most difficult of all were the US-ROK free trade agreement negotiations. These continued all through the period, with tough talking on both sides and against a backdrop of highly vocal and occasionally violent ROK demonstrations. Farmers defending their rice and large conglomerates defending their selling practices in the US market formed an unusual alliance against the negotiations. The two sides were negotiating against a strict timetable with a target date for agreement of 2 April 2007, so that US President Bush would be able to notify Congress of his intention to sign such a deal, but it was clear that there were many sticking points in areas such as intellectual property rights, financial services and rules of origin,[3] farm products and cars. The ROK negotiators accepted that there would have to be some give, especially when the radical *Hankyoreh Shinmun* published de-

---

[2] For background to the Lone Star case, see the article by James C. Schopf in this volume.

[3] The ROK wanted goods produced in the Kaesŏng special zone counted as being of ROK origin. Since Kaesŏng is in the DPRK, the US was not willing to accept this, and the issue was postponed for further consideration.

tails of their negotiating strategy in January 2007. With some fudging on sensitive issues, agreement was reached by the deadline to expressions of mutual satisfaction, including the expectation that two-way trade might rise by as much as twenty percent. It was clear, however, that there would be further negotiations before the new agreement could be ratified.

1.2 Relations with the People's Republic of China

Relations with the PRC produced no surprises. There were some desultory exchanges about alleged Chinese 'falsification' of history but these were less intense than in earlier years. The two countries continued to work closely on matters relating to the DPRK. President Roh visited the PRC in October 2006, soon after the DPRK's nuclear test. Roh and PRC President Hu Jintao expressed support for the UN Security Council resolutions of July and October on the DPRK's missile and nuclear tests, but agreed that the DPRK should not be isolated. They also indicated that their implementation of UN-imposed sanctions would be rather more limited than either the US or Japan would like. A further sign of good relations was talks between military representatives held in Seoul in January 2007, at which the two sides pledged to improve their military ties. More generally, anti-Japanese sentiments also provided common ground, both in relation to the DPRK and in wider concerns about Japanese politicians' wish to revise the constitution.

Trade continued to grow, reaching almost US$130 billion, up some twenty percent on 2005, and the possibility of a free trade agreement with the PRC was mooted.

1.3 Relations with Japan

The departure of Prime Minister Jun'ichirō Koizumi in September 2006 was welcomed by many in the ROK. Koizumi's insistence on actions such as visiting Tokyo's Yasukuni Shrine on 15 August 2006,[4]

---

[4] Tokyo's Yasukuni Shrine enshrines the spirits of all Japanese who have died in Japan's wars from 1868 to 1945, including those executed as war criminals after World War II.

the long-running dispute over the East Sea/Sea of Japan issue, and the equally long-running conflicting claims to the Tokdo/Takeshima/ Liancourt Rocks outcrop, had led to a souring of relations. The steadily hardening Japanese approach to the DPRK, shown by the call for very tough sanctions after the 4 July 2006 missile test, also caused anger in the ROK, and there were hopes that a new prime minister would lead to an improvement.

There were some signs of a possible better relationship. The two sides agreed to conduct a joint search exercise in September 2006 near the disputed islands in connection with Soviet-era dumping of nuclear waste. In January 2007, when leaders of China, Japan and the ROK met in Indonesia, there was even talk of a possible three-way free trade agreement, and the following month, the ROK defence minister made the first visit at that level to Tokyo since November 2003. But there was continued ROK wariness about Japan. The ROK minister for culture and tourism announced just before Koizumi stepped down that there would be no further relaxation of the rules on Japanese cultural manifestations; most restrictions had been relaxed in the 1990s, but it was still too soon to allow Japanese cartoons and TV shows.

Koizumi's successor, Shinzō Abe, was hardly an unknown quantity. He had built up his political position in recent years on the basis of hostility to the DPRK and a wish to see an end to the constitutional restrictions on Japan's armed forces, and as soon as he took office on 26 September, Ban Ki-moon, the ROK foreign and trade minister, called on him to 'squarely face up to history'. The hard Japanese line following the DPRK's October nuclear test did not improve matters, and neither did the Japanese view that the question of DPRK-abducted Japanese should be raised in the Six Party Talks, which the ROK preferred should concentrate on the nuclear issue. Indeed, President Roh specifically mentioned this in his New Year address, noting while he understood Japanese feelings on the abduction issue, Japan should concentrate on the main point. For good measure, Roh warned that Abe should not visit Yasukuni. Historical issues would not go away, however. In early March 2007, Abe, in response to questions in the Japanese Diet, appeared to contemplate withdrawing the 1993 cabinet secretary statement that had acknowledged Japanese government responsibility for the 'comfort women' system.[5] There was some at-

---

[5] 'Comfort women' is a euphemism to describe women and girls forced or persuaded into officially sanctioned brothels for the Japanese military from the 1930s

tempt at retraction, but when the Japanese and ROK foreign ministers met on Cheju island at the end of March, Song Min-soon told his Japanese counterpart that Japan should take full responsibility for its history.

1.4 Other international issues

Free trade agreements also feature in ROK relations with a number of other countries, without the problems that marked ROK-US negotiations, to the chagrin of some American commentators who feel that the opposition to the US-ROK free trade agreement is motivated by more than economic concerns. The ROK has concluded such agreements with a number of countries since the first such pact with Chile in 2004. Agreement was reached with the Association of Southeast Asian Nations (ASEAN), except for Thailand, in August; the ROK was not prepared to open its rice market to the Thais, but officials said that they expected that the new agreement would eventually extend to Thailand. Discussions were under way with Canada, and began with the European Union; the latter is already the second largest market for ROK goods, ahead of the US but after the PRC.

The need to guarantee energy supplies featured prominently in international activity; Korea Gas is the world's largest purchaser of natural gas, and agreement was reached with Qatar in November 2006 to increase the amount supplied. The same month also saw an agreement with Nigeria, under which the ROK will supply US$10 billion for railway construction in return for oil. The ROK and Indonesia agreed on closer energy/economic ties during President Roh's December 2006 visit. Energy matters are an additional factor for ROK interest in Iraq; Iraq re-opened its embassy in Seoul on 4 January 2007, thirteen years after it was closed following the first Gulf War. Energy issues also featured prominently in relations with Russia, and trade is also rising, albeit slowly.

President Roh had a busy year travelling. His visits included India, Cambodia, Australia and Indonesia. At the Asia-Europe Meeting (ASEM) summit in Helsinki in September, he proposed the establishment of a North East Asia Security System, but the proposal made

---

onwards. They came from most parts of the Japanese wartime empire, but the majority were Korean.

little impact. The ROK held talks on military co-operation with Israel in Tel Aviv in January 2007.

In October 2006, Ban Ki-moon, then foreign and trade minister, was elected to succeed Kofi Annan as UN secretary-general, and he took over the portfolio on 1 January 2007. This international recognition was much welcomed in the ROK. While paying tribute to his predecessor, the new secretary-general promised to undertake a thorough reform of the UN system. Ban had been an effective foreign minister but was relatively little known outside the ROK, and seemed to be slow in taking up his new role. There was some speculation that he might find it difficult to tackle DPRK issues, widely regarded as one of the most difficult tasks that he would face.

2 Democratic People's Republic of Korea

2.1 Six Party Talks and relations with the US

During 2006-07, the consequences of US economic controls imposed in 2005, missile tests in July 2006 and a nuclear test in October 2006 dominated the DPRK's relations with the rest of the world. The 2005 US allegations over alleged DPRK money laundering and counterfeiting of US currency, which lay behind the 2005 controls and which led to the freezing of DPRK-related accounts in the Macau-based Banco Delta Asia (BDA), halted all progress on the September 2005 agreement that had been reached in the Six Party Talks. The DPRK refused to cap its nuclear programme or to return to the Non-proliferation Treaty while these controls remained in place. The US, for its part, argued that once the Treasury investigation had begun, it had to run its course, which it proceeded to do, very slowly. Not only did the US action freeze DPRK government funds but it also hit Western businesses that operated in the DPRK, which used the same bank to transfer funds. For the DPRK, the affront probably was less in the amount of money involved than in the affront to its state sovereignty in the US action. One of its constant complaints was that the US refused to deal with it as a normal state, and here was another example of such an action.

DPRK verbal protests having produced no effect, the DPRK may well have sought to put pressure on the US by its missile tests in July. The tests themselves may have had a military purpose, and DPRK statements stressed that nobody would now dare attack the country. But they also appeared to express DPRK frustration at the refusal of the US to modify its position. The immediate result, however, was widespread condemnation, with even the PRC and the ROK joining in, though it soon became apparent that neither country intended the DPRK to be forced into a corner, a position also adopted by Russia. Yet still there was no change in the US position and the DPRK's funds remained frozen. The DPRK's next move, the 9 October nuclear test, produced similar wide-scale condemnation at the UN, but again, the PRC, Russia and the ROK, while supporting UN Security Council Resolution 1718 passed on 14 October 2006, again indicated that they were not prepared to follow the hard-line policies favoured by the US and Japan. A month later at the Asia Pacific Economic Cooperation (APEC) summit, US President Bush found a general unwillingness to condemn the DPRK's actions. The DPRK dismissed all criticism of both the missile and the nuclear tests in its usual strident manner, but at the same time indicated that a resolution of the frozen funds issue could lead to progress in other areas.

This relative lack of support, together with Republican loss of control over Congress, problems in Iraq and the departure of US Secretary of Defence Donald Rumsfeld, may have led to a reconsideration of US tactics towards the DPRK. There was pressure from both the PRC and the ROK for a more accommodating US approach. At first, the Six Party Talks, resumed in December in Beijing, seemed to make no progress. However, when the US and DPRK chief negotiators, Christopher Hill and Kim Kye Gwan, met in Berlin in January 2007, there seems to have been enough flexibility on both sides for an agreement to be reached at the reconvened Six Party Talks held in Beijing in February. The agreement was facilitated by separate talks between US Treasury officials and DPRK representatives, which appeared to pave the way for the freeing of the blocked funds. While the US refused to withdraw the claims about money-laundering and counterfeiting, it agreed that the funds blocked in the BDA could be released to another bank for onward transmission to the DPRK government,[6] for humanitarian and educational purposes. This caveat caused concern among the foreign businesses whose funds formed part of the US$25 million

---

[6] Some commentators speculated that the US authorities could not in fact assemble enough evidence to prove in a US court the charges against the DPRK.

frozen funds, but neither the US nor the DPRK paid much attention to complaints on the score.

The 13 February agreement[7] was complex and demanded fast action for it to be effective. Not only were the BDA funds to be released, and the DPRK's nuclear facilities at Yŏngbyŏn closed down, but a series of subcommittees were to set about solving issues such as the normalisation of relations with Japan and the US, all within sixty days. The US administration also faced much criticism for having 'rewarded' DPRK bad behaviour; John Bolton, former US ambassador to the UN, was particularly fierce in his condemnation of the new agreement, partly because while it capped the Yŏngbyŏn programme, it did not address the other nuclear issues, such as the question of a highly enriched uranium programme (which had began the current nuclear crisis in 2002), and what would happen to such nuclear weapons as the DPRK might have already constructed. Senior members of the administration, including both the president and Dr Rice, the Secretary of State, were dismissive, while a series of newspaper articles, presumably based on briefing from within the administration, implied that perhaps a mistake had been made in 2002, and that there was in fact no DPRK highly enriched uranium programme. The administration also played down newspaper reports of nuclear links between the DPRK and Iran.

After the 13 February agreement, there was some movement. The DPRK invited International Atomic Energy Agency (IAEA) inspectors back for the first time since 2003 and some of the subcommittees met. But difficulties soon emerged. Talks on the normalisation of relations with Japan and the US began; those with Japan lasted only a day. The chief DPRK negotiator, Kim Kye Gwan, gave a talk at Stanford University in February, and then went to New York for talks with Christopher Hill. Little progress was made and it was soon clear that the BDA blocked funds would cause problems. Although the DPRK repeatedly said that release of the funds was essential for progress, no funds were released; banks doing business with the BDA would fall foul of Section 311 of the US 2001 Patriot Act, and would not be allowed to do business in the US or with US banks. By the end of March 2007, it was increasingly likely that there would be no solution

---

[7] The agreement's provisions are summarised in the preceding survey article on relations between the two Koreas.

to this problem by the time the DPRK was due to cap its Yŏngbyŏn programme in mid-April.

2.2 Relations with the PRC

The PRC continued to be the main supporter of the DPRK during the period, supplying both food and fuel oil, but the relationship came under severe strain in the wake of the missile and nuclear tests. Chinese leaders had called on the DPRK not to conduct either test and expressed anger when the DPRK ignored them The PRC supported the July and October Security Council resolutions. There were even unverified reports that the Bank of China, taking a leaf from the US book, had frozen some DPRK bank accounts in August as a means of bringing pressure. But the PRC, while working behind the scenes to persuade the DPRK to return to the Six Party Talks, argued that sanctions should not be an end in themselves but should aim at getting the DPRK back to the negotiating table, and that the US needed to show some flexibility.

These were not entirely altruistic moves. The PRC is concerned that unrest on the Korean peninsula would have an adverse effect on its north-eastern provinces and their ethnic Korean minority; this also partly explains its unwillingness to encourage cross-border migration into these areas from the DPRK, and its willingness to return those who cross, despite growing international criticism of this policy.[8] The PRC fears that increasing the DPRK's isolation, which is one effect of punitive sanctions, would increase the volatility of the situation on the peninsula.

The PRC was not only the main supplier of aid to the DPRK but is also its main trading partner. Despite the many difficulties of doing business in the DPRK, a growing number of Chinese businesses have established links there in recent years, and there is an increasing Chinese business presence in the country. The DPRK is also a popular destination for Chinese tourists. These developments, together with the quarrel with the PRC over historical claims, which the DPRK shares with the ROK, have led commentators to argue that the PRC's long-term aim is to absorb the DPRK or at least part of it into China.

---

[8] See the article by Peter Beck et al. in this volume.

Although the PRC undoubtedly wants a compliant neighbour, it seems unlikely that it would seek to incorporate more minorities.

2.3 Relations with Japan

The DPRK cannot have expected much change in Japan's policy following the departure of Prime Minister Koizumi, since his successor was a well-known hawk on the abduction and other issues. Japan led the way in the call for sanctions after both the missile and nuclear tests, and when its original proposals were watered down, imposed tough sanctions of its own. The Japanese kept up pressure on Ch'ongnyŏn (Chōsen sōren), the pro-DPRK association of Koreans in Japan. The DPRK responded with denunciations and protests. When agreement emerged on resuming the Six Party Talks, the DPRK argued for a time that Japan was not fit to attend, an argument ignored by the other participants. Even after the 13 February agreement, Japanese leaders insisted that they would maintain their full range of sanctions and would not contribute to the proposed funding of new energy supplies for the DPRK, unless the abduction issue was resolved. The ROK denounced the Japanese position publicly; other members of the Six Party Talks were willing to do so in private, but to little effect. It was no surprise, therefore, when the talks on DPRK-Japan normalisation got nowhere.

2.4 Relations with Russia

The steady improvement in DPRK-Russian relations that began in the late 1990s continued, perhaps symbolised by the opening of an Orthodox church in Pyongyang in the course of the year. Russia tended to side with the PRC and the ROK in calling for a modification of US and Japanese policy towards the DPRK. Economic and technical co-operation was set to increase, and the first meeting since 2000 of the intergovernmental committee set up to foster this took place in late March 2007; the Russians said that there would never be such a long delay again. In January 2007, talks resumed—they were broken off in 2002—on the DPRK's Soviet-era debt; the DPRK apparently hoped that Russia would cancel the US$8.8 billion debt outright. There is also Russian interest in rehabilitating the DPRK railway system and supplying energy, but the Russians have problems over financing such programmes.

2.5 *Other relations*

Continued confrontation over the nuclear issue has affected the DPRK's relations with many countries, and there has been a major reduction in aid and contacts. Concern about human rights again led to condemnation at the UN Human Rights Commission in autumn 2006; for the first time, the ROK supported the European Union-sponsored motion. Heavy flooding in July and August 2006 led to the DPRK cancelling both the Arirang Mass Games, which it had hoped would be a major tourist attraction, and North-South joint celebrations to mark Liberation Day on 15 August. The floods prompted a modest reversal of the DPRK's position, adopted in 2005, of cutting back on international humanitarian aid in favour of development aid. The World Food Programme (WFP) was allowed to resume some operations, although on a smaller scale than before, and the International Red Cross also agreed to provide aid. The WFP appealed for US$102 million but only a fraction of this was forthcoming. In late autumn 2006, claims began to appear in the US press that the UN Development Programme (UNDP), which had operated in the DPRK since 1979, had broken UN rules on payments and staffing by making payments to the DPRK government in hard currency and accepting DPRK seconded staff in its offices.[9] The sums were relatively small, just under US$28 million between 1997 and 2006, but were described as being on a par with those that had gone missing in the Iraq 'food for oil' scandal. The UN investigated, concluding that normal procedures were followed as far as possible, and that monies passed to the DPRK could be accounted for. The DPRK refused to change its practices and suspended contacts with UNDP in March 2007.

---

[9] As in other Communist countries until very recently, the DPRK had insisted that foreign organisations including embassies and aid agencies should pay all bills in hard currency, and should only employ staff supplied through government agencies. These staff were not paid directly. What UNDP was doing in the DPRK was similar to what embassies, including both the US and the British, and aid agencies had done in many countries in the past, and the system survived in Vietnam and in the PRC until the mid-1990s.

Paek Nam Sun, the then DPRK foreign minister, went to the ASEAN Regional Forum Meeting in Bangkok in July 2006, but the DPRK was unhappy with the condemnation of its missile test. The nominal head of state, Kim Young Nam, attended the 14th Non-Aligned Movement (NAM) meeting in Havana in September, where he argued for a strengthening of the movement. Foreign Minister Paek died on 2 January 2007. He had been ill for some years, and real power in the ministry had long rested with a number of vice-ministers including Kang Sok Ju and Kim Kye Gwan. In any case, the Foreign Ministry is an executive body; major foreign policy decisions are made elsewhere.

ONLINE GRASSROOTS JOURNALISM AND PARTICIPATORY DEMOCRACY IN SOUTH KOREA

Ronda Hauben

ABSTRACT

This article explores how grassroots journalism and online participation embody the ideals of participatory democracy in the South Korean context. Since 2000, online alternative media in Korea have played a pivotal role in many political events including the 2002 candlelight protests against the SOFA, the 2002 presidential election campaign, and the 2005-06 exposure of the stem cell research fraud of Hwang Woo-suk. A Korean news website OhmyNews (www.ohmynews.com), founded in 2000, has played an important role in spearheading a challenge to the domination of public opinion and the public agenda by the conservative mainstream press. Drawing on the idea of the public sphere pioneered by Jürgen Habermas, this paper examines the creation of new online forms of organisation by netizens as part of the new public sphere made possible by the Internet.

1 THE PUBLIC SPHERE AND SOUTH KOREA

In the spring of 1996 Jürgen Habermas was invited to South Korea for two weeks to lecture and discuss his concept of a public sphere with Korean scholars. He gave several lectures and participated in workshops where the theoretical and practical aspects of his concept of a public sphere were applied to Korean society. The book *Habermas and the Korean Debate* (1998) edited by Han Sang-jin is a collection of the papers presented during Habermas' Korean seminar. The book includes a paper by Professor Park Hyeong-jun (1998) of Dong-A University. This paper is prescient in that it provides a general framework to view an important struggle that has been waged in Korean society over the past decade. Park focuses on the potential of the Internet to make possible the development of a 'new form of participatory democracy'. Already by the mid-1990s, Park noted, 'the quantity of political discussion in cyberspace is considerable' (Park 1998: 439). He describes how '[e]veryday dozens, or even hundreds, of political "pieces" appear in the major commercial BBSs [bulletin board systems]'.

Park believes that political discussion online represents a yearning for 'participatory democracy', and is a reflection of the 'citizens' desire to intervene in a certain political event or to participate in the decision making process' (Park 1998: 440). He anticipates that such democratic processes will develop in two different forms: where existing social movements plan to increase their online activity; and in the creation of new forms of online organisation by 'netizens'. He explains the need to pay attention to the possibility of online social movement activity as a form of what he calls 'electronic participatory democracy' (ibid.: 440-41). He argues that combining the characteristics of the autonomy of civil society and the Internet would lead to embracing a new collective identity on the part of people online. The new identity is 'a flexible and loose identity' which has 'great potentiality with regard to dispersing critical discourses' (ibid.: 441). Furthermore, the continuing development of the Internet would encourage non-hierarchical or horizontal social structures. Such developments will contribute to 'the possibility for the formation of a new public sphere' (ibid.: 442).

Park's paper about the potential for such a new sphere, for 'electronic participatory democracy' to gain a foothold in South Korea, provides the impetus for investigating subsequent developments. Fortunately, there is a rich body of theory and practice to refer to about the South Korean struggle for a more democratic society. The focus of this article is on the development of new online forms and processes, and the role of online grassroots journalism, particularly the online newspaper OhmyNews. It takes as a case study the exposure in 2005-06 of Hwang Woo-suk's fraudulent claims in stem cell research.

1.1 The global Internet and the netizen experience in Korea

Just as the citizen is the significant actor in the struggle for participatory democracy, the netizen is the empowered actor in the participatory democratic processes of the Internet. Describing the development of the netizen as a socially oriented identity, Lee Byoung-kwan writes (Lee Byoung-kwan et al. 2005: 58):

[Michael] Hauben (1997)[1] defined the term Netizen as the people who actively contribute online towards the development of the Internet ... In particular, Usenet news groups or Internet bulletin boards are considered an 'agora' where the Netizens actively discuss and debate upon various issues ... In this manner, a variety of agenda are formed on the 'agora' and in their activity there, a Netizen can act as 'a citizen who uses the Internet as a way of participating in political society ...'.

Recent developments in South Korea provide a laboratory where netizens have endeavoured to test the potential of the Internet to provide a new form of public sphere, as a means for the citizen to participate in public life and to create an impact upon the decision-making processes of society.

2 PARTICIPATORY DEMOCRACY IN THE KOREAN CONTEXT

In response to a question about why his organisation, People's Solidarity for Participatory Democracy (PSPD) included the word 'participatory democracy' in its name, Lee Tae-ho, the organisation's deputy general secretary, referred to the candlelight demonstrations in the former East Germany that had helped to bring down the Berlin Wall in 1989.[2] Lee said that the spirit of these demonstrations, contained in the slogan of the Germans, 'We are the people', is 'especially important', because it helps to illustrate what is meant by participatory democracy. 'For me personally', he explained, 'there is some continuity between the candlelight demonstrations in Germany and Korea.' With the end of the cold war, Lee elaborated, it becomes clear that there is no way to have democracy without the participation of the citizens.

Lee noted that even with the political reforms of June 1987 in South Korea, and the constitutional processes put in place to replace the military government, the power of the state remained strong and overpowering for the citizens. Without overcoming these obstacles it would not be possible to build democracy. So participatory democracy, he explained, is not just about the participation of citizens, but also involves observation and control over the aspects of state power by the citizens.

---

[1] Hauben, Michael (1997), 'The Net and Netizens: The Impact the Net has on People's Lives', in: Hauben and Hauben: 3-34.
[2] Interview with Lee Tae-ho, 18 July 2006.

Some scholars writing about the struggle for democratisation in South Korea explain that it was not until 1997, ten years after the June 1987 reforms, that there was an actual transfer of political power to opposition parties. At the time of this transfer, however, the conservative media remained as one of the arbitrators of the form that any reform of the political system would take. After June 1987, rather than the conservative media being curtailed, it emerged as an 'independent political institution' (Chang 2005a: 928. See also Choi 2005; Kang 2005). Other scholars emphasize the need to reform the conservative media. 'Without the reform of the media, no success of democratic reform is possible', argues Cho Hee-yeon, one of the founders of PSPD (Cho 2001: 4).

The three most powerful conservative newspapers are *Chosun Ilbo* (5 March 1920), *Donga Ilbo* (5 April 1920), and *JoongAng Ilbo* (22 September 1965). These three, each with circulation figures of around 2 million, have a combined market share of 70 per cent (Lee Eun-Jung 2004: 624). According to the *Sisa Journal* (3 January 2002), no politician has 'won elections against the will of these newspapers' (Lee Eun-Jung 2004: 634).

3 OhmyNews

OhmyNews began in February 2000 with the explicit objective of bringing about a shift in the balance of power of the media in South Korea. OhmyNews was started by Oh Yeon-ho, formerly a journalist for the *Monthly Mal,* an alternative magazine owned by the Citizen's Coalition for Democratic Media. Oh worked for *Mal* as a journalist for the decade following 1988. In July 1994, he published a story with indepth coverage of the 1950 No Gun Ri massacre of South Korean civilians by US soldiers during the Korean War. The mainstream conservative Korean press ignored the story at the time, though there was a reference to the *Mal* story in the progressive daily newspaper *Hankyoreh*.

Several years later, in 1999 some Associated Press (AP) reporters wrote about the incident. The mainstream Korean news media from the Korean Broadcasting System to *Chosun Ilbo* wrote articles based on the AP story, as if it were breaking news, explained Oh. Not only did the South Korean government take it up, but the AP reporters won a Pulitzer for their article. While the AP story included accounts from

US soldiers who had been involved, an element which had not been part of Oh's story, this experience led Oh to conclude that it was not the nature of the news that governed how much attention a story received, but the power of the news media organisation that determined what was to be considered as news (Oh 2005).

As a reporter for a small alternative publication, Oh experienced discrimination in his effort to cover stories. Nor did journalists for the mainstream conservative media treat him as a fellow journalist. Oh observed that power was maintained by the mainstream media via its ability to set the standards for what was considered news, news gathering and news distribution. With the creation of OhmyNews, Oh was determined to make fundamental changes in the process of news gathering, production and distribution. One basic change that OhmyNews instituted was to welcome netizens to become journalists. Describing his philosophy, Oh (2004a: 2) writes:

> Every citizen is a reporter. Journalists aren't some exotic species, they're everyone who seeks to take new developments, put them into writing, and share them with others. This common truth has been trampled on in a culture where being a reporter is seen as something of a privilege to be enjoyed. Privileged reporters who come together to form massive news media wielded power over the whole process of news production, distribution and consumption.

Readers could submit stories which would be considered by OhmyNews editors for publication. Articles which were accepted were fact-checked, edited and then published. Those who contributed articles were called citizen journalists or citizen reporters. The citizen reporters whose articles appeared in OhmyNews would be paid a small fee; the amount depended on whether the article appeared on the front page or elsewhere in OhmyNews. Oh explains that instead of the standard of most mainstream journalists, 'I produce and you read', OhmyNews had substituted, 'We produce, we read, we change the world together' (Oh 2004b). The concept of 'news' was transformed by OhmyNews. Articles could include opinions as long as the facts were accurate.

Oh started OhmyNews with a small staff of four reporters and limited resources. He was helped by online production of the newspaper, with the Internet providing a platform that would make possible readers' comments and discussion on articles and the means to distribute the newspaper. In order to produce this Internet newspaper, given its small staff, Oh adopted a strategy that he called 'selection and concentration'. The staff would decide on a focus for their coverage and put their resources into providing substantial coverage of these stories. Though at the beginning priority was given to news about politics, society and non-governmental organisations (NGOs), other sections, including international news, business and culture, were added as the newspaper developed (Oh 2005: 29)

In the business plan for the OhmyNews Foundation, several aspects of OhmyNews are explained in greater detail.[3] The long-term strategy is to produce 'an Internet daily newspaper superior to Digital Chosun'. OhmyNews will bring innovations to 'journalism culture by a revolution in news production, delivery and consumption culture', and will provide a 'pivot for the federation of reporter-like reporters'. News form and content will be transformed with the goal of 'destroy[ing] the standardized form of news report', striving for the 'best investigative reports', and reporting 'vivid sounds of the field: live reports, audio plus video, if possible'. The third aspect, after strategy and transformation of work methods, will be to 'fire arrows toward specific targets: attack corrupted and privileged areas'. The targeted audience is the 'Young N-generation, progressive activists, and reporters', including 'high school students, college students, 386 generation, NGO[s], local activists and reporters'. The philosophy proposed is labelled 'open progressive'. This means that 'We are to pursue open progressive perspectives, criticizing unproductive and stubborn progressives and supporting productive and conscientious conservatives.' While the group PSPD worked to build solidarity among civic activists as an NGO, OhmyNews also sought to create an 'NGO'—News Guerrillas Organization—for solidarity among 'news guerrillas'. Oh explains this term as follows (Oh 2004a):

> The dictionary definition of guerrilla is 'a member of small non-regular armed forces who disrupt the rear positions of the enemy'. Citizen reporters can be called guerrillas because they are not professional and regulars and they post news from perspectives uniquely their own, not those of the conservative establishment.

The goal in the business plan is to replace the 8:2 ratio between conservative media and progressive media in South Korea with a 5:5 ratio.

---

[3] Oh, Yeon-ho (2004c), *Daehanminguk Tuksanpoom, OhmyNews*, Seoul: Humanist, pp. 327-353, Translation from Korean into English by Lee Jin-sun.

4 2002 CANDLELIGHT DEMONSTRATIONS FOR TWO DEAD GIRLS

A number of articles in OhmyNews contributed to the success of the 2002 presidential campaign. One particular article which appeared in OhmyNews and other online sites provides an interesting example of the power of the netizen.

In June 2002, an armoured military vehicle driven by two US servicemen ran over and killed two Korean middle-school girls. At the time, however, most Koreans were focused on the World Cup celebrations taking place in Korea. By November 2002, the mood had changed, and there was a clear desire among many Koreans that the soldiers concerned should be punished. The Status of Forces Agreement (SOFA) between the US and the Republic of Korea provided that the soldiers be tried by US courts, not under Korean law, and they were found not guilty. A documentary about the trial and its outcome was shown on Korean television. A few hours after watching the documentary, an OhmyNews citizen reporter, using the name AngMA, posted a message on several forums on the Internet including one at OhmyNews, which read:

> We are owners of Korea. We are Koreans who deserve to be able to walk in Gwanghwamun[4]. I cried when I watched the TV documentary broadcast of the event, because until now I didn't understand those who struggle so strongly.
>
> It is said that dead men's souls become fireflies. Let's fill downtown with our souls, with the souls of Mi-seon and Hyo-soon. Let's become thousands of fireflies this coming Saturday and Sunday. Let's sacrifice our private comfortable lives. Please light your candle at your home. If somebody asks, please answer, 'I'm going to commemorate my dead sisters'. Holding candles and wearing black, let's have a memorial ceremony for them.
>
> Let's walk in Gwanghwamun holding a lighted candle. Let's commemorate the lives of Mi-seon and Hyo-soon, who were forgotten in the joy of June. Will the police prevent us? Even if they forbid it, I will walk in Gwanghwamun, even if the police attack me.
>
> We are not Americans who revenge [sic] violence with more violence. Even if only one person comes, it's ok. I will be happy to say hello. I will talk about the future of Korea in which Mi-seon and Hyo-soon can take a comfortable rest.

---

[4] Gwanghwamun is the area of Seoul where the US embassy is located. It was off limits for demonstrations.

> I'll go on, this week, next week, the following week. Let's fill Gwanghwamun with our candle-light. Let's put out the American's violence with our peace.[5]

AngMA posted this at three different online sites on 28 November 2002 at 04:00, five hours after he had seen the TV documentary. The next day he posted it at OhmyNews. Fifteen thousand people appeared at the first candlelight vigil for the two dead girls on 30 November. The rally was due to netizens and the Internet. The movement continued to develop and expand. So too did the online discussion and debate. By 14 December more than 100,000 people gathered in Gwanghwamun.

Song Yong-hoi (2007) chose this incident as the basis for a study of the media dynamics of five news publications, both online and print, progressive and conservative. Included in the study were the conservative *Chosun Ilbo* and *JoongAng* and the progressive *Hankyoreh*. The online newspapers OhmyNews and Pressian were the two online progressive newspapers included. The period of the study was from 13 June 2002, when the two girls died, to 31 December 2002.

Journalism researchers refer to the concept of 'framing' to indicate how a story is presented. Framing refers to 'a central organizing idea or story line that provides meaning to an unfolding strip of events, weaving a connection among them. The frame suggests what the controversy is above, the essence of the issue' (Gamson and Modigliani 1987: 143). In covering a news issue, two considerations are of special importance. The first is how much attention is devoted to the issue by the publication. The second is how the issue is presented in the publication. Song's findings indicate that in June 2002 there was substantially less coverage of the deaths in the conservative press, while the progressive press, both the print publication *Hankyoreh,* and the online publications, gave the incident more substantial coverage. For example, during the ten-week period immediately following the deaths, OhmyNews published 1,010 articles, and *Chosun Ilbo*, 96. After the US court verdict exonerating the soldiers, coverage in all the publications increased, with the greatest amount of coverage in OhmyNews. During this period, the period after the verdict until 31 December 2002, OhmyNews published 1,965 articles, *Chosun Ilbo*, 604 (Song 2007: 80-81).

---

[5] Message translated from Korean into English by Lee Jin-sun.

Song reports that the content of the articles differed in the different publications as well as the amount of coverage. The sources the journalist uses for an article are part of the mechanism of providing a particular frame for the article. The conservative and progressive publications differed on the sources quoted in their articles. The conservative publications drew on official Korean government sources sympathetic to the US government, portraying the protests as anti-Americanism. The progressive publications, both print and online, focused more on the demonstrations and the protest movement, referring to protest movement sources. The study indicated that in reading accounts of the same event it was at times difficult to recognise that the conservative and progressive publications were talking about the same event.

Another concept used in journalism studies is that of 'agenda-setting'. This refers to the fact that issues covered by the mainstream press are also issues that become part of the public agenda. When news is ignored by the mainstream press, it is less likely to get public attention. A focus of the demonstrations was the public demand for revisions of SOFA and for this issue to be part of the public agenda.

One question raised by the findings of Song's study is whether the extensive coverage in the progressive press was a contributing factor to the increasing numbers of people participating in the protests. Another question was whether the extensive coverage in the progressive press increased the coverage of the protests in the conservative press. Such questions are a basis for further study and investigation.

5 ROH MOO-HYUN'S ELECTION CAMPAIGN

The candlelight demonstrations of 2002 occurred during a period leading up to the presidential election campaign held that year. Developments in the election campaign were another part of the power struggle between the conservative print media and online discussion by netizens on the Internet. During the campaign, criticism in the print media stirred interest in Roh Moo-hyun, a candidate who was considered to be outside of the political mainstream. The narrow focus of the conservative print media was countered by a broad discussion online of the issues of the election. This discussion utilised a variety of online forms, including discussion groups, online polemics, and online journalism. Responses to the print articles were posted and distributed on the Internet.

On 12 May 2002, PSPD held an online poll to see which of several candidates was most popular. The poll included Rhee In-je, an advisor to the Millennium Democratic party (MDP) and a member of the National Assembly, Lee Hoi-chang, the head of the Grand National party (GNP), and Roh Moo-hyun, who appeared to be the candidate least likely to be able to win the election. Yet Roh won the PSPD poll.

The presidency election campaign started out, however, with the appearance that it would follow the form and practice of previous campaigns. The GNP candidate seemed destined for victory. In January 2002, he had visited the US and met with high-level officials, including Vice-President Dick Cheney. The GNP at the time held the majority of seats in the National Assembly, 150 out of 272, and had moreover scored a victory over the Millennium Democratic party of the incumbent president, Kim Dae-jung, in the June 2002 local elections, winning eleven of sixteen contests for mayors and governors (Steinberg 2005).

Up until March 2002, Roh was scoring far behind Lee according to polls such as one reported in *Chosun Ilbo* (5 March 2002), which gave Lee Hoi-chang 38.7 percent of the vote, and Roh 25.2 percent. In online publications, however, there were signs that the election was going to be more of a close race than was apparent in the print press. An online publication, *Digital Times*, as early as February 2002 showed Roh ahead of Lee (Yun Seongyi 2003: 220). The significant aspect of the election campaign for Roh was the fact that his candidacy was strongly opposed by the conservative print press. For example, during the primary election, the 'major newspapers almost everyday carried articles that both implicitly and explicitly criticized candidate Roh Moo-hyun' (Yun Young-min 2003: 148). Surprisingly, the attacks by the print media served to increase the public's interest in Roh and his campaign. As Yun suggests, '[a]s a result more and more voters must have wondered to themselves "Just who is this Roh Moo-hyun?"'(ibid.: 154). In his study of the activity on the Internet during the 2002 election, Yun documents the 'sharp increase in the number of visits to Roh's website' and judges 'that must have been the reason why "Roh Moo-hyun" became one of the most popular search terms in the news section of portal sites' (ibid.: 154).

Criticism of Roh by the major newspapers had a David and Goliath effect, with Roh being regarded as the brave David able to slay the more powerful Goliath (ibid.: 148). Attacks on Roh that appeared in the conservative print media were quick to draw responses and discussion in online newspapers and discussion forums. If there was a reference in the print media to a speech that Roh gave, the whole speech would be posted online with a response to the article that had appeared in the print media (Lee Eun-Jung 2004: 634). Similarly, online discussions were common, and supporters of Roh would send each other articles they found of interest. The online discussion and exchange of views found particular favour among the younger generations who had previously found politics uninteresting. A feedback loop developed between the articles published in the conservative major print publications and the comments and discussion that occurred online (Yun Young-min 2003: 163). To Lee Eun-Jung, the election of 2002 was 'a power struggle between the main print media and the Internet', and 'for the first time in Korean history, the power of the so-called netizen ... made itself felt' (Lee Eun-Jung 2004: 634, 632).

5.1 *Role of netizens in the election campaign*

Prior to the election, most experts would have assumed that it was impossible for Roh to win because of the Internet. But after the election, these same experts would agree that the Internet had played a significant role in the victory (Yun Young-min 2003: 163). Though he is cautious about claiming causality without further study, Yun proposes that the 'so-called experts' should exert caution when making their predictions about 'such events in the future' (Yun Young-min 2003: 163).

Summarising Roh's victory, Yun writes (ibid.: 143):

> Cyberspace is making it possible for citizens to choose a political position free from the influence of the mainstream press ... Public opinion, which has been almost exclusively minted by a few mass media, can no longer be hidden beneath the control of the press. The ... effect is expected to break the old equation, 'the opinion of the press = public opinion = prevailing opinion'.

Lee Eun-Jung agrees that something important happened: 'In a sense the netizens mobilized themselves into the political realm, exercising their power as citizens ...' (Lee Eun-Jung 2004: 635). She concludes that 'with their electoral revolution the netizens had transformed political culture in Korea' (ibid.: 638).

5.2 Nosamo: a new online institutional political form

Crucial to the victory of netizens in the 2002 election was the online fan club they created to build support for Roh. Nosamo was started by Lee Jeong Ki (User ID: Old Fox) on 15 April 2000. Nosamo, also transliterated as 'Rohsamo', stands for 'those who love Roh'. The fan club had members both internationally and locally, with online and offline activities organised among the participants. When Nosamo was created, a goal of the organisation was participatory democracy.

Explaining how the participatory process works, Kim Hee-kyung and her co-authors provide an example from Nosamo's experience (Kim Hee-kyung et al. 2004: 4):

> Their internal discussion making process was a microcosm of participatory democracy in practice. All members voted on a decision following open deliberations in forums for a given period of time. Opinions were offered in this process in order to effect changes to the decision on which people were to vote.

Such online discussion and decision-making was demonstrated when members of Roh's fan club disagreed with his decision to send Korean troops to Iraq in support of the US invasion. The fan club members held an online discussion and voted on their web site about the war in Iraq. They issued a public statement opposing the decision to send Korean troops to Iraq. Even though they were members of a fan club, they did not feel obliged to support every action of the Roh presidency.

Initially, Nosamo had 40 members. They shared certain political goals, which included challenging the domination of the conservative press over Korean politics. They also opposed regional loyalty as the basis for electoral success in Korean politics. The meeting launching Nosamo was held in an Internet café ('PC Bang' in Korean) in Taejŏn. Over 100 people attended and the meeting was broadcast live by OhmyNews. Instead of following the existing model of a political party organisation, Nosamo was organised at a local level, sponsoring local activities among its netizen population that included trips to the country's highest mountains, holding campfires on local beaches, and bicycling and walking between two 'regionally antagonistic' cities, Pusan and Kwangju (Kim Yong-ho 2003: 5). Nosamo's activities were mainly organised online but included many offline political and social activities. The fan club began to draw the attention of those who did not know of its online existence when members of Nosamo worked to help Roh Moo-hyun win the newly instituted primary in the MDP.

Trying to win mass support for the party, the MDP instituted its first open primary election to choose its presidential nominee. Rotating open primaries were held in different cities and provinces from January through April 2002. At first Roh was considered an underdog among the MDP candidates. He came in third in the first primary, but then second in the second primary. By the third primary, held in Kwangju, he came in first (Kim Yong-ho 2003: 6). Nosamo's online membership had found the means to gain support for Roh, helped by the open nature of the primary. In April 2002 Roh won the MDP's formal nomination, but had little formal support from the MDP organisation. Nosamo refashioned itself to provide a more formal organisational form for its presidential candidate. It used its online structure to raise funds for Roh and to organise and carry out a vigorous online and offline campaign. At one point, Roh made an agreement with another presidential candidate, Chung Mong-joon, to hold a televised debate, from which the winner would run against the GNP candidate. Though Roh had trailed Chung some of the time in the polls, and trailed the GNP candidate Lee through much of this campaign period, his Nosamo supporters made sure they were available to be polled about who won the debate. Roh emerged from the televised debate with a score of 46.8 percent in favour, to 42.4 percent for Chung.

OhmyNews and the netizens played a critical role in the hours leading up to the election scheduled for 19 December 2002. Oh and other OhmyNews journalists and citizen reporters covered the evening's events continuously throughout the night. As the election approached, Oh realized he had watched netizens supporting the Roh election phenomenon for two years. Oh wondered if it would be possible for netizens to succeed in their campaign for Roh given the opposition of the conservative media. He describes what happened. Around 22.30 the night before the election, Chung withdrew his support for Roh. *Chosun Ilbo* announced the event, urging voters to follow Chung's lead and withdraw their support from Roh. OhmyNews continually updated its coverage. Oh reports that the discussion boards on OhmyNews were flooded with comments. The article in OhmyNews about Chung's withdrawal of support received 570,000 hits in the ten hours following the announcement. With the hits it received later that day, making a total of 720,000, it set a record for the most hits on a single article in OhmyNews in one day (Oh 2003: 116-17, as described in Chang 2005a: 931). Instead of being dissuaded by Chung's action and *Chosun Ilbo*'s efforts to change the course of what would happen in the election, netizens rallied round Roh, discussing what to do about the turn of events, and urging their family, friends and others to vote. This episode led Oh to the conclusion that the importance of the 2002 election was that it was not based on support for Roh personally, but was a manifestation of 'the desire of young netizens for political reform' (Oh 2005: 66).

After the election victory, reporters from *Chosun Ilbo* and other conservative news media called to congratulate Oh and other OhmyNews reporters. According to Oh (2005: 70):

> OhmyNews did our job as the media by giving the Roh Phenomenon its worth as a news story. For example, on a scale of 100 we gave the Roh Phenomenon a 95 in terms of newsworthiness. Korea's conservative dailies, however, gave it only a 30. Through our own abilities, we did what the media naturally should have done. We rejected their standards and through on-the-spot coverage we were able to decide just how newsworthy the Roh phenomenon was.

On 19 December, Oh wrote that '[t]he power of the media dominated for 80 years by *Chosun Ilbo*, *Joong Ang Ilbo* and *Dong-A Ilbo* has finally changed. The power has gone from the printed newspaper and the professional journalists to the netizens and citizen reporters' (Oh 2005: 69-70).

During the 2002 presidential campaign, citizens found a way to turn the election campaign into a citizens' event. They became actively involved in debating and exploring the issues that were raised. It was not only the candidates or the elites and their newspapers that participated in the debates. On the contrary, articles in the conservative press about the Roh candidacy were subjected to scrutiny, and citizens could respond in both discussion forums and online newspapers. Citizens had reclaimed their role as participants in the election process, rather than being resigned to the status of passive observers. The citizenry also became watchdogs of the process, as well as participants. They were able to contribute to and spread the discussion among other citizens. The 2002 presidential campaign in South Korea was thus an important development in the democratisation of Korea. Out of the debate and discussion emerged a broader form of public opinion than had hitherto been available in Korea.

6 STEM CELL FRAUD AND THE NETIZENS: A CASE STUDY

Another important struggle developed in South Korea in the autumn of 2005. A research laboratory at Seoul National University (SNU) directed by the veterinary scientist Hwang Woo-suk published what were considered forefront research papers in the field of stem cell research. His papers, published in *Science* (vol. 303, no. 5664, 12 March 2004, pp. 1669-74, and vol. 308, no. 5729, 17 June 2005, pp. 1777-83, both papers subsequently retracted by *Science*), documented a technique for cloning stem cells, to produce patient-specific cell lines to use in the treatment of certain diseases, including Parkinson's disease and diabetes, and of injuries such as spinal column injuries. This research was heralded as providing hope for therapeutic treatment. Skillful in public relations, Hwang successfully cultivated journalists and other media contacts. He was treated as a national hero, and received funding and acclaim from the government of Roh Moo-hyun. Private commercial entities like Posco, South Korea's largest steel corporation, and Korean Airlines supported his work (Yoon 2005).

Even before Hwang's second paper appeared in *Science,* reporters for the US science journal *Nature* had visited Hwang's laboratory and learned that some of the ova used in his research may have been donated by women who worked as part of his research team. A woman who is in a subordinate position in a research project is considered to be at risk of being under pressure from her employer to make such a donation. Consequently, such donations are contrary to ethical guidelines requiring donations to be voluntary.

Following this investigation, questions about possible ethical violations in Hwang's research were raised in an editorial in the journal (*Nature,* vol. 429, no. 6987, 6 May 2004, p.1). A television documentary by PD Notebook, an investigative news programme on Munhwa Broadcasting Corporation (MBC), based on information from one of Hwang's former research colleagues, was produced in the fall of 2005 and aired on 22 November 2005. The documentary raised a number of ethical questions about the ova used in Hwang's research. The television programme promised a follow-up documentary that would raise further questions about possible fraud in the research. What followed, however, was a flurry of corporate, government and media support for Hwang. This included mainstream media like *Chosun Ilbo,* and government officials who formed an unofficial group called 'Hwang'gŭm

Pakchwi' ('golden bat') to support Hwang.[6] Supporters of Hwang created an online web site 'We love Hwang' to plan their defence of him. Only messages supporting Hwang could be posted on the site (Hong and Lee 2006).

After their programme on Hwang, the PD Notebook website was filled with messages of protest. In the process of investigations for a follow-up programme, the producers of PD Notebook had used a hidden microphone to tape an interview with one of Hwang's researchers, who admitted falsifying Hwang's data. The television interviewers, however, were accused of threatening the researcher they were interviewing, and a campaign was organised to induce the advertisers on PD Notebook to withdraw support from the programme. The follow-up programme was cancelled on 7 December 2005. Progressive media including OhmyNews and Pressian carried stories challenging the attack on PD Notebook. OhmyNews compared the attacks on PD Notebook and others who were raising questions about Hwang's work to activities, similar to those that took place in Nazi Germany. A few civic and labour groups also defended PD Notebook's investigation of the problems in Hwang's work.

At first Hwang denied any problems with his research. But after the first PD Notebook programme, he acknowledged that ova had been donated by two of the researchers in his lab, a procedure that is in violation under the Helsinki Declaration.

Those challenging Hwang's research could expect to become the object of a public attack. *Chosun Ilbo* took issue with OhmyNews and Pressian editorially for raising concerns about the research. President Roh promised continued support for Hwang, and the scientist's supporters claimed that the beneficial potential of his research, the promise that it could provide a cure for serious medical problems, was being properly treated as of more importance than possible ethical violations. The fact that a prestigious scientific journal such as *Science* had

---

[6] Ties with Park Ki-young, Science and Technology Advisor for the President, 'yielded a favourable environment for Hwang in the government, as a non-official group consisting of high-ranking government officials was created to support Hwang's research that includes not only Hwang and Park, but also Kim Byung-joon, Chief National Policy Secretary, and Jin Dae-jae, Information and Communications Minister. The group was dubbed "Hwang'gŭm Pakchwi", a loose acronym formed from each member's family names, which means "golden bat" in Korean' ('Hwang Woo-Suk' in: Wikipedia, online: http://en.wikipedia.org/wiki/Hwang_Woo-Suk) (accessed 25 April 2007).

published Hwang's research papers was offered as proof that the scientific community had verified his research.

On several online sites, however, there was continuing discussion about this research. At scientists' websites such as BRIC (Biological Research Information Centre),[7] scieng (Association of Korean Scientists and Engineers),[8] and the Science Gallery of DC Inside,[9] a photography web site, messages were posted and the questions raised by Hwang's research discussed. Just when it appeared that the attack on PD Notebook was succeeding, a post appeared on BRIC which would have a significant impact on the outcome of the controversy.

On 5 December 2005, a netizen with the log-in 'anonymous' posted a message entitled 'The show must go on' on the BRIC website. 'Anonymous' explained it was possible to access the website of the journal *Science* and download the pictures that Hwang had submitted in support of his research. 'Anonymous' reported that he had found two sets of duplicate photos in the collection of pictures. He invited others on BRIC to take a look for themselves. Many netizens responded to the post, verifying the claims. News of the duplicate photos quickly circulated online, and they were copied or linked to many other sites (Hong and Lee 2006). The following morning, another anonymous netizen challenged the claims that the DNA of the stem cells that Hwang claimed to have produced matched the DNA of the donors. The posts documenting the fabrication of Hwang's research results were widely distributed online. One netizen described how during this period, those online knew the news as it was happening online and only several days later would the news appear in the traditional media.[10]

The scientific community was watching the online discussion. Shortly after the post on BRIC on 5 December, Hwang sent an email to *Science* acknowledging that there were duplications in the photos he had submitted as the evidence for his research, but said this had been the result of a mix-up. He continued to assert that his research claims were valid. In response to these exposures of the problems in Hwang's articles, a group of young professors at SNU, his university, called for an investigation. A panel was formed, and, after investigating Hwang's work and examining the notes and records that were

---

[7] http://postech.ac.kr/ (accessed 25 April 2007).
[8] www.scieng.net (accessed 25 April 2007).
[9] http://www.dcinside.com (accessed 25 April 2007).
[10] Discussion with Kim Hee-won, August 2006.

made available, concluded that there had been no cloning of stem cells, i.e. no patient-specific stem cells had been produced by Hwang's laboratory. The critique presented by netizens had been proven accurate.

This controversy offers insight not only into the actions of the online community of netizens, but also into the constraints the conservative mainstream media works under. Son Byung-kwan's review of the book, *The Country of Hwang Woo-Suk* (publisher: Bada) by Lee Sung-joo, a journalist who worked for 13 years at *Donga Ilbo*, describes the role of Lee's chief editor in censoring the exposure of Hwang's fraudulent work (Son 2006a, 2006b). The newspaper's policy was to report the story in a way that was 'neither ahead nor behind' other mainstream news organisations. Articles that Lee wrote were rejected or not published until the news was stale, and he was reassigned to another beat to prevent him from continuing to follow the story. The chief editor directed the newspaper to intensify the criticism of MBC PD Notebook instead of reporting the revelations of fraudulent scientific claims against Hwang (Son 2006a, 2006b).

Lee's experience was corroborated by staff reporter Kim Hee-won of the *Hankook Ilbo* in a paper he presented in August 2006, in which he documents some of the mechanism that led to the lack of press coverage of the exposure of the fraud until late in the struggle. Kim's paper is based on interviews with six journalists who were working for broadcasting, newspaper or news agencies during or just before the Hwang affair (Kim Hee-won 2006). Kim describes how Hwang had cultivated contacts with mainstream reporters and media organisations. Once the fraud began to be unravelled, reporters who had such contacts recognised that covering the story would jeopardise their relationships with Hwang and his laboratory. When advertisers pulled their ads from PD Notebook in response to public pressure, other news organisations worried about the negative impact articles exposing Hwang might have on their advertisers. One reporter described how his news organisation cultivated both 'pro-Hwang' and 'anti-Hwang' unofficial channels of information. This was reflected in the internal controversy within the organisation and in swings in the nature of its coverage. A reporter from another news organisation explained that his editor did not want any open challenge to Hwang, as 'opinion leaders' in business had encouraged the editor to refrain from printing articles that would discredit Hwang. Another reporter referred to internal discussion about what to do once the duplicate photos had been revealed. At first, however, there was no change in coverage. Still another reporter described how his organisation decided to take its time in order to be 'accurate' about its reports and so the media organisation did not expose the Hwang fraud.

This series of events demonstrates the developing power of the online media in Korea and how this is presenting a serious challenge to the power of the traditional print media. The online sites of scientific researchers including BRIC, scieng and Science Gallery of DC Inside, were able to stand up against the attacks from the government and media establishment, including online forums set up to defend Hwang. The netizens of BRIC, scieng and DC Inside were supported by others in the online community, by the discussion and linking of articles on other online forums and blogs, and by online media like OhmyNews and Pressian. One blogger explained that the hierarchy within Korean scientific laboratories makes it difficult for young researchers to speak up and to fight abuse. Yet problems could be pinpointed and then treated seriously via anonymous posts and online discussion.

7 Conclusion

Certain general characteristics emerge which point toward some general concepts in the development of online journalism. The non-hierarchical form of the online experience contrasts sharply with the hierarchical institutional forms that many Koreans face offline. Similarly, the ability to speak up and express one's opinions contrasts with other aspects of Korean life and experience. Discussion and debate online have functioned as catalysts for offline organisation and demonstrations. Describing the rich array of online forms, Chang Wooyoung writes (Chang 2005b, as quoted in Chang 2006: 3) that:

> [T]he progressive camp has taken initiatives in the cyberspace by using various types of online media including PC communication communities, closed user groups (CUGs), independent Internet newspapers, political webzines, portal sites for social movements, fan clubs sites of political leaders, and 'anti' sites.

Yet when one reads analyses of what is happening in terms of democratisation in Korea, the focus is more commonly on the weakness of the political party structures, or the danger of a strong civil society developing without an adequate institutional structure (Choi 2005; Kim Sun-hyuk 2000). There is little attention to the online new democratic processes and the potential they represent for creating new democratic forms (Park 1998).

Several of the online posts presented in this paper provide examples of the ability of netizens to breach the boundary between the concerns of the individual netizen and the social purpose that characterises citizenship. By the messages they have posted netizens have been able to have an impact on social issues they deem important. Their concerns have been reflected from the grassroots upward. Other netizens build on their concerns or distribute their posts to others. Interactive participation and discussion among netizens is critical and provides a basis to begin to construct a modern theory and practice of participatory democracy.

The form created for Nosamo is a form that encouraged participation and provided the basis for citizens to affect developments in their society. Similarly, the processes pioneered by OhmyNews and other online media offer a design expanding the news and views that define public opinion and the public agenda. Netizens participating on BRIC, scieng and the Science Gallery of DC Inside collaborated to examine the claims in a scientific paper, claims which the peer review process of the journal *Science* had failed to adequately evaluate. Such new online forms and processes need to be documented and analysed, not ignored or blindly admired.

OhmyNews, Nosamo and science related web sites like BRIC are examples of forms created or utilised by netizens. These are examples of changing institutional forms made possible by the Internet. South Korea, a society where there is much broadband access and democratic ferment, is an environment where such new institutional forms can be explored and lessons learned about their nature and the potential for crafting new democratic processes. Such lessons can be helpful elsewhere if the details are known and lessons shared.

REFERENCES

Chang, Woo-young (2005a), 'Online Civic Participation, and Political Empowerment: Online Media and Public Opinion Formation in Korea', in: *Media, Culture, and Society*, 27 (6), pp. 925-35

Chang, Woo-young (2005b), 'The Political Dynamics of Online Journalism: With a Focus on "Political Webzines"', in: *Media and Society*, 13 (2), pp. 157-88

Chang, Woo-young (2006), 'The Structural Transformation of Cyber Public Sphere in Korea: From the Prominence of Progressive Camp to Equilibrium between the Progressive and Conservative Camp', unpublished paper

Cho, Hee-yeon (2001), 'The Role of NGO's in the Democratic Transition', in: *Asia Solidarity Quarterly*, 3 (Winter), pp. 124-44, http://www.peoplepower21.org/publication/pub_view.php?article_id=4485 (accessed 4 July 2007)

Choi, Jang-Jip (2005), *Democracy after Democratization: the Korean Experience*, Seoul: Humanitas

Gamson, William and André Modigliani (1987), 'The Changing Culture of Affirmative Action', in: *Research in Political Sociology*, 3, pp. 137-77

Han, Jongwoo (2002), 'Internet, Social Capital, and Democracy in the Information Age: Korea's Defeat Movement, the Red Devils, Candle Light Anti-U.S. Demonstration and Presidential Election During 2000-2002', draft paper, September 2002. Online: http://sai.syr.edu/facultypapers/Han%207-29-03.pdf (accessed 25 April 2007)

Han, Sang-jin (1998), *Habermas and the Korean Debate*, Seoul: Seoul National University Press

Han, Sang-jin (2004), 'Confucian Tradition and the Young Generation in Korea: The Effect of Post-Traditional Global Testing', paper prepared for the International Symposium Dialogue among Youth in East Asia Project, Yingjie Exchange Center of Peking University, Delivered 14 January 2004

Hauben, Michael and Ronda Hauben (1997), *Netizens: On the History and Impact of Usenet and the Internet*, Los Alamitos CA: IEEE Computer Society Press/John Wiley and Sons

Hauben, Ronda (2005), 'The Rise of Netizen Democracy: A Case Study of Netizens' Impact on Democracy in South Korea', unpublished paper. Online: http://www.columbia.edu/~rh120/other/misc/korean-democracy.txt (accessed 19 April 2007)

Hong, Sungook and June S. Lee (2006), 'Science Communication and the Role of the Media in Hwang Scandal', unpublished paper

Kang, Myung-koo (2005), 'The Struggle for Press Freedom and Emergence of "Unelected" Media Power in South Korea', in: John Erni and S. K. Chua (eds.), *Asia Media Studies: Politics of Subjectivities*, London: Blackwell Publishing, pp. 75-90.

Kim, Hee-won (2006), 'Why Media Support a Scientific Fraud', paper presented at the EASTS Conference, 3-5 August 2006. Online: http://sts.nthu.edu.tw/easts/agenda.htm (under Kim's name but not this title, accessed 24 April 2007)

Kim, Heekyung Hellen, Jae Yun Moon and Yang Shinkyu (2004), 'Broadband Penetration and Participatory Politics: South Korea Case', in: *Proceedings of the 37th Annual Hawaii International Conference on System Sciences*, Honolulu: IEEE Conference Proceedings, pp. 1-10

Kim, Sun-hyuk (2000), *Politics of Democratization in Korea: the Role of Civil Society*, Pittsburgh: University of Pittsburgh Press

Kim, Yong-ho (2003), 'Political Significance of the 2002 Presidential Election: Outcome and Political Prospects for the Roh Administration', in: *Korea Journal*, 43 (2), pp. 230-256

Lee, Byoungkwan, Lancendorfer, Karen M., and Lee, Ki Jung (2005), 'Agenda-Setting and the Internet: the Intermedia Influence of Internet Bulletin Boards on Newspaper Coverage of the 2000 General Election in South Korea', in: *Asian Journal of Communication*, 15 (1), pp. 57-71

Lee, Eun-Jung (2004), 'E-democracy@work: The 2002 Presidential Election in Korea', in: Steven Gan, James Gomez and Uwe Johannen (eds.), *Asian Cyberactivism: Freedom of Expression and Media Censorship*, Singapore: Friedrich Naumann Foundation, pp. 622-42

Oh, Yeon-ho (2004a), 'The Revolt of the 727 News Guerillas: A Revolution in News Production and Consumption', in: *OhmyNews* 19 February 2004. Online: http://english.ohmynews.com/articleview/article_view.asp?no=153109&rel_no=1 (accessed 25 April 2007)

Oh, Yeon-ho (2004b), 'The End of 20th Century Journalism', speech to 2004 conference of the World Association of Newspapers, Istanbul, 31 May 2004, in: *OhmyNews* 1 June. Online: http://english.ohmynews.com/articleview/article_view.asp?article_class=8&no=169396&rel_no=1 (accessed 25 April 2005)

Oh, Yeon-ho (2004c), *Daehanminguk Tuksanpoom, OhmyNews*. Seoul: Humanist, pp. 327-353, Translation from Korean into English by Lee Jin-sun

Oh, Yeon-ho (2005), 'OhmyNews: A Unique Product of Korea', Unpublished English translation, 7 January 2005

Park, Hyeong-jun, (1998), 'The Informatization and Computer Mediated Communication in Korea: An Application of Habermas "Public Sphere Theory"', in: Han, Sang-jin (ed.), *Habermas and the Korean Debate*, Seoul: Seoul National University Press, pp. 421-44

Park, Seung-gwan, and Jang, Gyeong-soeb (2001), *Media Power and Agenda Dynamics*, Seoul: Communications Books

Son, Byung-kwan (2006a), 'How Media Promoted Hwang Myth', in: *Ohmynews International*, 27, March 2006. Online: http://english.ohmynews.com/articleview/article_view.asp?menu=c10400&no=281880&rel_no=1 (accessed 25 April 2007)

Son, Byung-kwan(2006b), 'Book Reveals More to Hwang Scandal: Author (Part 2)' in *OhmyNews International*, 27 March 2006, Online: http://english.ohmynews.com/articleview/article_view.asp?no=281883&rel_no=1 (accessed 25 April 2007)

Song, Yonghoi (2007), 'Internet News Media and Issue Development: A Case Study on the Roles of Independent Online News Services as Agenda-Builders for Anti-US Protests in South Korea', in: *New Media and Society*, 9 (1), pp. 71-92

Steinberg, David I. (2005), 'The Evolution of Political Party System and the Future of Party Politics in the Republic of Korea', in: Alexandre Mansourov (ed.), *ROK Turning Point*, Honolulu: Asia-Pacific Center for Security Studies, pp. 118-40

Yoon, Chang-hee (2005), 'Stem cell controversy being felt by sponsors', *JoongAng Ilbo*, 16 December 2005, http://joongangdaily.joins.com/article/view.asp?aid=2658162 (accessed 4 July 2007)

Yun, Seongyi (2003), 'The Internet and the 2002 Presidential Election in South Korea', in *Korea Journal*, 43 (2), pp. 209-29

Yun, Young-min (2003), 'An Analysis of Cyber-Electioneering: Focusing on the 2002 Presidential Election in Korea', in: *Korea Journal*, 43 (3), pp. 141-64

THE LONE STAR SCANDAL: WAS IT CORRUPTION?

James C. Schopf

ABSTRACT

The Lone Star scandal emerged as one of the biggest Korean news stories of 2006. The foreign fund faced allegations of corruption, of bribing financial authorities for favours through the below-market purchase price of publicly held shares in Korea Exchange Bank. To facilitate the deal, the Ministry of Finance and Economy and the Financial Supervisory Commission were accused of improperly providing Lone Star with an exception to the bank law's ban on takeovers by non-bank financial institutions, of failing to issue a notice of prompt corrective action, of limiting the bidding, and of breaking normal bureaucratic decision-making protocol. Applying a functional definition and approach to measure corruption, favours (rent) and legal infractions serve as indicators to help us determine whether or not corruption took place during the Lone Star takeover. Analysis reveals that while some laws and procedures were liberally interpreted, a lack of rent in the takeover signifies absence of large-scale corruption, particularly trivial in comparison to graft under previous Korean authoritarian regimes. The overly aggressive investigation of Lone Star can best be explained, therefore, as part of a hostile political reaction to the power of foreign capital and the demands of globalisation.

1 EXAMINING THE PROBLEM

The Lone Star bribery case has captured South Korean newspaper headlines for over a year since it broke in February 2006—an apparent case of corruption, allegedly involving the below-market price sale of publicly owned shares in Korean Exchange Bank (KEB) to the Lone Star Fund in return for bribes. The case has incited great controversy, pitting the supreme prosecutor of the Republic of Korea (ROK), the Board of Audit and Inspection (BAI) and South Korean opposition parties against Lone Star, the Ministry of Finance and Economy (MOFE), the Financial Supervisory Commission (FSC), KEB management and much of the foreign investor community. While the prosecutor, in an investigation launched on 13 March 2006, has alleged that Lone Star participated in a serious case of elite corruption, Lone Star and its supporters maintain the fund's innocence, claiming that allegations of scandal were merely part of a broad political backlash against foreign investors. Whose claims are accurate? And, if Lone Star is indeed guilty, how does this incidence of Korean corruption measure up to those in the recent past? According to Transparency International's Corruption Perception Index (CPI), corruption appears to be a fairly common occurrence in Korea. Is the Lone Star scandal noteworthy only because a foreign firm was caught 'playing by Korean rules'?

This paper will seek to answer whether Lone Star, MOFE and the FSC are guilty, as alleged, of committing large-scale 'transactive corruption,' that is, exchanging rent for private favours.[1] In fact, the evidence, I would argue, reveals that corruption in the Lone Star takeover of KEB appears relatively mild, paling in comparison, for instance, to corruption under previous Korean authoritarian regimes, in particular Chun Doo-hwan's corrupt exchange of rent for bribes through the industrial rationalisation programme of the 1980s. While evidence indicates that laws and procedures were liberally interpreted, distorted and perhaps even broken to allow for Lone Star's ownership bid, an absence of rent signifies a lack of large-scale corruption. The overly aggressive investigation of Lone Star can best be explained as part of a hostile Korean response to the power of foreign capital and the demands of globalisation. The first section of the article will introduce a functional definition and approach to measure corruption. These tools will then be applied to the recent Lone Star Scandal, with rent and legal infringement serving to indicate whether or not corruption has taken place. After a brief comparison with the large-scale corruption typical under past Korean authoritarian rule, the article will examine the politics behind the Lone Star Scandal.

---

[1] Transactive corruption refers to a mutual arrangement between a donor and a recipient, actively pursued by and to the mutual advantage of both parties (Alatas 1990: 9).

2 Defining and Measuring Corruption

2.1 *Definitions*

A definition and method by which to measure corruption are crucial to resolving whether Lone Star's takeover of KEB qualifies as major graft, and to compare it with previous instances of elite corruption in Korea. This article adopts what Michael Johnston terms a 'modern' definition of corruption, focusing on the behaviour of government officials and politicians, as opposed to more 'classic' notions of corruption, which concern social morality (see Heidenheimer et al. 1989: 9). Among commonly accepted 'modern' definitions of corruption are legalistic ones, which classify a corrupt act as the violation of official regulations in return for bribes or status gain,[2] and the patron-agent-client model of corruption, which defines as corrupt an instance in which an agent (bureaucrat or politician) defies the will of the patron (in a democracy, the public) to make a deal with a client. Here, we adopt the most commonly used and accepted definition, Transparency International's simplification of the patron-agent-client model, with corruption as 'the misuse of public power for private gain' ('private' from the perspective of the agent, that is, the government official or politician). The legalistic definition of corruption can serve to identify an agent's breach of public trust for private return, since laws and rules in a democracy are usually designed to direct the agent to serve the public. This article also examines elite or 'grand' corruption, as opposed to lower-level bureaucratic graft, and corruption which is 'transactive', involving an exchange of government-provided rents (returns above market level) for either bribes (so-called market corruption) or loyalty (so-called parochial corruption) (see Alatas 1990: 3).

2.2 *Measuring corruption*

We must also measure corruption in order to determine its possible presence in the Lone Star takeover. One of the more common general

---

[2] Nye establishes the legalistic definition of corruption as 'a behavior which deviates from the formal duties of a public role because of private regarding (personal, close family, private clique) pecuniary or status gains' (Nye 1967: 419).

approaches to measuring corruption is to rely on indices, such as the Business International Index (BII) and Transparency International's Corruption Perception Index (CPI), which measure the perceptions of business people, foreigners, or the general populace towards the prevalence of corruption in society. Not only is this method inappropriate for the study of a single case such as the Lone Star takeover, but there is the strong possibility that perceptions of the interview subjects will be biased, as the great majority base their opinion of corruption on information obtained through the media, rather than through direct experience. An increase in media corruption coverage, then, if unrelated to the actual incidence of corruption, can distort public perceptions.[3] In the ROK, democratisation freed the press to cover corruption stories, which shot upward from an annual average of 8.8 under authoritarian rule to 771 stories under democracy.[4] Perception indices recorded a corresponding rise in Korean and foreign awareness of Korean corruption from 5.7 in 1980 to 5 in 1996, according to the BII. Transparency International's CPI dropped Korea from 27th in 1995 to 50th most corrupt state in 1999. When corruption reporting is so clearly divorced from instances of actual corruption, as in the Korean case, or a single case is in question, such as the Lone Star takeover, another more accurate method must be applied that directly measures corruption.

To qualify as a case of transactive corruption, in keeping with Transparency International's corruption definition, rent, in the form of assets or capital at below market prices, should be provided in return for something that maximises the private gain of the office holder, usually bribes or political loyalty. The existence of rent (or favours), then, is a necessary, but alone insufficient condition for the existence of corruption, since rent can also be offered as an incentive for firms to take an otherwise unprofitable action to advance the public interest,

---

[3] Such was the case in the United States, when an increasingly competitive television news industry intensified crime reporting to boost ratings. This manoeuvre led to a sharp rise in the perception of crime as a serious problem—5 percent in June 1993 named crime as the nation's most important issue, against 31 percent who did in February 1994 (Jackson and Naureckas 1994), while murder rates fell by over 41 percent in the 1990s. FBI, 'Unified Crime Reports, 1999, Table 1, Index of Crime, United States, 1980-1999'. Online: http://www.fbi.gov/filelink.html?file=/ucr/Cius_99/w99tbl01.xls.

[4] These figures relate to the average annual number of stories per year in the major South Korean daily *Chosun Ilbo* that included the word 'corruption'—'부정부패,부정비리', or '비리'. Authoritarian rule includes the Park *yushin* and Chun regimes (1973-87), with democracy represented by the years 1987 to 2004.

for instance, by stimulating economic recovery or fostering industrial revitalisation.

The first step to distinguish cases of transactive corruption in industrial restructuring is to identify whether rent has been transferred. It is not uncommon, however, for firms to deny receiving rent, instead alleging that financial assistance is merely fair compensation for taking on worthless assets. In the case of Chun Doo-hwan's industrial rationalisation, takeovers proceeded according to the 'takeover first, settle accounts later' principle, providing new owners control over target firm management and an opportunity to manipulate on-site inspections, to lower the purchase price and demand compensation from compliant state-controlled banks.[5]

Instead of analysing the results of on-site inspections, invariably a source of friction between the new and old owners, this article, employing comparative statics analysis, seeks to measure rent by comparing the purchase price to the market's estimation of target firm value, and comparing the firm's market value before and after the public release of takeover terms, in order to gauge the amount of government financial assistance, if any. Market capitalisation (the price multiplied by the number of shares) is employed to measure firm value. Relevant industry indexes are then utilised to control for alternate sources of share price variation. Increases in firm value are attributed to the provision of financial support only in cases where the firm's share prices diverge from the industry index.[6]

3   THE LONE STAR TAKEOVER OF KOREA EXCHANGE BANK: WAS IT CORRUPTION?

Applying the legalistic and Transparency International definitions of corruption can help us determine whether Lone Star's purchase of KEB qualifies as a case of corruption. According to Transparency In-

---

[5] Bank financial favours were subsidised by 3 percent loans from the Bank of Korea. In the first rationalisation case (of the Kukje Group), when a bank resisted (Korea First Bank) it was overruled by the president.

[6] On the basis of discussion with professionals in the Korean securities market, this study selects as a time horizon the interval from one week preceding a relevant event to two weeks afterwards. Examining the interval before the event takes into account the possibility of news leaks, particularly likely with regard to the release of financial statements, the preliminary drafts of which must receive firm approval prior to final release.

ternational's definition—the misuse of public office for private gain—Korean government officials at MOFE and FSC, and managers representing government interests at KEB must have abused their authority by selling publicly owned KEB shares at below market price to Lone Star in return for bribes. The crucial evidence in this type of transactive corruption is bribes to officials and bank management, and rent to Lone Star. Along the way, officials may have broken laws, rules or bureaucratic procedures to facilitate their scheme.

The supreme prosecutor's office and Board of Audit and Inspection alleged numerous legal and procedural violations during the Lone Star takeover of KEB. MOFE and the FSC were accused of breaking the bank law by providing Lone Star with an exception to prohibitions on majority ownership of a Korean bank by non-bank financial institutions (NBFI), even though KEB was not bankrupt as measured by its Bank for International Settlements (BIS) ratio. The financial authorities were charged with breaching administrative procedure by failing to issue a prompt corrective action (PCA) before granting Lone Star an exception and by limiting the bidding in the purchase of KEB, while MOFE was accused of exceeding its authority by pressuring the FSC and state-run Export-Import (EXIM) Bank of Korea to conform to its position. Officials breached procedure, the prosecutor alleged, to make a self-serving deal, exchanging rent, in the form of below market-priced KEB shares, in return for bribes.

Financial ministry officials do indeed appear to have taken an expansive interpretation of the bank law to allow a foreign NBFI such as Lone Star to take over KEB, although they were within precedent. However, the amount of rent provided to Lone Star was negligible at best and did not come close to the level of favours provided by Korea's authoritarian regime in the 1980s. The vigorous movement against the Lone Star takeover, therefore, appears motivated more by political opposition to over-dependence on foreign investment and globalisation than by criminal wrongdoing.

3.1 Assessing the evidence against Korean financial authorities

The question is to examine the legal merit behind accusations against Korean financial authorities, that they broke the bank law by approving an unqualified NBFI takeover, failed to follow procedure by not issuing a PCA, improperly limited the bidding, and allowed improper interference between financial agencies.

3.1.1 *Application of the bank law exception provision*

The prosecutor and BAI charged that the FSC had improperly granted Lone Star an exception to article 15 of the bank law, which limited NBFIs, such as Lone Star, to a 10 percent ownership stake in any Korean bank. The law's objective had been to prevent *chaebŏl* dominance of the financial sector and to ensure long-term oriented ownership. The prosecutor and BAI alleged that an exception could not be applied to KEB, which was not an insolvent financial institution according to its BIS ratio, and that FSC broke administrative procedure by granting an exception without first issuing a PCA.

The BAI claimed that KEB upper management, particularly its president, Lee Kang-won, vice-president, Lee Dal-yong, and bureau chief, Cheon Yong-jun, had provided the Financial Supervisory Service (FSS) with an unrealistically pessimistic forecast of KEB's end of 2003 BIS ratio in order to qualify the bank improperly as an insolvent financial institution, eligible to be taken over by an NBFI such as Lone Star, under article 2 of bank law enforcement ordinance 8 (Kang Jin-gu 2006). The BAI and prosecutor alleged that Lee Kang-won had discarded the most optimistic of Samil Accounting's three KEB asset forecasts for the May 2003 end of year, submitting to the FSC on 21 July 2003 the neutral and pessimistic forecasts, the latter with a 6.16 percent BIS prediction (*Hankook Ilbo*, 8 November 2006).[7] Following limited discussion, the FSC lowered its KEB forecast to 6.16 percent from an earlier forecast of 8.44-9.14 percent, providing, at an internal meeting on 25 July, the basis for unofficial FSC approval of Lone Star's request for a bank law exception (*Hankyoreh Shinmun*, 7 November 2006a).[8] The FSC officially approved the exception on 5 September 2003, concluding that with a BIS ratio of 6.16 percent, KEB's financial foundations could deteriorate and damage the bank's financial health.[9] The BAI charged, however, that KEB management simul-

---

[7] Samil Accounting's three plans estimated KEB's capital at 1.5288 trillion, 1.0584 trillion, and 588.7 billion won respectively.

[8] At the time Baek Je-heum, bank supervisory bureau chief at the FSS, was reported to have said that '6.16 percent is not credible' (Lee 2006).

[9] The FSC discussed a bank inspection division #1 document titled 'Prospects for KEB finances' with neutral and pessimistic 2003 KEB BIS ratio forecasts of 9.3 percent and 6.2 percent respectively.

taneously forwarded data to the KEB board of directors that yielded a BIS prediction of 10 percent, and from February 2003 had officially estimated its end of 2003 BIS at above 8 percent. Critics also complained that the pessimistic scenario contained unrealistically large loan loss reserves, and alleged fabrication of data, since fewer losses were predicted for some KEB borrowers under the pessimistic than the neutral scenario. The BAI concluded that with a BIS ratio of 9.56 percent during the first half of 2003—over 8 percent since the 1997 IMF crisis—KEB was not insolvent and did not qualify for a bank law exception.

MOFE and FSC defended the accuracy of their KEB BIS forecasts based on Samil's pessimistic scenario, arguing that KEB's loan loss reserves were not excessive (Kim Jae-ho 2006).[10] MOFE maintained that if KEB had not increased capital in October 2003, it was likely it would have gone bankrupt through the November 2003 LG Card incident and the bankruptcy of KEB Card, while the FSC pointed out that even with Lone Star's 1.1 trillion won capital infusion, KEB's BIS level of 9.3 percent at the end of 2003 was below the original 10.2 percent pessimistic prediction, and could have dropped to 4.4 percent without the Lone Star funds (Park and Kwon 2006).

The BAI also argued that the FSC had violated administrative procedure by granting an exception to Lone Star without first issuing a PCA to assist the bank to normalise operations under provision 10 of the financial industry structural reform law (Kim Young-bae 2006). Instead, MOFE and the FSC relied on article 2 of bank law enforcement ordinance 8, which provides an exception to the 10 percent NBFI share-holding limit, 'to reorganize a bankrupt financial institution or in cases in which special grounds are recognized'. BAI pointed out that the financial authorities had not legally designated KEB as a bankrupt financial institution.

The FSC response can be gleaned from the minutes of a FSC bank supervisory department meeting of 25 July 2003, which discussed a confidential document produced by the department, entitled 'Investigation of KEB's inducement of foreign capital'. The FSC acknowledged that KEB was not bankrupt, 'but considering its potential losses, its financial conditions could continue to deteriorate'. Applica-

---

[10] KEB's KEB Card loan loss reserve rate of 34.4 percent was similar to LG Card's 36.5 percent and Woori Card's 33.5 percent, and close to the actual amount of bad loans.

tion of the special grounds clause to restructure a weak financial institution could thereby be justified. The FSC also referred in the meeting to the precedent set by past exceptions granted to the bank law, which had allowed foreign Newbridge Capital and Carlyle, both NBFIs, to take over Korea First Bank and KorAm Bank in July 1999 and July 2000 respectively, 'neither of which had been bankrupt at the time of sale' (Lee Jung-hwan 2005). MOFE and FSC also claimed that issuing a PCA could destroy confidence and possibly result in KEB's collapse, hurting the Korean economy. Considering uncertain financial market conditions and KEB's financial difficulties, MOFE explained that it had no choice but to issue the exception (*Seoul Economy*, 20 June 2006).

The FSC's proper application of the bank law exception appears to boil down to whether KEB's condition warranted 'special grounds' under enforcement ordinance 8. The vagueness of what constitutes 'special grounds', however, grants officials excessive discretion and invites abuse. For instance, should authorities decide on the basis of actual or predicted BIS ratio? One possible standard of insolvency risk might be whether KEB's predicted BIS ratio would fall below the 8 percent international standard. By that measure, KEB looks to have been a borderline case, with financial performance ranking near the bottom of the Korean financial industry. KEB's end of 2003 BIS ratio of 9.3 percent exceeded only Chohung Bank, which had just been taken over by Shinhan Bank, and placed KEB near the 8 percent BIS limit without Lone Star's 1.1 trillion won capital infusion. On the other hand, KEB President Lee Kang-won and the FSC appear to broken protocol by accepting Samil Accounting's pessimistic scenario as the BIS forecasting standard, with Lee simultaneously reporting a much more optimistic forecast to his own board of directors. There were public goods grounds for KEB management and the FSC to bend rules to push through the Lone Star deal, however, since a Lone Star capital injection was likely to raise KEB share value, helping the state bank EXIM to recoup public funds injected into KEB and avoid any additional injection of public funds.

3.1.2 *Limited bidding*

The prosecutor and BAI also charged that KEB management and sales agent Morgan Stanley, in order to deliver favours to Lone Star, failed to openly announce the KEB sale or seek out as many interested investors as possible. The BAI argued that despite KEB's January 2003 privatisation plan calling for the transparent sale of its government-held shares, President Lee Kang-won, with MOFE's tacit consent, had already reached a secret agreement with Lone Star in December 2002, after the fund had suggested a takeover in October.[11] The BAI and prosecutor claimed moreover that KEB ignored Samsung Securities request for an open sale of shares, that Lee Kang-won did not contact any interested investors, contrary to his October 2004 claim to the National Assembly to have contacted 14 foreign banks, and that Morgan Stanley failed to follow a formal sales procedure, only contacting three banks in March 2003 to assess interest in KEB: the Hong Kong and Shanghai Banking Corporation, Standard Chartered Bank, and Newbridge. With a memorandum of understanding (MOU) with Lone Star close at hand, the contacts were a mere formality, in contrast to the 88 banks approached by Morgan Stanley in the October 2002 Chohung Bank sale (*Naeil*, 26 June 2006). The BAI also claimed that Lee had ignored Dubai Bank's interest in investing 600 billion won in the bank in June 2003, presumably because KEB's April MOU with Lone Star granted the fund exclusive negotiation rights.[12]

MOFE claimed that no bank had expressed interest in investing in KEB, neither KEB's major private shareholder Commerzbank, nor major foreign banks contacted by MOFE, including Bank One, BNP (Banque Nationale de Paris) Paribas, Crédit Suisse First Boston, JP Morgan Chase, Rabo Bank, HSBC, and Standard Chartered Bank. These all cited KEB's numerous bad loans and poor prospects for the Korean financial market and economy for their lack of interest (Kang Jin-gu 2006). Only Newbridge Capital submitted a confidential proposal for merger with Korea First Bank (KFB), and negotiations were simultaneously conducted with both funds until May 2003, when Newbridge withdrew intent to invest. Dubai Bank, according to MOFE, had only proposed investing US $300 million (360 billion won), much less than Lone Star's 1.1 trillion won (*Financial News*, 21 June 2006). MOFE argued that a fully transparent sale of KEB would

---

[11] BAI First Assistant Director-General Ha Bok-dong presentation of the intermediate results of the BAI investigation of KEB sale to the National Assembly Legislation and Judiciary Committee. Secretariat of the National Assembly (2006), 260th National Assembly, Extraordinary Session, 'Record of the Legislation and Judiciary Committee, 4th session', pp. 7-12, 26 June 2006. Online: http://likms.assembly.go.kr/kms_data/record/data2/260/pdf/260ba0004b.PDF#page=2.

[12] Secretariat of the National Assembly (2006).

have exposed the bank's severe capital shortage, leading to a run on deposits and instability in the Korean financial market. After KEB's shareholders had approved attracting investment through a limited competitive sale, MOFE said, public announcement of the sale was cancelled (Kim Jae-ho 2006).

Comment: KEB's board of directors is legally entitled to select their most preferred method of sale and clearly had an incentive to avert a crisis of confidence set off through exposure, which could have hurt KEB's value. On the other hand, transparency is also undeniably important as a mechanism to prevent collusion. In KEB's case, however, after a number of banks had been contacted and the press had disclosed rumours of a KEB sale in January 2003, it appears clear that any interested party would not have been excluded from entering a competitive bid.

3.1.3 *Bureaucratic interference*

The BAI and prosecutor also charged MOFE with exceeding its authority in the KEB Lone Star sale by pressuring the FSC to approve the deal and by hiding negotiations from the KEB board of directors and shareholders. The BAI and prosecutor argued that Byeon Yangho, policy head of MOFE's finance bureau, had played a central role in securing KEB for Lone Star, first persuading MOFE to approve, then influencing the FSC, EXIM and the KEB board of directors to complete the sale. The prosecutor claimed that after being approached by Lone Star in late 2002, Byeon actively promoted the Lone Star sale through various measures: sending Lee Kang-won a simulated sale of 51 percent of KEB shares to Lone Star for one billion US dollars in November 2002, instructing MOFE officials to 'solve the problem of Lone Star's qualifications to takeover KEB by any method' (*Kookmin Ilbo*, 7 November 2006), approving the KEB Lone Star MOU in March 2003 without consulting the FSC, and insisting, as chair of a July 2003 policy meeting of government financial institutions, that Lone Star receive the bank law exception, despite an internal MOFE report that 'it would be difficult to apply the exception regulation to Lone Star' (*Hankyoreh Shinmun*, 7 November 2006b).

The BAI argued that MOFE pressure prevented the FSC from independently assessing Lone Star's qualifications for a bank law exception and overrode checks and balances in the financial policy system. MOFE's vice-minister, Kim Jin-pyo, told Bloomberg Press that

Lone Star would take over KEB before the FSC could consider the case, and MOFE sent an official letter requesting FSC approval the day after Lone Star's application. Baek Je-heum, bank supervisory bureau chief at the FSS, allegedly ordered reluctant lower-level officials to lower KEB's predicted BIS and unofficially approved Lone Star's takeover request in mid-July, citing KEB's potential bankruptcy, without investigating Lone Star's qualifications or the accuracy of the BIS ratio forecast. Lone Star then completed the takeover in August, electing five new executives to the board of directors prior to official approval. The FSC hastily granted this in September, despite unresolved questions about Lone Star's ethical standards, financial stability and management structure.[13]

The prosecutor and BAI also claimed that Byeon and MOFE had exceeded their authority in overruling the state bank EXIM's opposition to Lone Star's request in June 2003 for a call option in the KEB sales contract and had allowed Lone Star to purchase EXIM shares at a later date; furthermore, that KEB President Lee, with tacit MOFE approval, had independently proceeded with the MOU, on-site inspection and formal investment proposal, only consulting the board of directors and KEB majority shareholders EXIM and Commerzbank in the final stages of the sale.[14]

In its response, the FSC rejected the BAI assertion that it had met Lone Star's request for an oral commitment without full investigation, arguing that 'the results of the July 25, 2003 meeting to discuss Lone Star qualifications ... did not comprise a legal verbal promise.' Such a promise in any case could not be provided under the bank law, since only an FSC general meeting could legally render a decision (*Seoul Economy*, 20 June 2006). FSS working-level officials who had assessed KEB's BIS ratio denied being forced deliberately to reduce their projection (*Korea Herald*, 12 April 2006). MOFE noted that its official duties included supervising EXIM, which justified intervening, with consultation from Morgan Stanley, when negotiations between EXIM and Lone Star stalled over the issue of the call option (*Seoul Economy*, 20 June 2006).

Comment: MOFE's successful persuasion of the FSC to adapt its position on the Lone Star KEB takeover is evidence of bureaucratic politics, but not proof of corruption. The political leadership has the

---

[13] Secretariat of the National Assembly (2006).
[14] Secretariat of the National Assembly (2006).

prerogative to delegate authority to various bureaucratic ministries as it sees fit, and may have granted more authority to MOFE.

4 RENT TO LONE STAR?

The prosecutor alleged that all of the legal and procedural violations by KEB management and financial authorities were part of a scheme involving transactive corruption—to deliver rent through below-market-priced publicly owned KEB shares in return for bribes. To measure corruption, therefore, what is required is to assess the amount of rent to Lone Star and determine if bribes were paid to government officials.

The prosecutor claimed that Lone Star's takeover price reflected unfounded fears of KEB going bankrupt, based on the unrealistic 6.16 percent BIS prediction—a 'giveaway price'—representing a favour of at least 344.3 billion won (Kang Jin-gu 2006). The BAI claimed that Morgan Stanley used the 6.16 percent BIS prediction to modify initial on-site inspection asset and debt values, arriving at a negotiation sales price level of 4,245 won per share, only 0.85 times book value, below Chohung Bank's recent takeover price of 1.66 book value. The BAI argued that KEB management instructed accounting firm Samil to exclude results from a second on-site inspection in April, which had revealed a 462.1 billion won rise in KEB's net asset value to 1.5288 trillion won, due to recovery of primary corporate borrowers, SK Global, Hynix and Hyundai Shipping, whereupon KEB decided not to renegotiate the price with Lone Star.[15] The BAI also criticised the inclusion of a call option in the contract, which allowed Lone Star to purchase more shares at a later date.

Lone Star, MOFE and FSC defended KEB's sale price of 4,250 won per share, noting that it was 15 percent above the July 2003 market share value (3,729 won), and included a price of 5,400 won paid for old shares, a 45 percent management premium. The FSC countered the BAI by calculating KEB's price as 2.44 times book value, compared to only 2.33 for Chohung, and pointed out that KEB was paid entirely with cash, compared to only 51 percent for Chohung. MOFE explained that mounting losses at KEB Card and fears of a KEB bankruptcy without capital injection kept KEB share values down in July,

---
[15] Secretariat of the National Assembly (2006).

preventing upward adjustment in KEB's price to match rising Hynix share values (Kang Jin-gu 2006). In fact, the 15 percent premium paid by Lone Star compares favourably with other recent Korean bank takeovers, above the 11 percent and 5.7 percent premiums paid by Carlyle and Citibank respectively to take over KorAm, and much better than the tremendous subsidies provided for Newbridge's takeover of KFB.

Table 1 Korean bank takeover premiums

Takeover bank	Target bank	Date of takeover	Stake size	Price per share (in won)	Market price previous month (in won)	Premium
Citibank	KorAm	24/02/2004	36.6%	15,500	14,664	5.7%
Carlyle	KorAm	14/11/2000	36.6%	6,800	6,115	11%
Standard Chartered	Korea First	12/01/2005	48.56%	16,511	Not traded	--
Newbridge	Korea First	03/07/1999	51%	5,000	2,645	89%*** (-57%)
Hana	Seoul	19/08/2002	100%	5,654	Not traded	--
Shinhan	Chohung	01/03/2003	80.04%	6,150	4,927	25%
Lone Star	KEB	01/10/2003	51%	4,245	3,70	15%

Source: KSE Data Base.

*** The sale of KFB to Newbridge Capital contained an indemnification clause, obligating the Korean government to buy back non-performing KFB loans in the first two years after the deal (three years for loans to debt-workout firms). So, even though KFB shares had been trading at 2,645 won, the government injected 1.02 trillion won into KFB after the purchase. Newbridge may have paid a 235 billion won premium (purchasing 51% of shares for 500 billion won), but they received 520 billion won in government subsidy, or a 57% return. The press termed the sale 'a fire sale' and Lee Hun-jae, former chairman of the FSC (1998-2000), finance minister (2000 and 2004) and acting prime minister (2000 and 2004) later called the terms of the sale regrettable.

MOFE also insisted that the call option included in the deal reflected the interests of the majority shareholders as much as those of Lone Star, which had demanded a call option of 5,000 won and all the profits from any rise in share value. Instead, the call option allowed EXIM and Commerzbank to share in possible share increases by stipulating a future sale for the higher of two prices, one a weighted average of new shares and old shares purchased, and the other the average market share price. MOFE insisted that EXIM's board of directors had independently decided to offer the call option to Lone Star (*Newsmaker*, 20 June 2006a).

As evidence that KEB shares had sold at market price, MOFE and Lone Star pointed out that even if one argued that MOFE had illegitimately influenced EXIM and BOK's decision to sell, Commerzbank, a private party to the transaction with abundant commercial and banking experience, had acted to further its own best interest by freely approving the terms of the deal. Two permanent and two outside directors represented Commerzbank on the board of directors during the Lone Star negotiations, providing authority over KEB management. MOFE pointed out that Commerzbank had approved selection of Lone Star in April 2003 and actively participated in negotiations over the price and conditions of the purchase, reviewing and approving reports on the main conditions of the purchase from KEB management in June and July of that year. MOFE added that Commerzbank had sent letters confirming their earlier approval of the sale to Lee Kang-won, president of KEB, and to Park Chong-gun, chair of the National Assembly finance and economy committee, in October 2005 and February 2006 respectively (*Newsmaker*, 20 June 2006b).

Minutes[16] from a board of directors' meeting of 29 August 2003 appear to show Commerzbank's satisfaction with the sales terms to Lone Star. Commerzbank's two directors, KEB Deputy President Manfred Drost and Managing Director Hans-Bernhard Merforth, forecast increasing KEB losses and opposed delaying the sale for fear that Lone Star would recalculate and request a price deduction. An anonymous KEB labour union member mentioned that Commerzbank, concerned by KEB Card's financial difficulties and the North Korean nuclear weapons programme, had been warning throughout 2003 that KEB losses would exceed the level of 2000, when capital had been reduced (*Financial News*, 23 April 2006). A Commerzbank presentation in 2003 to international investors in Germany presented the sale of KEB shares as part of a wider restructuring strategy to sell off loss-making banks following divestment in Erste Bank, Deutsche Börse, Crédit Agricole and Buderus. Commerzbank had struggled with losses

---

[16] These minutes were presented before the National Assembly on 23 April 2006.

of €215 million in the fourth quarter of 2002, and needed to raise its Tier I BIS ratio to over 7 percent from 6 percent to 6.7 percent.[17]

Commerzbank was not alone in expecting further deterioration in KEB's finances after the takeover. The Korean press erroneously reported in July 2003 that Lone Star was negotiating with the government over a 'put back option' clause in the contract to guard against future drops in KEB share value, by allowing Lone Star to sell back shares at a predetermined price (*Newsmaker*, 29 July 2003). Interestingly, critical press reports of the Lone Star takeover in 2003 focused on Lone Star's possible violations of the bank law and notoriety as a speculative fund—not the takeover price (*Korea Times*, 8 August 2003; *Newsmaker*, 29 July 2003; Chung 2003).

Participants in negotiations between Lone Star and KEB noted that KEB's market-traded share value influenced negotiations more than on-site asset inspections. An effective means for KEB management to lower Lone Star's purchase price would be to disseminate pessimistic BIS ratio predictions to lower market appraisal of KEB's value. To the contrary, however, throughout 2003 President Lee publicised KEB's positive performance and higher actual and predicted BIS ratio, while successfully maintaining secrecy around the lower BIS predictions submitted for MOFE and FSC approval of a bank law exception. Lee Kang-won announced at a July 2003 shareholders' meeting that he 'didn't agree that KEB was bankrupt ... that this year is looking much better', citing increased net interest profit of 10.2 percent, a 25 percent rise in commission fee profits, and a doubling of before-tax profits to 200 billion won (Lee Jung-hwan 2005). In an October 2003 press briefing, Lee Kang-won trumpeted KEB's July and August net profits of 156.5 billion won (US$135.97 million) and predicted a net profit for the third quarter of 2003 (*Korea Herald*, 11 October 2003). Press reports throughout 2003 only referred to BIS ratios of 9 percent and above for KEB; none mentioned the 6.16 percent BIS projection (*Korea Times*, 8 August 2003, 30 October 2003).[18]

---

[17] Presentation by Dr Eric Strutz, Commerzbank's CEO, 'Investors' Day 2003, Financials: Facts and Figures', 10 September 2003 at Glashütten (Taunus), Germany.

[18] The June 2003 BIS was believed to be 9.3 percent, forecast to rise to 11.9 percent in October following the takeover.

5 BRIBES FROM LONE STAR?

The prosecutor charged that Lone Star had bribed Byeon Yang-ho (MOFE's finance bureau policy chief), and KEB top management to attain rent through a below-market price purchase of KEB shares. KEB President Lee Kang-won allegedly received 710.5 million won in severance pay for early retirement, and 720 million won in consultation fees, thereby exceeding KEB's permissible limit, and was appointed as a consultant and outside board member to KEB after the takeover by Lone Star (*Donga Ilbo*, 8 November 2006). Lee Dal-yong, former KEB vice-president, received 875 million won in severance pay compensation (Kim Ji-hyun 2006). The prosecutor charged that Byeon Yang-ho was paid off later with a 40 billion won (US$43 million) KEB investment in his private fund, Vogo Investment. The prosecutor alleged further that Lone Star had provided lawyer Ha Jong-seon[19] with 2 billion won (US$2.13 million) to lobby government officials to facilitate the KEB sale, although no evidence existed of Ha passing on the funds.

Lee Kang-won's alleged compensation exceeded KEB internal regulations, and therefore appears suspicious, although the compensation could have been provided as compensation for Lone Star breaking an earlier pledge to maintain his position. Or, Lee could have been paid off simply for forwarding a pessimistic BIS prediction to help Lone Star qualify for the takeover, apart from the issue of takeover price. Lone Star's alleged payment to Byeon is harder to grasp, however. Why would Byeon take on such great risk in return for the vague promise of future compensation—investment two years later in a private investment fund he had yet to establish? Forty billion won was only a drop in the bucket for Vogo Fund, which was large and profitable enough to purchase BC Card, Korea's largest credit card company. It is also highly implausible that a single medium-level government official such as Byeon should have determined MOFE's position on the controversial Lone Star KEB takeover and have persuaded the FSC and EXIM to follow. Yet the prosecutor cleared higher-ranking officials of involvement, such as MOFE head Kim Jin-pyo, Kwon O-kyu, Blue House senior secretary for national policy, and Lee Hun-jae, former minister of finance and FSC head.

---

[19] Ha was president of Hyundai Marine and Fire Insurance, and worked for Lone Star as a lawyer during its takeover of KEB.

If one were to assume that Lone Star did receive a large amount of rent in the takeover, one could entertain the possibility that the Roh administration was complicit, instructing the prosecutor to limit investigation to Byeon and Lee Kang-won. Large successful bribery cases in democratic Korea, however, usually involve dozens of high-level politicians and officials (31 in the case of the infamous Hanbo bribery case, for instance), as the diffusion of authority under democracy increases the number of veto players. Opposition party members on important committees in the National Assembly must be bought off, and have ample interest to expose the administration's involvement. Their silence makes this scenario highly unlikely.

6 COMPARISON WITH THE CHUN INDUSTRIAL RATIONALISATION

The lack of rent to Lone Star is striking in comparison to the tremendous illicit favours gained by cronies under previous Korean authoritarian regimes, such as Chun Doo-hwan's restructuring, from 1981 to 1987, of the construction, shipping, steel, and textile industries. The Chun dictatorship provided seven trillion won in financial assistance through the industrial rationalisation programme in the form of write-offs and postponed repayment of interest and principal, and new preferential interest rate loans to 57 firms it designated to take over others. Firms were not required to pay a takeover price in four of the seven largest takeovers, which represented an immediate gain of US$20 million to US$40 million, while financial assistance drove up the values of takeover firm shares in the short time surrounding public release of the takeover terms, even with share indices controlling for other possible contributing factors.

In contrast to Chun's claim that assistance represented compensation to well-managed firms to take over poorly run, non-viable operations, to help revive struggling industries and to preserve jobs, analysis of five key measures of financial performance reveals that target firms outperformed the firms designated to take them over in four of the five largest cases. A look at Chun's record of bribe receipts reveals that the largest rent recipients under industrial rationalisation had also shouldered the greatest bribe burdens, both overall and in their respective industries (see Table 2).[20] Many large rent recipients also had marriage ties with Chun's elite, notably Daelim and Daewoo, both rumoured to be on the verge of bankruptcy (see Table 3). Chun, therefore, had clearly allocated rents in return for private gain, either to increase the receipt of bribes or to consolidate the support of his ruling elite.

---

[20] With assistance from the People's Solidarity for Participatory Democracy (PSPD), I filed a freedom of information request with the National Assembly administrative affairs office on 19 May 1998, under the newly passed Korean Freedom of Information Act. My request covered several hundred thousand pages of sealed documents detailing the exchange of bribes under the Fifth Republic that had been provided by various ministries to National Assembly members participating in the 150th General Assembly's closed-session 38th Special Inquiry into Corruption, held in 1988. Following an initial rejection, I appealed on 13 July with assistance from the PSPD, and in August 1998 the National Assembly's freedom of information deliberative committee granted my request. The information released to me came as the first application of the Korean Freedom of Information Act for classified National Assembly documents.

Table 2 The Chun industrial rationalisation: winners, loser, financial support and rent

Losing group	Winning group	Debt terms: #yrs deferred/ #yrs repayment/ interest rate	Price paid per share	Post support share value*	Gain from target	Gain from own share rise	Total gain
Kukje Affiliate Union Steel	Dongkuk	US$229 million credit guarantee Write off	2,517 won	4,120 won	US$22 million	? Not publicly traded	US$22 million +
Kukje Commerce	Hanil	US$218.8 million: Write off US$218.8 million: 15/15 US$263.2 million: 12/10 US$70.3 million: 10/10/10% New loans	1 won	821 won	US$43.09 million	US$47.3 million	US$90.4 million
Kukje Commerce	Kukdong	US$165 million: Write off US$74 million: 15/5 US$90.8 million: 15/10 US$64.85 million: 10/10/10% New Loans	80 won	821 won	US$8.133 million	US$9.367 million	US$17.5 million
Daehan Sunjoo	Hanjin	US$494.7 million: Write off US$438.8 million: 15/15 US$235 million: 5/5/5% New Loans	419 won	860 won	US$15.403 million	? Not publicly traded	US$15.403 million +

Losing group	Winning group	Debt terms: #yrs deferred/ #yrs repayment/ interest rate	Price paid per share	Post support share value*	Gain from target	Gain from own share rise	Total gain
Namkwang	Ssangyong	US$169.7 million: Write off US$169.5 million: 15/10 US$62.6 million: 10/10 New Loans	Free	1,690 won	US$27.699 million	? Not publicly traded	US$27.699 million +
Daelim	Samho	US$340.7 million: 10/15 US$48.1 million: 3/0 US$34.4 million: 20/0 US$111.7 million: 10/10/10% New Loans	Free	1,590 won	US$42.297 million	US$558.778 million	US$601 million
Daewoo	Kyungnam	US$554 million: 15/15 US$235 million: 12/5/10% New Loans	1/100 won	1,695 won	US$33.149 million	US$269.916 million	US$303 million

*Average value two weeks following support.

Sources: Debt terms from Government of the Republic of Korea, Ministry of Finance (MOF), *Reorganization of Infeasible Firms*, a compilation of documents from the MOF, Bank of Korea, Bank Supervisory Board, and main banks, in: National Assembly, *Fifth Republic Corruption Hearings*, July 1988, p. 323; FOI requested materials, prices from *FOI Request Material*; Gains calculated from *KSE Data Base*; Bribes per asset data from National Assembly, *1988 Investigation into Fifth Republic Corruption*, requested materials which include: National Tax Office, *Confirmation of the Record of the Tax Treatment of Political Donations*, February 1989; Blue House, *New Village Movement Donation List*, February 1989; and, for direct political contribution data, Government of Korea, High Court, *Chun Doo-hwan Trial Documents*, 16 December 1996.

Table 3 Performance, bribes and family ties, 1979-84

	Affected Groups	A	B	C	D	E	Top Firm	Elite Ties	Bribe Per Asset	Industry
W	Dongkuk	55	27	18	9	36		Four ministers One ambassador	.021 (1st Overall)	Steel
L	Union	82	73	73	46	91	***		.0007	
W	Hanil	78	33	22	67	33		Two KMA presidents Roh Tae-woo NA DJP member	.038 (3rd Overall)	Textiles
L	Kukje	60	60	80	40	60	***		.0007	Shoes
W	Hanjin	43	0	0	0	0		One minister	.01331 (1st in Industry)	Shipping
L	Daehan Sunjoo	71	29	29	43	14	***		0	
W	Ssangyong	14	11	11	89 (19)	43 (17)			.00426 (8th of 40 in Industry)	Construction
L	Namkwang	46	52	51	16	32	***		0	
W	Daelim	68	30	24	22	76	***	Brother-NA chairman Chun's brother employed by group	.00497 (9th of 40 in Industry)	Construction
L	Samho	35 (55)	19	16	19 (38)	22			0	

THE LONE STAR SCANDAL: WAS IT CORRUPTION? 105

	Affected Groups	A	B	C	D	E	Top Firm	Elite Ties	Bribe Per Asset	Industry
W	Daewoo	* please see note						Brother is deputy prime minister Roh Tae-woo	.00475 (13th of 40 in industry)	Construction
L	Kyungnam	24	33	23	60	22	***		0.00016 (bottom of industry)	
W	Kukdong	95	97	95	89	95			.027 (2nd Overall)	Construction

Source: Bribes per asset data from National Assembly, *1988 Investigation into Fifth Republic Corruption*, requested materials, which include: National Tax Office, *Confirmation of the Record of the Tax Treatment of Political Donations*, February 1989; Blue House, *New Village Movement Donation List*, February 1989; and, for direct political contribution data, Government of Korea, High Court, *Chun Doo-hwan Trial Documents*, 16 December 1996. Financial statistics were gathered from *Annual Analysis of Firms*; family tie data from *Chaeböl and Chaeböl Families*.

Financial Rankings are % of industry firms below the firm.
*** Best Performer
A = Sales/Assets
B = Profit/Financial Cost
C = Earnings/Assets
D = Current Ratio
E = Debt/Asset
L = Loser
W = Winner

* Daewoo Corporation, a trading firm, also contained the group's smaller construction operations. In mid-February 1985, rumours of Daewoo's collapse led to a 20 percent fall in share value and prompted the group to issue a disclosure denying that Daewoo had become a target of Chun's industrial rationalisation programme, or had entered into non-payment. From *Chosun Ilbo*, 'Daewoo Disclosure says no Truth to Rumour of Non-Payment', 22 February 1985 [in Korean].

7 A POLITICAL EXPLANATION

Lone Star may have been guilty of over-compensating a former bank president to help secure an exception to the bank law, as two other NBFIs had done before. The KEB price was in line with other contemporary Korean bank takeovers, though, so it appears unlikely that Lone Star received rent through the deal. Why then, has the Lone Star case provoked so much interest, prompting investigations from the National Assembly, BAI, and the prosecutor, and motivating assignment of over 80 attorneys in the prosecutor's office for 11 months of mostly fruitless investigation? To understand why, one must examine underlying political motives behind the scandal.

Opposition to Lone Star's takeover bid began with the KEB Card labour union, which found allies among progressive non-governmental organisations (NGOs) and the opposition political parties. Revelation of the fund's tremendous tax-free profit in 2006 turned popular opinion against Lone Star, strengthened the anti-Lone Star forces and prompted the first of several National Assembly probes into the takeover.

Soon after Lone Star's takeover, the KEB union reacted to Lone Star's violation of a promise not to change bank management by threatening a strike and blocking access to a meeting of the board of directors to elect a new president (*Korea Times*, 11 November 2003). KEB Card union's opposition to Lone Star stemmed from the fund's layoff of 54 percent (over 1000) of KEB card workers following the merger between KEB and KEB Card in November 2003. A former KEB Card employee, Chang Hwa-shik, also former vice-chairman of the Korean Federation of Clerical and Financial Labor Unions, responded by establishing an anti-Lone Star NGO, Spec Watch, in August 2004, with backing from national labour leaders and academics. Spec Watch, with 5,050 petitioners, then filed suit against Lone Star in the Seoul Administrative Court in October 2004, arguing that the takeover should be ruled invalid for violating the bank law. Spec Watch later protested against the alleged low price of the takeover, sought equal acquisition rights for domestic NBFIs, and expressed a general hostility to foreigners taking over major Korean firms (Choe and Kim 2006).

Spec Watch's opposition to Lone Star was encouraged by growing popular resentment toward foreign investors. This stemmed initially from the Korean taxpayers' repayment of loans provided by the International Monetary Fund (IMF) to ensure repayment of private foreign lenders. Concern grew about a perceived outflow of national wealth, as foreign investors cashed out lucrative profits from the sale of Korean firms and property acquired during the crisis at depressed prices under a weak Korean won. The 1.151 trillion won and 701.7 billion won profits (thanks to 8.4 trillion won in combined Korean government support) earned by foreign funds Newbridge and Carlyle, through their purchase and sale of Korea First Bank and KorAm Bank, respectively, would now be topped by Lone Star's 4.5 trillion won profit from the sale of KEB to Kookmin Bank. Lone Star, already a record profit earner through Korean real estate speculation, further incensed Korean public opinion by evading taxes on the KEB sale, by locating company headquarters in Belgium, a tax haven (*Korea Times*, 31 October 2006).

As popular opposition to Lone Star mounted with the impending KEB sale, Spec Watch found a sympathetic audience from National Assembly opposition parties—the conservative Grand National Party (GNP), the leftist Democratic Liberal party (DLP), and the smaller Democratic and People First parties—who charged that the Roh Moo-hyun government was complicit in the case and complained about an outflow of national wealth through the KEB sale. The opposition was pleased to turn the Lone Star KEB sale, Roh's first successful inducement of foreign investment, against the government. Supportive Assemblymen, including some from the ruling party, provided Spec Watch with evidence for its case against Lone Star, and initiated probes into the Lone Star KEB purchase (Choe and Kim 2006). Opposition to Lone Star also conformed to the pro-*chaebŏl* policy of the GNP, which sought to eliminate limitations on domestic NBFI ownership of banks, and to the pro-labour, nationalistic outlook of the progressive DLP (Kim Jae-ho 2006).

Spec Watch joined the National Assembly finance committee in charging Lone Star employees involved in the KEB takeover, prompting the prosecutor's September 2005 investigation. The National Assembly finance and economy committee followed in October 2005 with a parliamentary inspection of the approval of the takeover by the FSC and the FSS. As Lone Star proceeded with the KEB sale to Kookmin Bank, following expiration of a two-year required ownership period in February 2006, the four National Assembly opposition parties attempted to block the sale, first through a legally flawed draft resolution demanding government suspension of the sale. In March

2006, a four-party investigatory committee, consisting of 29 members, asked the BAI to investigate the KEB sale, while the National Assembly's finance committee requested that the prosecutor investigate the KEB sale yet again. By August 2006, the anti-Lone Star coalition widened with the addition of the Korean Alliance against the Korea-US FTA. (This alliance against the proposed free trade agreement included progressive NGOs, labour representatives, academics and the press.)

8 Conclusion

The prosecutor, in December 2006, charged Lone Star with corruption, alleging that the fund had bribed the financial authorities to receive favours through the below-market purchase price of KEB. To facilitate the deal, MOFE and FSC were accused of improperly providing Lone Star with an exception to the bank law's ban on NBFI takeovers, of failing to issue a PCA, of limiting bidding, and of breaking normal bureaucratic decision-making protocol. A closer look at the takeover, however, reveals that other banks had been informed about the bidding; issuing a PCA might have damaged KEB's value; and bureaucratic politics fail to constitute evidence of corruption. KEB's projected BIS level without capital infusion placed it near the 8 percent insolvency standard. KEB thus qualifies as a borderline case, a judgment call for financial authorities eager to follow the precedent established by the takeover of KorAm and Korea First banks by foreign NBFIs Carlyle and Newbridge. Most importantly, though, Lone Star received no rent from the takeover. Corruption, therefore, if it existed, was of a fairly mild variety, particularly when compared to previous graft in Korea under the Chun regime. Political factors, namely popular hostility to foreign capital in the wake of the IMF crisis, combined with the effective influence of financial unions, civic groups and opposition parties can better account for the disproportionate attention paid to the Lone Star scandal.

Elements of Korean democracy may have made the exchange of bribes for rent less likely, by increasing transparency and accountability and by expanding the winning coalition, thus reducing incentives and increasing the cost and risks for firms and politicians to engage in corruption. While democracy has helped prevent leaders from reallocating private property for private gain, democratic governments also show a tendency to redistribute private property to the general public. Populist pressures do appear to have contributed to the Lone Star scandal. Liberal democracies also possess a judicial system to uphold private property rights, however, and indeed the Seoul courts have demonstrated independence in the Lone Star case by rejecting several of the prosecutor's requests for arrest warrants. This is where Lone Star's best hope lies for a fair outcome in the case that in July 2007 was still proceeding. One clear lesson from the Lone Star scandal is the pressing need to revise ambiguously worded clauses in the bank law, which can help to reduce excessive bureaucratic discretion and help prevent any future such fiascos.

REFERENCES

Alatas, Syed Hussein (1990), *Corruption: Its Nature, Causes and Functions*, Aldershot UK: Avebury
Cho, Jae-hyon (2006), 'Headed to Lone Korea?', in: *Korea Times*, 8 November 2006
Choe, Kye-wan and Kim Kyung-hwan (2006), 'Lone Star Fund: A Korean Investor Must Be Named', in: *Hankyoreh 21*, 29 June 2006 [in Korean]
Chung, Kil-gun (2003), 'Negotiations to Induce Capital from the US Fund Lone Star', in: *Economy 21*, 27 June 2003 [in Korean]
Donga Ilbo, 'President Lee Kang-won Promised to Keep Job Five Days before the Contract ... Suspicions of Back Dealing', 8 November 2006 [in Korean]
Financial News, 'Commerzbank Predicted KEB Insolvency Beforehand', 23 April 2006 [in Korean]
Financial News, 'Looking Back at 2003, KEB ... Recall Issuance of 300 Billion Won ABS', 21 June 2006 [in Korean]
Hankook Ilbo, 'Resilient Investigation into the KEB Give-Away Sale', 8 November 2006 [in Korean]
Hankyoreh Shinmun, (a) 'KEB Giveaway Price Sale: "Not a Policy Mistake but Collusion"'; (b) 'Warrant Issued For Former MOFE Bureau Chief Byeon Yang-ho', 7 November 2006 [in Korean]
Heidenheimer, Arnold J., Michael Johnston and Victor T. LeVine (1989), 'Terms, Concepts, and Definitions: An Introduction', in: Arnold Heidenheimer, Michael Johnston and Victor T. LeVine (eds), *Political Corruption: A Handbook*, New Brunswick NJ: Transaction, pp. 8-9
Jackson, Janine and Jim Naureckas (1994), 'Crime Contradictions', in: *Extra!*, May/June 1994
Kang, Jin-gu (2006), 'MOFE and FSC Directly Oppose the BAI: "There was no Choice"', in: *Newsmaker*, 20 June 2006 [in Korean]
Kim, Jae-ho (2006), 'MOFE's and FSC's Unusual Direct Opposition to the KEB Investigation', in: *Chosun Ilbo*, 21 June 2006 [in Korean]
Kim, Ji-hyun (2006), 'KEB Sale Illegal and Abnormal, Prosecutors Say', in: *Korea Herald*, 8 December 2006
Kim, Young-bae (2006), '"Lee Hun-jae Gate": Is this an Imaginary Tale?', in: *Hankyoreh 21*, 29 June 2006 [in Korean]
Kookmin Ilbo, 'President Lee Leads the KEB Sale: Financial Authorities Collude', 7 November 2006 [in Korean]
Korea Herald, 'KEB Rises on CEO's Upbeat Forecast', 11 October 2003
Korea Herald, 'Inspectors Expand Probe into KEB', 12 April 2006
Korea Times, 'Lone Star's Eligibility for KEB Takeover Questioned', 8 August 2003
Korea Times, 'Lone Star Completes Takeover of KEB', 30 October 2003
Korea Times, 'KEB Union Challenges Lone Star', 11 November 2003
Korea Times, 'Harmonizing Nationalism and Globalization', 31 October 2006
Lee, Jung-hwan (2005), 'Amazing, Lone Star's Advanced Financial Techniques', in: *Economy 21*, 26 September 2005 [in Korean]
Lee, Woo-seung (2006), 'The Prosecutor Decides to Request an Arrest Warrant for Kim Suk-dong or Byeon Yang-ho', in: *Segye Ilbo*, 8 November 2006 [in Korean]
Naeil, 'The Sale of KEB to Lone Star: Pre-Emptive Protection', 20 June 2006 [in Korean]
Newsmaker, 'Speculative Fund KEB Sale Approved', 29 July 2003 [in Korean]

Newsmaker, (a) 'Was there a Crisis Three Years Ago or Not? Standard for Judging the KEB Sale', (b) 'MOFE: "If Capital Hadn't Been Expanded KEB Would Go Insolvent"', 20 June 2006 [in Korean]

Nye, Joseph S. (1967), 'Corruption and Political Development: a Cost-Benefit Analysis', in: *American Political Science Review*, 61 (2), pp. 417-27

Park, Seung-hyu and Kwon Jae-hyun (2006), 'Those Related to the KEB Sale to be Summoned this Week', in: *Newsmaker*, 20 June 2006 [in Korean]

Seoul Economy, 'MOFE: "The KEB Sales Price Was Correct"', 20 June 2006 [in Korean]

CHANGING PERCEPTIONS OF INWARD FOREIGN DIRECT INVESTMENT IN POST-CRISIS KOREA (1998-2006)[1]

Judith Cherry

ABSTRACT

This article analyses trends in inward foreign direct investment (IFDI) in post-crisis Korea, focusing on the problems facing the Korean government in its efforts to attract higher levels of inward FDI by changing both the nation's 'hardware' (laws, regulations, institutions and systems) and its 'software' (attitudes, mindsets and actions). The article uses European investors in Korea as a case study; the major theme that emerged in the interviews carried out with executives was that there are significant mismatches between the speed and effectiveness of the reforms made to Korea's IFDI 'hardware' and 'software'. These reflect, to a great extent, the disparity between the speed at which Korea has emerged as a major player and key trading partner in the global economy, and the rate at which mindsets and attitudes have altered—in terms of Koreans' attitudes towards foreign participation in their economy, their perceptions of the world and their place in it, and foreigners' views of Korea.

The past thirty years have seen a dramatic increase in global flows of foreign direct investment, with both inflows and outflows rising from around the US$18 billion mark in the early 1970s to the US$450 billion level by the late 1990s. Since the 1990s, investment flows to developing countries have been facilitated by a shift in perceptions of inward foreign direct investment away from the negative and unwelcoming attitude adopted in the 1970s and 1980s to a much more positive assessment of the potential benefits of IFDI and the contribution it can make to economic development and growth.[2] This shift in percep-

---

[1] This article contains excerpts from Judith Cherry (2007), *Foreign Direct Investment in Post-Crisis Korea: European Investors and 'Mismatched Globalization'*, London: Routledge. Relevant fieldwork was carried out with financial support from the British Academy, which the author gratefully acknowledges.

[2] The beneficial effects of IFDI can be felt in areas as diverse as fixed capital formation, technology and skills transfer, productivity and efficiency, international com-

tion was particularly evident in East Asia, where some countries opened their markets to foreign investors in the hope of attracting the capital, technology and expertise needed to enhance their firms' competitiveness in global markets (Kim Zu Kweon 2003: 86-90). In Korea,[3] however, the negative perceptions of IFDI, the passive and reactive attitudes of successive governments towards inward investment promotion, and the controlling and restrictive nature of their IFDI policies remained largely unchanged for the first 35 years of the country's economic development. It was only after the financial crisis of 1997 that the government took active steps to increase Korea's attractiveness as a host for inward investment, reflecting a new perception of the role that foreign investors could play in helping the country recover from the crisis and creating a firm foundation for sustainable growth in the future.

This article begins with a brief overview of past inward foreign direct investment in Korea, providing the context for the analysis of inward investment in post-crisis Korea (1998-2006) that follows. Using European investors in Korea as a case study, the analysis focuses on the problems facing the Korean government in terms of its efforts to attract higher levels of IFDI by changing both the nation's 'hardware' (its laws, regulations, institutions and systems) and its 'software' (the attitudes and actions of its people).

1 INWARD FOREIGN DIRECT INVESTMENT IN PRE-CRISIS KOREA (1962-97)

Between 1962, when the first case of inward foreign direct investment was notified to the Korean authorities, and the outbreak of the Asian financial crisis in 1997, IFDI notifications remained at comparatively low levels, achieving a cumulative total of US$24.6 billion during the 35-year period, to be invested in 10,452 projects (see Table 1).[4] Although legislation providing for the inducement of foreign direct in-

---

petitiveness, employment and national wealth, trade and the balance of payments situation, and economic concentration (Hood and Young 1979; Kim Mi-a 1999: 81; Invest Korea 2004: 1). For a more detailed discussion of the positive and negative effects of inward foreign direct investment, see Cherry (2006).

[3] In this article, 'Korea' refers to the Republic of Korea (South Korea).

[4] The Korean Investment Notification Statistics Center provides IFDI data for this period (1962-97) on a notification basis only.

vestment was enacted in the early 1960s, the Park Chung-hee government showed a strong preference for commercial loans over IFDI as a means of financing its economic development plans. Accordingly, FDI inflows were controlled and restricted, and inward investment notifications registered just US$150 million in 195 projects between 1962 and 1969. However, the shift in Korea's economic policy in the 1970s away from labour-intensive light industrial manufacturing sectors towards the development of heavy and chemical industries necessitated an easing of the restrictions on IFDI projects that could bring in the capital, technology and skills needed for the successful transformation of the economy.

As inward investment increased in the 1970s, the influx of foreign capital (particularly from Japanese investors seeking lower production costs in Korea) exacerbated concerns about the possible negative effects of IFDI in terms of foreign domination of the economy and the erosion of Korea's economic sovereignty. This in turn prompted the government to tighten the laws once again, giving priority to joint ventures in which foreigners' shares were capped at 50 percent (Maigov 2001: 22). These new restrictions, combined with rising wage levels in Korea, led to a decline in IFDI notifications; between 1974 and the first major revisions to IFDI policy a decade later, annual notifications stayed well below the US$300 million level, dropping as low as US$79 million in 1976 (Investment Notification Statistics Center 2006). By the end of 1983, the cumulative value of investment notifications since the beginning of the 1970s stood at US$2.2 billion to be invested in 2,367 projects (see Table 1).

Table 1 Korean inward foreign direct investment: 1962-1997
(Notification basis: in cases, millions of dollars, percent)

	Notification volume	% of total	Notification value	% of total
1962-1969	195	1.9%	149.9	0.6%
1970-1983	2,367	22.6	2,174.7	8.8
1984-1992	3,730	35.7	7,839.8	31.8
1993-1997	4,160	39.8	14,481.9	58.8
Total	10,452	100.0	24,646.3	100.0

Source: Investment Notification Statistics Center 2006.

From the mid-1980s, the Korean government implemented a series of measures aimed at deregulating and liberalizing IFDI and improving the country's business and investment environment in order to make Korea a more attractive host for investment by foreign multinational corporations (MNCs). The weakening of the preference seen in previous years for commercial loans over IFDI as a means of financing economic development was prompted by both domestic and external factors. In the late 1980s, Korean companies found their international competitiveness eroded (principally by high wage increases) and faced a growing challenge at the low end of the global market from newly industrializing economies that still possessed the competitive advantage of low-cost labour. The switch to the technology-intensive, high value-added production necessitated by these developments required access to the advanced technology, skills and know-how possessed by multinationals from the major industrialized economies of the world.

In addition, the Korean government's reliance on overseas borrowing in the 1960s and 1970s had resulted in a rapid increase in the country's total foreign debt, which had soared from US$89 million in 1962 to US$40.4 billion in 1983 (SaKong 1993: 258-9). The US government's policy of maintaining high interest rates and a strong dollar, which had the effect of increasing both the principal and interest on loans from American financial institutions, and the debt crisis in Latin America prompted a re-evaluation of the Korean government's policy of restricting inward foreign direct investment. Finally, the Korean government was coming under increasing pressure to open its markets to foreign—principally American and European—goods and services. In the words of one Korean scholar, the government shifted its attitude to one of a 'cautious welcome' for inward investment, with rigorous approval procedures but generous benefits for those who did invest (Jung 1987: 271).

The measures to promote IFDI achieved some degree of success, as notifications broke through the US$1 billion mark in 1987 and cumulative investment reached US$7.8 billion between 1984 and 1992, with total volume in excess of 3,700 projects (see Table 1). Inward investment was boosted by the economic boom of the late 1980s, the gradual liberalization of the domestic market, and increased investment activity in the service sector ahead of the 1988 Olympic Games. Annual notifications remained above the US$1 billion mark until 1989; thereafter, the economic problems facing Korea and affecting domestic firms, including slower economic growth, union militancy, rising production costs and excessive red tape, caused IFDI notifications to fluctuate between US$800 million and US$1.4 billion through to the end of 1992 (Investment Notification Statistics Center 2006).

The liberalization and deregulation measures implemented by the Kim Young-sam government as part of its *segyehwa* (globalization) policy had a significant impact on inward investment activity in Korea in the early- to mid-1990s. Almost 60 percent of the IFDI notifications made between 1962 and 1997 occurred during Kim's five-year term of office, reflecting the increasing attractiveness of the Korean market and the new opportunities for foreign multinationals created by the ongoing revision of IFDI-related laws and regulations. Nevertheless, Korea continued to lag behind its regional competitors in terms of attracting inward investment, and on the eve of the 1997 crisis the Kim Young-sam government maintained to a significant degree the restrictive and passive attitude towards IFDI that had been adopted by its predecessors.

Inward foreign direct investment activity in Korea during the pre-crisis period was dampened by a number of factors, most important of which was the government's preference for foreign capital in the form of loans rather than IFDI. This in turn reflected the state's desire to control the allocation of financial resources to domestic firms by channelling funds through the state-guided domestic financial sector, and resulted in IFDI policies that sought to regulate and manage inward investment, rather than encourage and promote it. Another significant deterrent was the negative public sentiment that prevailed in some sectors of society regarding foreign participation in the Korean economy; specifically, concerns that increased levels of inward investment might lead to foreign domination of the economy and an erosion of Korea's economic sovereignty. In addition, during the 1960s, Korean academics cited the weakness of the local economy, the low levels of demand for advanced and sophisticated technology in light industrial, labour-intensive manufacturing industries, and the reliance of Korean firms on the mature technology embedded in the outdated machinery they imported from overseas as factors depressing inward investment activity (Kim Pyŏng-sun 2002: 14; SaKong 1993: 119; Song 2004: 15). Finally, in the late 1980s, foreign investors were discouraged by the economic problems facing Korea and affecting domestic firms, including slower economic growth, union militancy, rising production costs and excessive red tape.

2 INWARD FOREIGN DIRECT INVESTMENT IN POST-CRISIS KOREA (1998-2006)

One of the most dramatic changes that occurred in the wake of the 1997 financial crisis in Korea was the shift in government policy and attitudes towards inward foreign direct investment. Having been regarded as a second-best option for financing development from the 1960s through to the late 1990s, IFDI took on a new significance and attraction for policy makers. There was a growing consensus that Korea had to make concerted efforts to attract higher levels of inward investment in order to recover from the crisis, enhance the international competitiveness of domestic corporations and ensure future growth. In addition to helping Korea in the short term by providing much-needed injections of capital and acquiring insolvent or struggling Korean corporations, foreign investors could make a valuable longer-term contribution to replenishing Korea's depleted foreign exchange reserves, boosting production, increasing exports, enhancing productivity and creating jobs and wealth.

Following the inauguration of Kim Dae-jung as president of the Republic of Korea in February 1998, the new government implemented the reform programmes mandated by the International Monetary Fund (IMF) as a condition of its rescue package. The proposed reforms in the corporate, financial and public sectors and in the labour market were crucial in two respects: firstly, as a means of building an economic structure that could withstand any further external shocks and of helping local corporations develop into world-class enterprises and, secondly, as a way of creating a business environment that would attract substantial amounts of high-quality inward foreign direct investment. In addition to these programmes of reform and restructuring, the government also took swift and decisive action to promote and encourage inward investment. In November 1998, the Kim administration enacted the Foreign Investment Promotion Act with the stated aim of attracting US$20 billion in IFDI by 2002 and placing Korea in the top ten host nations for inward investment in the world.

The shift in policy from 'passive liberalization to active promotion' also involved the establishment of new institutions, major revisions to IFDI-related regulations, the full-scale liberalization of investment sectors, the revamping of incentives, and the creation of an investment environment capable of attracting internationally competitive MNCs (Kim June-Dong 2003a: 24; Hwang 1999: 3; Kim Pyŏng-sun 2002:

24). Institutional changes had begun with the establishment in April 1998 of the Korea Investment Service Centre, which was charged with the task of providing a one-stop service for potential investors, offering assistance in all investment-related matters ranging from the application process to labour issues, taxation and legal matters (Pak 2003: 13; Kim Suk 2000: 292). The Office of the Investment Ombudsman was established in October 1999 to resolve any problems experienced by foreign investors in their business and daily lives, with 'home doctors' providing one-to-one assistance for investors in matters such as obtaining business permits and raising grievances with the authorities (Park 2003: 229-30).

In terms of IFDI-related regulations, investment procedures were greatly simplified, the range of institutions to which notifications could be made was expanded, and the government increased the number of industries open to foreign investment (Kim Suk 2000: 292-4). Among the most important regulatory changes was the complete liberalization of mergers and acquisitions transactions; this move, along with the elimination of the ceiling on foreign equity ownership in the stock market in May 1998, gave foreign companies far greater access to Korean assets than ever before. Another highly significant move was the complete liberalization of the Korean real estate market in July 1998 and the revision of the Foreigners' Land Acquisition Act to allow foreign nationals to purchase land in Korea (Park 2003: 229). In the immediate post-crisis period, the Kim government also expanded the range of tax incentives available to foreign investors and took steps to improve the working environment, enhance transparency in the workplace, strengthen the protection of international property rights, and bring Korean business practices into line with international standards (Pak 2003: 13; Kim Suk 2000: 294).

The impact of these changes on inward investment levels was dramatic: after rising to US$8.9 billion in the year following the IMF bail-out, IFDI notifications soared above the US$15 billion mark in 1999 and maintained that level the following year (see Table 2). Actual levels of investment also experienced rapid growth, doubling from US$5.3 billion in 1998 to more than US$10 billion in 1999 and 2000. Although the government's liberalization measures and its more positive approach to IFDI promotion were clearly a factor in the surge in inward investment, IFDI levels were also boosted by the fall in stock and asset prices caused by the depreciation of the Korean currency which, combined with the large number of business put up for sale as a result of bankruptcy or restructuring, created substantial investment opportunities for foreign multinationals (Yu 2002: 91).

Table 2   Korean inward foreign direct investment: 1997-2002 (Notification/actual invested basis: in millions of dollars, cases, percent)

	Notification value	Year-on-year increase	Notification volume	Actual value*	Year-on-year increase
(1997)	(6,970.9)	(117.7%)	(1,110)	---	---
1998	8,852.6	27.0	1,401	5,308.0	71.7%
1999	15,531.4	75.4	2,103	10,851.0	104.4
2000	15,249.6	-1.8	4,144	10,238.0	-5.7
2001	11,286.2	-26.0	3,344	5,055.0	-50.6
2002	9,092.6	-19.4	2,409	3,804.0	-24.8
Total	60,012.4		13,401	32,256.0	

* Actual value statistics from Invest Korea database: none available prior to 1998.
Source: Investment Notification Statistics Center 2006; Invest Korea 2007.

Given the temporary nature of some of the key factors fuelling inward investment after 1998—exchange rate fluctuations, the fall in stock prices and the rush to sell off assets—the investment boom of the late 1990s was short-lived. In 2001, notifications dropped by 26.0 percent to US$11.3 billion and declined by a further 19.4 percent to reach US$9.1 billion in 2002. A similar trend was seen in the value of actual investments, which peaked at US$10.9 billion in 1999 before dropping to US$5.1 billion in 2001 and US$3.8 billion in 2002, the final year of the Kim Dae-jung administration. Before looking at the reasons for this reversal in Korea's fortunes, it will be useful to identify and explain trends in inward investment between 1998 and 2002 and highlight the concerns that were being expressed over the quality of foreign investment entering Korea.

One of the most significant trends in Korean IFDI after the crisis was the continuing 'tertiarization' of inward investment: the shift away from investment in manufacturing to a focus on the service sector in general and the financial sector industries in particular. In 1997, investment in service industries had accounted for 62.5 percent of the total value of IFDI notifications in Korea; the corresponding share for manufacturing was 36.0 percent. Investment in the service sector declined immediately after the crisis as a consequence of the recession in the domestic economy, falling levels of disposable income, declining demand for service industry products and concerns about the country's economic prospects. However, it increased again after 1999 with the rapid recovery of the Korean economy, the restructuring of the financial sector, and the further liberalization of the tertiary sector. By 2001, the service sector had regained its dominant position in terms of inward FDI, accounting for a 64.1 percent share of the value of notifications—a sharp contrast with the share of 25.8 percent taken by the manufacturing sector in the same year (Investment Notification Statistics Center 2006).

Another important trend in post-crisis IFDI during the Kim Daejung administration was the increasing level of mergers and acquisitions (M&A) activity following the lifting of the government's ban on hostile takeovers. In many cases, Korean firms experiencing liquidity problems or facing bankruptcy received injections of cash from a foreign partner aiming to gain a controlling share of the business; in others, Korean conglomerates approached foreign multinationals with offers of assets for sale. The share of total IFDI notifications accounted for by M&A transactions rose from 10.0 percent in 1997 (US$700 million) to 15.0 percent in 1999 (US$2.3 billion) before falling back to 8.4 percent in 2000 (US$1.3 billion) (Investment Notification Statistics Center 2006). The rise in the share of total IFDI accounted for by M&A transactions came at a time when concerns were being expressed about the quality of inward IFDI in terms of both the relative decline in manufacturing investment and the increase in M&A deals, which might result in streamlining and job losses (compared with greenfield investments, which are guaranteed to create employment).

The third major trend between 1998 and 2002 was the emergence of European nations—principally the member states of the European Union—as major investors in Korea. Prior to the crisis, IFDI was dominated by firms from the United States; American firms maintained their leading position in 1998, despite the small decline in the value of their notifications from US$3.2 billion in 1997 to US$3.0 billion. Investment by Japanese companies remained well below that of American and European firms, fluctuating between a low point of US$504 million in 1998 and peak of US$2.5 billion two years later. In 1999, Europe became the leading investor region, with notifications of

US$6.4 billion, compared with US$3.7 billion from the United States and US$1.7 billion from Japan. Over the five-year period, European firms accounted for the largest share of cumulative investment in Korea: 31.3 percent (US$18.8 billion), compared with shares of 30.0 percent for the United States (US$18.0 billion) and 11.5 percent for Japan (US$6.9 billion) (Investment Notification Statistics Center 2006).

Two trends that were giving Korean government officials cause for concern during this period were the increasing proportion of IFDI accounted for by new, rather than additional, investments and the move towards smaller-scale projects. With the exception of 2000, the share of total IFDI accounted for by foreign multinationals making additional investments in their Korean subsidiaries fluctuated around the 40 percent mark. A higher proportion of notifications to re-invest might be taken as an indication of a strong degree of satisfaction on the part of investors regarding their business operations in Korea and a positive view of Korea's future economic prospects. Finally, immediately after the crisis, the share of all investment notifications accounted for by projects valued at less than US$10 million was just over 90 percent. The trend towards small-scale projects continued and increased through to 2002, by which time 96 percent of all projects notified to the Korean authorities were valued at less than US$10 million; during this period, fewer than 45 projects in any year were valued at more than US$100 million (Investment Notification Statistics Center 2006).

The downturn in IFDI notifications and actual investment levels in 2001-02 prompted a vigorous debate in government and academic circles seeking to identify and remove the remaining barriers to inward investment. In the immediate post-crisis period, reports detailing the positive role that foreign investors had played in Korea's recovery from the crisis[5] (Chang 2001; Ch'oe 1998; KIEP 1998) and upbeat media coverage about the benefits of IFDI appeared to reflect a view that the Korean government's efforts to induce foreign capital were justified in terms of the beneficial effects seen in the domestic economy. Indeed, people who expressed negative views about IFDI were regarded as 'ultranationalists' or people who were out of touch with the needs of the times (Yang 1999: 34). However, as the Korean economy began to recover, exchange rates stabilized and the most ur-

---

[5] For a detailed discussion of the role played by foreign investors in Korea's post-crisis economic recovery, see Cherry (2006).

gent phases of the financial and corporate restructuring programmes were completed, the old exclusionist sentiments began to resurface. Negative reports about the activities of foreign firms circulated, fuelling deeply rooted concerns about 'fire sales' of Korean companies, an outflow of national wealth and the possible domination of the domestic economy by foreign multinationals (Kim Chin-jung 2000: 70-72; Ch'oe 2003: 99). These sentiments contributed to a 'weakening of the social consensus' that foreign investors should continue to play a role in the future growth of the Korean economy (Kim June-Dong 2003a: 1-2, 23).

Externally, the most important factors underlying the decline in IFDI levels were the stagnation of the global economy and FDI flows and the emergence of the People's Republic of China (PRC) as a major competitor in terms of attracting inward investment (Mun 2004: 21; Kim June-Dong 2003a: 18, 2003b: 198). Other factors included economic uncertainties following the terrorist attacks of 11 September 2001, and tensions between the United States and Iraq on the one hand and the US and North Korea on the other (Samsung Economic Research Institute 2003: 6). Domestic media reports of anti-American sentiment and demonstrations focusing on the US military presence in Korea further increased uncertainty among investors from the United States (Duerden 2002; O 2003: 369).

Inward FDI activity was also dampened by dissatisfaction among foreign investors experiencing problems with the Korean business and investment environment. The main focus of investor complaints was the lack of transparency and consistency in implementing the laws and regulations relating to inward investment. The situation was exacerbated by a lack of assistance from some bureaucrats, poor information flows, low levels of co-operation within and among government departments and agencies, and the Kim administration's failure to check whether or not the proposed improvements to the regulatory systems had actually been implemented. Other complaints included the lack of adequate investor relations management and post-investment support services, the weakness of overseas promotion regarding potential investment sectors and the Korean investment and business environment, and the inferiority of the incentives provided by the Korean government (Samsung Economic Research Institute 2003: 7; Kim Chin-jung 2000: 65-6, 68-70). Investors were further troubled by rapidly rising labour costs and low productivity, and the lack of labour market flexibility and high levels of union militancy presented problems for investors wishing to streamline the workforces of companies they had acquired (Song 2004: 24; Kang 2002: 35-6; Kim Chin-jung 2000: 62). Finally, foreign investors had concerns about the management and business culture in Korea; these focused on problems arising from debt-financed business expansion by Korean firms, the lack of transparency in corporate and financial governance, problems in obtaining credible financial and corporate information, the preference for business relationships based on personal connections rather than economic principles, and the 'widespread' bribery and corruption (Kim Chin-jung 2000: 63, 71-2).

As we have seen, the downturn in IFDI notifications came at a time when the Korean economy was showing signs of recovery, with gross domestic product (GDP) and *per capita* GDP both returning to pre-crisis levels of US$546.9 billion dollars (at current prices) and US$11,499 respectively. There had also been a spectacular recovery in usable foreign exchange reserves, which had increased from US$8.8 billion dollars at the end of 1997 to US$121.4 billion by the end of 2002 (KOSIS 2007; Invest Korea 2007). While there had been concerns about the 12.7 percent decline in exports in 2001 (to US$150.4 billion), export growth became positive once more in 2002, rising by 8 percent to reach US$162.5 billion, the second highest level in Korea's history (KITA 2007).[6] The recovery in these key economic indicators prompted the question: would the Korean government be as keen to promote inward investment now that the immediate dangers associated with the 1997 crisis appeared to have passed? Given the reluctance of successive governments in the past to open up the Korean market fully to foreign goods and services, the continuing dissatisfaction expressed by existing investors about barriers to their operations in Korea, and the weakening of the social consensus regarding the desirability of increased levels of IFDI, it seemed entirely possible that efforts to boost inward investment might begin to weaken with the upswing in Korea's economic fortunes. The change of government in 2003 was a potential watershed: the point at which IFDI promotion policies and systems could be further enhanced to stem the decline in inward investment, or the point at which attention could be re-focused on other policy issues.

---

[6] The highest level of exports recorded in any one year up to this point was US$172.3 billion in 2000 (KITA 2007).

Following President Roh Moo-hyun's inauguration in February 2003, the Korean government confounded sceptics by continuing with and even intensifying efforts to attract inward foreign direct investment. The policy of taking further action to improve the Korean business and investment environment and thus boost IFDI was closely linked with the Roh administration's key policy objective of transforming Korea into a business hub for Northeast Asia. For the new government, success in achieving its goal of developing the country into a regional logistics base, a financial hub and a centre for the headquarters of global multinational companies would depend to a great extent on its ability to complete the process of transforming Korea into an attractive host nation for inward foreign direct investment (Krause 2003: 33-4). The Roh government demonstrated its commitment to boosting Korea's performance in terms of attracting inward investment by re-launching the national investment promotion agency, Invest Korea, in November 2003. Invest Korea's mission was to create an investor-focused promotional system and provide support and incentives for investment in specific industrial sectors, targeting in particular the cutting edge investment needed to advance Korea's economic goals.

The new agency lost no time in clarifying its position on IFDI promotion and setting its agenda: in the immediate post-crisis period, the aim of Korea's inward investment policy had been simply to attract as much foreign capital as possible in order to stabilize the foreign exchange market, replenish the nation's depleted foreign exchange reserves and promote reform and restructuring. Five years on, Korea's situation and requirements had changed but the national investment promotion policy had not evolved in response to those changes. Invest Korea now aimed to link its IFDI promotion activities and the provision of investment incentives to the broader goal of enhancing Korea's international competitiveness, identifying target investment industries to which incentives and preferential funding could be applied (Invest Korea 2004).

Although the value of IFDI notifications continued to fall during the first year of the Roh administration, declining by almost 30 percent to reach the US$6.5 billion mark, the following year saw investment flows nearly double, with the value of notifications soaring to US$12.8 billion. After shrinking by almost 10 percent the following year and falling to US$11.6 billion, notifications declined by a further 2.9 percent in 2006, remaining just above the US$11 billion mark (see

Table 3). In contrast, the value of *actual* investments increased by almost 35 percent to US$5.1 billion in 2003, jumped a further 81 percent to US$9.3 billion in 2004 and then edged up to US$9.6 billion in 2005, before declining by 2.5 percent to US$4.4 billion in the first six months of 2006. The volume of IFDI also remained fairly stable, fluctuating between 2,600 and 3,700 cases per annum between 2003 and 2006 (MOCIE 2007; Invest Korea 2007).

Table 3 Korean inward foreign direct investment: 1998-2006 (Notification and actual invested basis: in millions of dollars, cases, percent)

	Notification volume	Notification value (A)	Increase	Actual value (B)*	Increase	(A)-(B)
1998	1,401	8,852.6	27.0	5,308.0	71.7%	3,544.6
1999	2,103	15,531.4	75.4	10,851.0	104.4	4,680.4
2000	4,144	15,249.6	-1.8	10,238.0	-5.7	5,011.6
2001	3,344	11,286.2	-26.0	5,055.0	-50.6	6,231.2
2002	2,409	9,092.6	-19.4	3,804.0	-24.8	5,288.6
2003	2,600	6,470.6	-28.8	5,130.0	34.9	1,340.6
2004	3,110	12,792.0	97.7	9,262.0	80.5	3.530.0
2005	3,707	11,563.5	-9.7	9,643.0	4.1	1,920.5
2006	3,108	11,232.8	-2.9	4,372.0	-2.5	
Total	12,525	42,058.9				

* Actual investment statistics available only for the period 1998-6/2006.
Source: MOCIE 2007; Invest Korea 2007.

The fall in investment notifications in 2003 was attributed by the Ministry of Commerce, Industry and Energy (MOCIE) to the global economic slowdown, the resulting decline in FDI inflows to most countries of the world (with the exception of China and Vietnam), and negative investor sentiment brought about by the war in Iraq (*Invest Korea Journal* 2003a, 2003b, 2004b). As IFDI activity recovered in 2004, Korean government officials ascribed the rise in capital inflows to the increase in global M&A activity as the recovery of the world economy got underway and, closer to home, to the concerted efforts made by Invest Korea to increase levels of inward investment. However, MOCIE warned that, despite the improvement in performance, factors including skyrocketing oil prices, global terrorism and strained domestic labour-management relations could dampen inward investment activity in the short term (*Invest Korea Journal* 2004a, 2004b, 2005). In 2005, with notifications declining by almost 10 percent, MOCIE cited the strength of the Korean won, the rise in international energy prices and the reduction in investment incentives in Korea as factors depressing IFDI activity (Duerden 2003; *Invest Korea Journal* 2006).

However, seen over a ten-year period, the trend was more encouraging; in the nine years following the 1997 crisis, the average annual value of IFDI notifications was US$11.3 billion. Following the initial decline in FDI inflows under the new government, annual notifications equalled or exceeded that average amount in 2004 (US$12.8 billion), 2005 (US$11.6 billion) and 2006 (US$11.2 billion). Furthermore, the gap that has always existed between notifications and actual investments narrowed considerably, falling from US$5.3 billion in 2002 to US$1.3 billion in 2003. After widening to US$3.5 billion in 2004, the discrepancy shrank to US$1.9 billion the following year, indicating a growing trend for foreign multinationals to follow through on their investment proposals (MOCIE 2007; Invest Korea 2007).

This period saw a continuation of four key trends in IFDI already observed during the Kim Dae-jung administration: investor preference for the service sector, the dominance of European firms, the increase in levels of M&A activity, and the predominance of small-scale investments. During the Roh administration, with the exception of strong performance in 2004, the share of total notifications accounted for by manufacturing companies fluctuated between just 26 and 38 percent of the total, with the service sector taking a share of around 60 percent. On a cumulative basis during this period, the Europeans once again took the largest share of IFDI, with notifications valued at US$16.4 billion or 39.0 percent of the total; the cumulative value and shares for the United States and Japan were US$10.4 billion (24.6 percent) and US$6.8 billion (16.1 percent) respectively (MOCIE 2007). The share of total FDI inflows accounted for by M&A transactions, which had stood at just 7.8 percent in 2002, rose sharply during the early part of the Roh Moo-hyun administration, reaching 42.9 percent of investment notifications during 2005 (US$5.0 billion out of a total of US$11.6 billion). There was a corresponding decline in the share accounted for by greenfield investments which, having peaked at 90.0 percent in 2002 (US$8.2 billion out of US$9.1 billion), accounted for less than 60 percent of notifications made during 2006 (US$6.7 billion out of US$11.2 billion) (MOCIE 2007).

Finally, investment activity continued to be dominated by small-scale projects; immediately after the crisis, the share of all investment notifications accounted for by projects valued at less than US$10 million was over 90 percent. The trend continued in 2003, with the share increasing to 96.7 percent and remained at a similar level through to the end of 2006, with fewer than 25 projects in any year valued at more than US$100 million. The increase in small-scale projects was due in part to the emergence of the PRC as a key investor in Korea—important in terms of volume rather than size. The PRC's share of the volume of investment notifications increased steadily, rising from 0.2 percent in 1990 to 27.3 percent ten years later (1,165 cases out of 4,275) before settling into a range of 11 to 23 percent between 2001 and 2006. However, there was better news for the authorities in terms of the tendency of foreign investors to re-invest in their businesses in Korea; between 1998 and 2002, the share of total IFDI accounted for by foreign MNCs making additional investments fluctuated around the 40 percent mark. During this period, the share accounted for by additional investments ranged from 43 percent to 66 percent, indicating a higher degree of satisfaction with and greater confidence in the Korean investment and business environment (MOCIE 2007).

As in the previous period, the stagnation in investment notifications resulted in a wide-ranging debate on ways to enhance further Korea's attractiveness as a host for inward investment. In early 2006, the government took action once again to regenerate the national investment promotion agency and appointed Chung Tong-soo, an American citizen who had trained as a lawyer and worked in the US Department of Commerce, as the new head of Invest Korea. The new chief executive made it clear that he viewed Invest Korea as just one element of the national drive to promote IFDI and emphasized the fact that other government ministries and agencies also had a key part to play in the process. Thus the role for Invest Korea as it went forward would be one of facilitator and co-ordinator, seeking to improve collaboration between ministries and between central and regional governments in matters relating to inward investment. Chung also suggested that Invest Korea needed to improve its relationship with the foreign business community and establish itself as a vital resource for foreign investors (*Invest Korea Journal* 2006: 10).

Analyses of foreign investors' perceptions of the Korean business and investment environment carried out at this time revealed that almost a decade after the financial crisis, foreign investors in Korea still faced a number of all-too-familiar problems and challenges in their daily working life. Korean and foreign commentators identified the same barriers to investment: the regulatory framework, including the lack of transparency of regulations and the inconsistency in their interpretation and implementation, particularly in the areas of taxation and intellectual property rights; union militancy and the high costs of labour; the challenges posed by the unfamiliar business environment despite attempts at reform; anti-foreign capital sentiment; and Korea's poor image among foreigners as a place to live, invest and do business. Furthermore, potential investors were often exposed to negative reporting about the Korean business environment and the exclusionist sentiments that lingered in some quarters of Korean society (Song 2004: 32-5; Weisbart 2004).

None of these barriers was new; indeed, many of these complaints and criticisms had been made by Korean analysts and foreign investors both before and after the 1997 crisis. In the immediate post-crisis period, the Kim Dae-jung government had taken action to enhance Korea's business and investment environment and to resolve the problems that had long plagued foreign investors. The approach taken by the Kim Dae-jung administration was one of changing Korea's 'hardware' by reforming and restructuring the corporate, financial and public sectors, addressing issues relating to the labour market, and implementing measures to bring the country's systems, institutions and regulatory framework into line with international best practice. Despite the Kim government's considerable achievements in these areas and notwithstanding the initial boom in post-crisis IFDI, the Roh Moo-hyun administration continued to face complaints from foreign investors and actual FDI inflows remained below the US$10 billion level each year. With the 'hardware' updated, it was time to focus attention on the 'software' of IFDI promotion by considering the impact on inward investment of the attitudes, mindsets and behaviour of the Korean people and foreign investors, and to consider the long-standing complaints and problems from a new, socio-political-cultural perspective.

3 CASE STUDY: EUROPEAN INVESTORS IN KOREA

In 2006, I carried out a series of 40 in-depth interviews with European businessmen, members of the Delegation of the European Commission to the Republic of Korea (DELKOR), and officials and members of the European Chamber of Commerce in Korea (EUCCK). The interviewees included expatriates with a wide range of experience in Korea (from less than one year to more than 30 years), representing a variety of nationalities and a broad spectrum of businesses, stretching from manufacturing to services and from major multinational corporations to small- and medium-sized enterprises.[7] The interviews sought to analyze changes in the business and investment environment since the 1997 crisis, assess Korea's advantages as a host for inward investment, identify obstacles to investment and the smooth running of business operations, and make suggestions for overcoming those obstacles and boosting IFDI levels.

In terms of barriers to inward investment, a major theme of the interviews was that there were significant mismatches in Korea between the speed and effectiveness of the reforms carried out on the 'hardware' of inward FDI (regulations, systems and institutions) and the changes seen in the 'software' (culture, business practices and attitudes). The European executives and officials highlighted a number of key areas—including regulations, labour relations, human resources and Korea's image—where disconnections between policy and implementation, the speed of change and resistance to reform, and perception and reality acted as a hindrance to the business operations of existing investors and as a possible deterrent to potential investors.

The greatest source of concern for many European investors in 2006 was the 'massive mismatch' between, on the one hand, the policies adopted by the Korean government and the regulatory framework created in order to support those policies and, on the other, the actual implementation of those policies and regulations by working-level officials. For many interviewees the problem lay in the fact that the necessary legislation and regulations did exist (and in many cases were as robust as any in the industrialized nations of the world) but either were not enforced or were implemented in an inconsistent and non-transparent manner. This made day-to-day operations and rela-

---

[7] As the interviews were carried out on the condition of strict anonymity, no references are given for the quotations used in this section.

tions with the Korean bureaucracy 'extremely time consuming and frustrating'.

A common complaint among European investors was the ambiguity of, and large number of grey areas in regulations, which gave lower-level bureaucrats leeway to make arbitrary decisions and interpret legislation in an inconsistent manner. This, they felt, could be explained to a great extent by the presence of forces of resistance within institutions and organizations, including bureaucrats reluctant to relinquish their power base or have their authority diminished by more transparent regulations that were not open to a variety of interpretations. At a broader policy level, investors highlighted the contrast between the government's general commitment to liberalizing and deregulating the economy, abiding by international codes of practice and creating a more favourable investment environment, and decisions taken by individual ministries and agencies which aimed to protect Korea's interests but, in fact, undermined the government's credibility among investors.[8] Furthermore, consistency in the implementation of key policies was undermined by the rapid turnover amongst high-level government officials, some of whom served less than a year in office.

In the area of labour relations, many interviewees expressed concern about the annual wage negotiations, which could be stressful and emotionally charged for companies with active and sometimes aggressive unions. Investors also commented on the dramatic manner in which union leaders and members made their demands, which often contributed to an increase in the tensions between foreign managers and their workers. Many felt that the excessive wage demands made by union leaders and employees reflected an assumption that foreign employers would not relocate operations to a country with lower labour costs (as many Korean firms were already doing) and therefore showed a lack of awareness of the realities of global business and the choices facing 'footloose' multinationals. Moreover, the unions appeared not to realize that the drama surrounding high-profile wage negotiations created a negative image of Korean union militancy that could act as a deterrent to potential foreign investors. However, as some interviewees observed, it might simply be that promoting inward

---

[8] An excellent example of this was the enactment of 'anti-tax treaty shopping' legislation in 2006, in the wake of the controversy over the US private equity fund Lone Star's exemption from Korean withholding tax when repatriating its profits through its subsidiary in Belgium. See Cherry (2007) and the article by Schopf in this volume for more details.

investment was not high on the bureaucrats' and union officials' agenda and that they saw little reason to change their attitudes and actions to suit foreign investors. This in turn suggested a persisting scepticism about the contribution that foreign investors could make to the continuing economic development of the country.

In discussions about the quality of human resources and education in Korea, many investors noted the contrast between the quantity of education and training received by their employees and the quality of that education in terms of the acquisition of job-related skills such as creative and lateral thinking, problem solving and fluency in foreign languages. In the eyes of many interviewees, this was the result of the focus on memorization and rote learning in the Korean education system, which continued to be strongly influenced by the Confucian values of respect for seniority and authority and observance of rigid hierarchies. After the 1997 crisis, when Asian values had come under attack, there had been high levels of interest in Western management techniques. However, a decade later there was an obvious discrepancy in some areas of corporate Korea between those early efforts to bring business and management systems into line with international best practice and the limited achievements in terms of a switch away from more traditional approaches to management that were based on Confucian values and beliefs.

The persistence of deeply-entrenched educational methods, management systems and business culture characteristics reflected to some degree the belief among those who resist change that the Korean approach remained valid in the new global business environment. It might also stem from a desire to hold on to more familiar values and systems in a rapidly-changing global business environment. Finally, interviewees identified a mismatch between the Koreans' perceptions of themselves and their place in the world and the general lack of knowledge about Korea in other parts of the world (including Europe). This they attributed to the underdevelopment of Korea as a tourist destination for non-Asian travellers and the weakness of official marketing activities aimed at highlighting the country's attractions as a tourist destination and investment location.

During the interviews, it became apparent that the impact of each of the negative factors identified by European executives could vary greatly among existing investors and also between existing and potential investors. For companies that were well-established and profitable, the challenges they faced on a day-to-day basis were serious and time-consuming but were viewed by many as merely part of doing business in Korea, and one investor even referred to them merely as 'irritants'. However, in terms of promoting inward investment, these issues could become much more significant as they might discourage existing investors from re-investing in and expanding their operations. In addition, the absence of positive news stories about Korea, the lack of knowledge and understanding of the social and cultural issues underpinning Korean business, and the inability to put key issues in the context of Korea's highly accelerated economic development could create and exaggerate negative perceptions of the country, the market and the people. While some potential investors would be undeterred by these issues and would focus on the competitive advantages of Korea, others might well question the wisdom of investing in a country portrayed by some sections of the media and described by some disgruntled and dissatisfied expatriates as hostile to foreign capital, with militant unions and an alien business culture.

In the eyes of most of the European executives and officials interviewed, the answers to these problems were more political and sociocultural than economic in nature. In the area of policy and regulation they felt that there was a need to create monitoring systems that could ensure that government policy was being implemented rather than undermined or discredited. They suggested that the government should consider lengthening the terms of office for key ministers and even for the president in order to facilitate greater consistency between the formulation and implementation of policy. Education could play a crucial role in bringing about the changes suggested by interviewees, in terms of reforming the national education system so that it would support the development of global managers. In a more general sense, it was felt to be important to educate government officials, regulators, the media and the public about the significance of globalization and the benefits that foreign investment has already brought and can continue to bring to Korea. Negative perceptions of Korea overseas could be challenged and overcome by proactive marketing and public relations activities. Foreign investors could play their part by becoming culturally aware, making determined efforts to understand Korean society and culture, and engaging with the government in discussions on enhancing and promoting Korea's advantages as a host for inward investment.

In addition to improving the investment environment and attracting more high-quality IFDI, many of the changes suggested by foreign investors would benefit the Korean nation as whole, contributing to the building of a strong and highly competitive economy. Greater consistency in the implementation of policy and regulations would help domestic and foreign businesses equally, and changes in education would benefit the nation in terms of fostering a creative and talented workforce with the skills to work as global managers either in Korea or overseas. However, the interviewees recognized that these reforms would inevitably take time and that some changes, including shifts in attitudes and perceptions, could not simply be legislated for by the government—in short, there were few, if any, quick fixes. Thus for foreign investors, the challenge was one of developing short- to medium-term strategies for dealing with day-to-day problems in the workplace, until such time as the problems they had highlighted were recognized and addressed.

4 Conclusions

The decade since the 1997 financial crisis has seen a dramatic shift in the Korean government's attitudes towards and policies regarding inward foreign direct investment. The creation of regulations and systems that aim to promote and encourage, rather than regulate and control FDI inflows resulted in significant improvements to Korea's IFDI 'hardware' and an investment boom in the immediate post-crisis period. At the end of the 1990s, the problems that had faced foreign investors for decades were addressed, in as much as legislation and regulations were revised, new support institutions were established, investment sectors were liberalized and incentives were enhanced. However, the decline in FDI inflows in the early years of the 21st century and the levelling off of investment values in recent years suggest that there is still work to be done if the Korean government wishes to attract even more high-quality inward foreign direct investment to Korea. The challenges ahead include thoroughly embedding the new systems and practices introduced after the crisis, addressing the problems facing existing foreign investors from a 'softer' socio-cultural perspective, identifying and removing the remaining barriers to investment, and convincing the Korean people of the many and varied benefits that can derive from higher levels of foreign participation in the domestic economy.

REFERENCES

Chang, Yun-jong (2001), *Oegugin chikchŏp t'ujaŭi ilsŏgojohyokkwa punsŏk* [An analysis of the 'killing five birds with one stone' effect of inward foreign direct investment], Seoul: Sanŏp Yŏn'guwŏn

Cherry, Judith (2006), 'Killing Five Birds with One Stone: Inward Foreign Direct Investment in Post-Crisis Korea', in: *Pacific Affairs*, 79 (1), pp. 9-27

Cherry, Judith (2007), *Foreign Direct Investment in Post-Crisis Korea: European Investors and 'Mismatched Globalization'*, London: Routledge

Ch'oe, Chun-uk (1998), 'Oegugin chikchŏp t'ujaŭi yŏk'al' [The role of inward foreign direct investment], in: *Chaejŏng P'orŏm* [Financial Forum] (April), pp. 44-55

Ch'oe, Sŏng-hwan (2003), 'Han'guk kyŏngjeŭi naeil: hoebogin'ga changgi ch'imch'ein'ga?' [Korea's economic future: recovery or long-term stagnation?], in: *Wŏlgan Chosŏn* [Korea Monthly], 24 (12), pp. 92-101

Duerden, Charles (2002), 'FDI surge continues in December', in: *Invest Korea Journal* 20 (1). Online: http://www.ikjournal.com (accessed 1 December 2006)

Duerden, Charles (2003), 'Fourth-quarter capital inflow slumps 63.7 pct.', in: *Invest Korea Journal*, 21 (2). Online: http://www.ikjournal.com (accessed 1 December 2006)

Hood, Neil, and Young, Stephen (1979), *The Economics of Multinational Enterprise*, London: Longman

Hwang, Chin-u (1999), 'Oegugin chikchŏp t'ujae taehan myŏt kaji ohae' [A few misconceptions about inward foreign direct investment], in: *Hanhwa Kyŏngje* [Hanhwa Economy], March, pp. 2-11

Invest Korea (2004), *Adapting to a Changing Economic Environment: Toward a New Foreign Direct Investment Policy*, Seoul: Invest Korea

Invest Korea, 'Facts and statistics'. Online: http://www.investkorea.org (accessed 17 February 2007)

Invest Korea Journal (2003a), 'Foreign investment dips on year, soars on month', 21 (6). Online: http://www.ikjournal.com (accessed 1 December 2006)

Invest Korea Journal (2003b), 'First quarter FDI slumps as global investor sentiment turns negative', 21 (3). Online: http://www.ikjournal.com (accessed 1 December 2006)

Invest Korea Journal (2004a), 'Third quarter FDI highest in three years', 22 (6). Online: http://www.ikjournal.com (accessed 1 December 2006)

Invest Korea Journal (2004b), 'FDI almost triples in first quarter', 22 (3). Online: http://www.ikjournal.com (accessed 1 December 2006)

Invest Korea Journal (2005), 'Committed to reform', 23 (1). Online: http://www.ikjournal.com (accessed 1 December 2006)

Invest Korea Journal (2006), 'FDI surpasses US$11 billion for second straight year', 24 (3). Online: http://www.ikjournal.com (accessed 1 December 2006)

Investment Notification Statistics Center. *Oegugin t'uja t'onggye* [Inward foreign direct investment statistics]. Online: http://www.mocie.go.kr/index.jsp (accessed 24 November 2006)

Jung, Ku-hyun (1987), 'Oegugin chikchŏp t'ujaŭi hyokkwawa chŏngbuŭi chŏngch'aek' [The effect of inward foreign direct investment and government policy], in: *Daeu Kyŏngje Yŏn'guso Sanŏpgwa Kyŏngnyŏng* [Daewoo Economic Research Institute Industry and Management], 44, pp. 271-90

Kang, Ji-Eun (2002), 'EU Investment in Korea: An Empirical Analysis', Master's dissertation, Hankook University of Foreign Studies, Seoul, ROK

Kim, Chin-jung (2000), 'Oegugin chikchŏp t'uja yuch'i hwalsŏnghwa pangane kwanhan yŏn'gu' [A study of plans to activate the attraction of inward foreign direct investment], Master's dissertation, Kyunghee University, ROK

Kim, June-Dong (2003a), *Inward Foreign Direct Investment into Korea: Recent Performance and Future Agenda*, Seoul: Korea Institute for International Economic Policy

Kim June-Dong (2003b), 'Inward Foreign Direct Investment into Korea: Recent Performance and Future Tasks', in: James M. Lister (ed.), *Raising the Bar: Korea as a Global Economic Player*, Washington D.C.: Korea Economic Institute, pp. 195-220

Kim, Mi-a (1999), 'Kungnae oegugin chikchŏp t'ujaŭi kungmin kyŏngjejŏk hyokkwa' [The effects of inward foreign direct investment on the Korean economy], in: *Muyŏk'ak Hoeji* [Trade Studies Journal], 24 (2), pp.79-93

Kim, Pyŏng-sun (2002), 'Oegugin chikchŏp t'ujaŭi sŏngjang yuhyŏnggwa yuch'i chŏngch'aege kwanhan yŏn'gu' [A study of growth patterns and attraction policy of inward foreign direct investment], in: *Han'guk Pukpang Hak'oe Nonjip* [Korean Northern Society Collection of Theses], 10, pp. 7-30

Kim, Suk (2000), 'Oegugin chikchŏp t'uja yuch'ijŏngch'aekŭi hyŏnghwanggwa chŏngch'aekchŏk kwajee taehan yŏn'gu' [The current status of policies to attract inward investment and policy issues], in: *Sahoegaebal Yŏn'gu* [Social Development Review], 16, pp. 273-99

Kim Zu Kweon (2003), 'Is Trade or FDI the More Important Contributor to Globalization?', in: H. Peter Gray (ed.), *Extending the Eclectic Paradigm in International Business: Essays in Honor of John Dunning*, Cheltenham: Edward Elgar, pp. 83-91

KIEP (Korea Institute for International Economic Policy) (1998), *Kyŏngjenan kŭkpogŭi chirŭmgil: oegugin t'uja*. [The shortcut to overcoming economic difficulties: Inward foreign investment], Seoul: Korea Institute for International Economic Policy

KITA (Korea International Trade Association), 'Trade statistics by country'. Online: http://global.kita.net (accessed 12 February 2007)

KOIS (Korean Statistical Information System), 'Statistical database'. Online: http://kosis.nso.go.kr/eng/index.htm (accessed 17 February 2007)

Krause, Lawrence B. (2003), 'Can Korea Become a Hub for Asia?', in: James M. Lister (ed.), *Raising the Bar: Korea as a Global Economic Player*, Washington D.C.: Korea Economic Institute, pp. 29-37

Maigov, Salambek (2001), 'The State's Role in Creating an Investment Climate', in: *Russian Politics and Law*, 39 (3), pp. 20-28

MOCIE (Ministry of Commerce, Industry and Energy), *Oegugin t'uja t'onggye* [Inward foreign direct investment statistics]. Online: http://www.mocie.go.kr/index2.html (accessed 17 February 2007)

Mun, Shi-jin (2004), 'Oegugin chikchŏp t'ujaŭi ipchi kyŏltchŏgwŏnine kwanhan yŏn'gu' [A study of factors determining the choice of location in foreign direct investment], Master's dissertation, Pusan University, ROK

O, Su-gyun (2003), 'Oegugin chikchŏp t'uja yuch'i hwaktae pangane kwanhan yŏn'gu' [A study of plans to expand the attraction of inward foreign direct investment], in: *Kŭktong Chŏngbo Taehakkyo Nonjip* [Collection of Theses from Keukdong College], 10, pp. 363-89

Pak, Yŏng-gŭm (2003), 'What Does Korea Need to Do to Induce More Foreign Direct Investment?', Master's dissertation, Ewha Woman's University, Seoul, ROK

Park, Yoon-shik (2003), 'FDI into Korea: The Past as Prologue', in: James M. Lister (ed.), *Raising the Bar: Korea as a Global Economic Player*, Washington D.C.: Korea Economic Institute, pp. 221-38

SaKong, Il (1993), *Korea in the World Economy*, Washington D.C.: Institute for International Economics

Samsung Economic Research Institute (2003), *Oegugin chikchŏp t'uja pujinŭi wŏnin'gwa ch'ŏbang* [Reasons and remedies for the stagnation of foreign direct investment], Seoul: Samsung Economic Research Institute

Song, Ŭi-dal (2004), *Oegugin chikchŏp t'uja: 21segi kŭllobŏl t'ŭrendŭ* [Inward foreign direct investment: a 21st century global trend], Seoul: Sallim

Weisbart, Mike (2004), 'Curing Korea's FDI phobia', in: *Korea Times* (28.11.2004). Online: http://times.hankooki.com/1page/opinion/200411/kt2004112815424645 510.htm (accessed 8 February 2006)

Yang, Sŏng-su (1999), 'Oejayuch'i, idaeronŭn kollanhada' [As it stands, the attraction of foreign capital is in trouble], in: *Chugan Han'guk* [Korea Weekly], 8 July 1999, pp. 33-6

Yu, Ch'ang-gŭn (2002), 'Han'gugŭi kŭmnyungwigiwa oegugin chikchŏp t'uja' [The financial crisis in Korea and inward foreign direct investment], in: *Yŏngsan Nonch'ong* [Yŏngsan University Collection of Theses], 5, pp. 78-99

EMERGENCE OF CHINA AND THE ECONOMY OF SOUTH KOREA

Joon-Kyung Kim and Chung H. Lee

Abstract

The emergence of China as a major player in the global economy has had many consequences for the economy of South Korea and has serious implications for that country's future prospects and economic relationship with China. This paper examines the changes in the export structure of the two economies that have taken place since the establishment of formal diplomatic relations in 1987 and their effect on the South Korean economy. It specifically examines whether the rise of China and its 'catching-up' with Korea has caused the 'hollowing out' of Korea's corporate sector.

China is now the most important destination for Korean exports and a major supplier of its imports. While it has become a serious challenger of South Korea in world markets for manufacturing exports, China is now an important bilateral trade partner for the country. Furthermore, South Korea has become an important parts supplier for China's manufacturing firms and has thus indirectly benefited from the growth of China's manufacturing exports. The growing bilateral trade and deepening of production networks may be taken as a sign of growing economic interdependence of the two economies.

1 Introduction

Rapid economic development in China and its emergence as a major trading nation of the world since the late 1970s have brought the two Northeast Asian economies—China and South Korea—closer together. Their bilateral trade has increased steadily in both volume and variety of goods traded since 1987, when China and South Korea (henceforth Korea) established a formal diplomatic relationship. In 1989, for instance, Korea's merchandise exports to China amounted to US$1.3 billion, while its merchandise imports from China were US$472 million. By 2006, Korea's merchandise exports to and imports from China grew to US$69.5 and US$48.6 billion respectively. China has also become one of the major host countries for Korea's overseas investment: in 2006 alone, Korea invested US$3.3 billion in China, and by the end of that year its total cumulative stock of investment in China stood at US$13.7 billion.

For Korea, China has now become its major competitor for market share in world markets as well as its major trade partner, as it has been gaining a comparative advantage in many of the manufacturing industries, especially labour-intensive ones, in which Korea used to take the lead (Kim and Lee 2003; Kim, Kim and Lee 2006; Nam 2004; Song 2000).[1] In fact, China's gain in comparative advantage in those industries is seen by some observers in Korea to have put the country in a 'nutcracker' situation (Booz-Allen and Hamilton 1997; *International Herald Tribune*, 28 March 2007) or between two 'neighboring whales' (*Digital Chosun Ilbo*, 29 January 2007), as it is being squeezed between price-competitive China and technologically advanced Japan. Obviously, even if this is true, it will be temporary and of short duration provided Korea succeeds in gaining a comparative advantage in technologically advanced sectors and thus sustain economic growth. If not, the situation will persist with long-term adverse consequences for the Korean economy.

Further complicating the economic relationship between the two economies is the fact that Korea is now a major supplier of parts and components in the manufacture of Chinese exports and thus benefits from the rapid expansion of those exports in third markets. As pointed out by Ravenhill (2006) in the case of ASEAN's relationship with China, Korea has also begun to partake in a new trade 'triangle' that has emerged with China's rapid industrialization.

The paper is hereafter organized as follows: Section 2 examines the trends and characteristics of the overall export structure of the two economies for 1992 and 2004 and shows that China's export structure has 'caught up' with that of Korea, its exports displacing Korean exports to Japan and the United States, Korea's two major trading part-

---

[1] The situation in which Korea now finds itself with respect to China parallels that in which Japan was before the 1940s. According to Howe (1996), the Japanese economist and theoretician Akamatsu Kaname (1896-1974) characterized the Japanese economy as being challenged by the 'newly industrializing economy' of China but lagging behind the West. Akamatsu saw Japan's situation as a transitional phase that required both the domestic and international processes of adjustment but was made difficult by the West with its entrenched trading position in East Asia.

ners. Section 3 reports on the trends and characteristics of China-Korea bilateral trade, showing that the bilateral trade of these two countries has increased more rapidly than their respective trade with the rest of the world. Section 4 examines trade in parts and components and cross-border production networks connecting the two economies, and section 5 looks into Korean investment in China and its effect on bilateral parts trade. Section 6 examines changes in the profitability of Korean manufacturing industries, which we take to be a harbinger of Korea's comparative advantage. Section 7 concludes the paper.

2 CONVERGENCE IN EXPORT STRUCTURE

How has the emergence of China affected Korea's exports to the rest of the world? Is China catching up with Korea in export structure? To answer questions such as these, we classify exports from the two countries into four technological groups—low-technology, medium-low technology, medium-high technology, and high-technology products.[2] As can be seen in Table 1, the two countries, especially China, went through major changes in export structure between 1992 and 2004.

Over the span of twelve years China's export structure shifted from low technology toward technologically more sophisticated products. In 1992, more than a half of its manufacturing exports were in low-tech products such as textiles, apparel and footwear, while the exports of medium-high and high-tech products accounted for only 12.4 and 10.9 percent respectively. By 2004, the share of low-technology exports declined to 31 percent, while the share of medium-high tech and high-tech exports rose to 19.6 and 34.2 percent respectively. In the high-tech product group, computers and office products, and radio, TV and communication equipment increased the most in terms of ex-

---

[2] For this purpose we regroup trade data using the International Standard Industrial Classification (ISIC). The four technology groups are thus comprised of the following ISIC sectors; 15-22, 36 and 37 for the low technology group; 23, 25-28 and 351 for the medium-low technology group; 24 (excluding 2423), 29, 31, 34 and 35 (excluding 351 and 353) for the medium-high technology group; and 353, 2423, 30, 32 and 33 for the high technology group. The non-manufacturing group consists of 01-14.

Table 1 Export distribution and revealed comparative advantage (RCA) by technology group

	China				Korea			
	Share (%)		RCA		Share (%)		RCA	
	1992	2004	1992	2004	1992	2004	1992	2004
Manufacturing								
High technology and ICT products	10.9%	34.2%	0.56	1.46	25.8%	39.2%	1.33	1.63
–Aircraft and spacecraft	0.5%	0.1%	0.14	0.07	0.9%	0.2%	0.28	0.11
–Pharmaceuticals	1.3%	0.8%	0.74	0.25	0.4%	0.3%	0.26	0.11
–Computers and office products	1.3%	14.9%	0.30	2.85	4.0%	9.0%	0.91	1.73
–Semiconductor, electronic valves	0.8%	3.7%	0.26	0.78	10.6%	11.0%	3.62	2.30
–Radio, TV, communic. equip.	4.5%	11.7%	1.24	2.44	8.5%	15.3%	2.31	3.19
–Precision, medical, optical instr.	2.6%	2.9%	0.75	0.81	1.3%	2.4%	0.39	0.65
Med-high technology	12.4%	19.6%	0.36	0.62	20.4%	35.2%	0.60	1.10
–Electrical machinery	3.3%	5.6%	0.87	1.35	2.2%	3.2%	0.59	0.77
–Chemical products	4.1%	3.9%	0.56	0.49	7.2%	10.2%	0.99	1.26
–Motor vehicle and trailer	0.8%	2.0%	0.07	0.20	5.8%	13.6%	0.50	1.33
–Other transport equipment	0.7%	1.0%	1.26	1.87	0.2%	0.2%	0.35	0.29
–Home appliance and machinery	3.5%	7.1%	0.32	0.80	5.0%	8.0%	0.46	0.91
Med-low technology	10.7%	12.4%	0.83	1.03	18.7%	17.3%	1.45	1.43
–Shipbuilding and repairing	0.6%	0.5%	0.61	0.71	5.4%	6.4%	5.77	8.45
–Coke, petroleum products	0.9%	0.8%	1.30	1.24	0.2%	0.1%	0.30	0.20
–Rubber and plastic products	2.0%	2.6%	0.83	1.04	2.8%	2.4%	1.15	0.96
–Non-metallic mineral products	1.9%	1.7%	1.31	1.36	0.8%	0.6%	0.52	0.44
–Basic & fabricated metal products	5.3%	6.7%	0.71	0.98	9.7%	7.7%	1.30	1.12
Low technology	53.4%	31.0%	2.43	1.74	31.6%	8.8%	1.44	0.49
–Textiles, apparel, footwear	37.5%	20.6%	4.42	3.13	25.4%	6.1%	2.99	0.92
–Food, beverages, tobacco	6.4%	2.6%	1.08	0.49	2.1%	1.1%	0.35	0.20
–Wood and paper products	2.0%	1.6%	0.45	0.51	1.0%	0.6%	0.22	0.19
–Other misc. manufacturing prod.	7.5%	6.3%	2.43	2.11	3.2%	1.0%	1.03	0.35
Non-manufacturing products	11.2%	2.6%	1.34	0.22	1.5%	0.4%	0.18	0.03

Source: UN COMTRADE.

port share between 1992 and 2004. The combined share of these exports increased from less than 6 to 26 percent between those two points.[3]

During the same period Korea also experienced a steady increase in the export shares of both high- and medium-high technology products—from 25.8 to 39.2 percent and from 20.4 to 35.2 percent respectively. Among the high-tech products the largest increase took place in radio, TV and communication equipment—from 8.5 to 15.3 percent—while the share of automobile exports, one of the medium-high tech products, more than doubled. In contrast, the shares of both low- and medium-low technology products decreased, with the steepest decline taking place in low-tech products. Indeed, the export share of textiles, apparel and footwear alone, which had been Korea's major exports up through the early 1990s, decreased from 25.4 percent in 1992 to 6.1 percent in 2004, indicating a rapid loss of Korea's comparative advantage in this group of products.

The changes in China's export structure described above suggest that it has been following other East Asian countries in the 'catching-up product cycle' development that began with Japan in the early 20th century. With China catching up with Korea in industrial development, we would expect a convergence in their export structure and increased competition for exports in world markets. To see how the two countries have fared in this competition, we compare the shares of imports from China and Korea for 1992 and 2004 in four markets—the rest of the world, Japan, the United States, and the European Union (EU) (Figure 1). It is clear that China made significant gains in the market share for all products in Japan and the United States, while Korea made no gain at all. In low-tech industries, China increased its market share in Japan, the United States, and the EU, while Korea's market share in all those markets declined absolutely. Even in medium-low tech industries China made significant gains in market share in Japan and the United States at the expense of Korea, whereas in the EU both China and Korea increased their market share, albeit the former more than the latter (Figure 2).

---

[3] Although computers and office products, and radio, TV and communication equipment are classified as high-tech products, the technology involved in their production in China may be of a simple assembly type used at plants of foreign multinational enterprises. Thus 'Made in China' is not necessarily the same as 'Made by Chinese'.

Figure 1   Import share of China and Korea in major markets

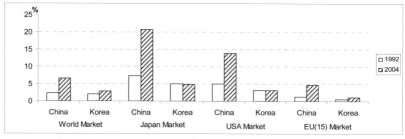

Source: UN COMTRADE.

Figure 2   Import share of China and Korea in major markets: low and medium-low technology industries

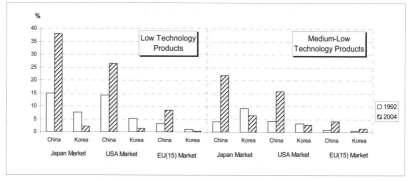

Source: UN COMTRADE.

Figure 3   Import share of China and Korea in major markets: high and medium-high technology industries

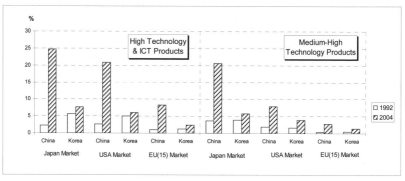

Source: UN COMTRADE.

In contrast, in high- and medium-high technology products Korea increased its market share in all the major world markets although, during the same period, China's share also increased (Figure 3). It is difficult to tell whether Korea would have increased its market share more in the absence of competition from China, but the data presented so far suggest that, while suffering a loss in market share in low- and medium-low technology products to China, Korea has managed to increase its market share in high- and medium-high tech products sufficiently enough to expand its share of total world exports—from 2.0 in 1992 to 2.8 percent in 2004. Some of this increase was, as we point out in the following section, due to an expansion of bilateral trade between the two countries.

3 EXPANDING BILATERAL TRADE

While Korea has been losing its market share for some of its exports in third markets to China, its bilateral trade with China has been expanding. In fact, the increase in Korean exports for the last decade was mainly due to an increase in its exports to China, as the latter's share of Korean exports increased from 3.5 percent in 1992 to 19.6 percent in 2004 (Table 2). This is as to be expected, since rapid economic growth in China has been accompanied by a rapid increase in its trade with the rest of the world, including that with Korea. What is thus of greater interest is whether trade between the two has increased more rapidly than their respective trade with the rest of the world. To answer this question we calculate the export- and import-intensity indices for China and Korea respectively, for the period 1992-2004 (reported in parenthesis in Table 2).[4]

Between 1992 and 2004, Korea's export-intensity with respect to China rose from 1.6 to 3.2, while its import-intensity remained the same. This increase in the export-intensity with the import-intensity remaining stable indicates the growing importance of China as Korea's export destination, albeit not as a source of its imports.

---

[4] The export intensity of country A with respect to country B is the ratio of B's share of A's total exports to B's share of world total imports. If it is greater than 1 it suggests that A is more closely tied with B in trade than the latter is with the rest of the world. The import intensity index is similarly calculated and has the same implication.

Table 2 Growing trade interdependency between China and Korea Share (percent) and trade intensity (in parenthesis)

	1992	1994	1996	1998	2000	2002	2004
China's share in Korea's exports	3.5%	6.5%	8.8%	8.3%	10.7%	14.6%	19.6%
	(1.6)	(2.4)	(3.3)	(3.2)	(3.1)	(3.2)	(3.2)
China's share in Korea's imports	4.6%	5.3%	5.7%	6.7%	8.0%	11.4%	13.2%
	(2.0)	(1.8)	(1.9)	(1.9)	(2.0)	(2.2)	(2.0)
Korea's share in China's exports	2.8%	3.6%	5.0%	3.4%	4.5%	4.8%	4.7%
	(1.3)	(1.5)	(1.7)	(2.0)	(1.8)	(2.0)	(1.9)
Korea's share in China's imports	3.3%	6.3%	9.0%	10.7%	10.3%	9.7%	11.1%
	(1.6)	(2.7)	(3.6)	(4.2)	(3.7)	(3.6)	(3.7)

Source: UN COMTRADE.

During the same period China's import-intensity with respect to Korea increased from 1.6 to 3.7, indicating both a growth rate of Chinese imports from Korea much higher than that from the rest of the world and the growing importance of Korea as a source of China's imports. China's export-intensity with respect to Korea also increased rapidly from 1.3 to 1.9, pointing to a bilateral trade that is expanding faster than their respective trade with the rest of the world.

The growth of bilateral trade between Korea and China is in itself a sign of increasing interdependence between the two economies, which is greater than suggested by the trade data presented in Table 2. The fact is that much of the bilateral trade is in parts and components and the growth in that trade suggests growing cross-border production networks spanning the two economies. In the following section we investigate in greater detail trade in parts and cross-border production networks.

4 TRADE IN PARTS AND CROSS-BORDER PRODUCTION NETWORKS

The increase in the export- and import-intensities discussed above, itself a measure of expanding bilateral trade between the two economies, may be due to their geographical proximity, but obviously that alone cannot account for such a rapid increase. We examine here whether expanding cross-border production networks have contributed to the increase in the bilateral trade between the two countries. Expanding production networks, which may be a consequence of international fragmentation of production processes, imply increasing parts trade between the two countries (Gaulier, Lemoine and Ünal-Kensenci 2005; Ando and Kimura 2003).

Tables 3 and 4 report the destinations and sources of parts trade for Korea and China in 1992 and 2004 for the industries in which much parts trade takes place. In 1992, China accounted for a meagre 0.9 percent of Korea's total parts exports, but in 2004 it accounted for 26.9 percent (Table 3). Increases in computers and office products; radio, TV and communication equipment; precision, medical and optical instruments; and electrical machinery were all from less than 2 percent to more than 30 percent. Even in motor vehicles and trailers the increase was from 0.9 percent in 1992 to 29.7 percent in 2004. This increase in parts trade, which is much greater than the increase in Korea's total exports from 3.5 to19.6 percent during the same period, is a sign of the growing importance of parts exports from Korea to China. It also indicates that China has become a major assembler of parts and components manufactured in Korea for many of its high- and medium-high tech products and that Korea has become an indirect beneficiary from China's growing exports to the world markets. In contrast, China has yet to become a major supplier of parts for Korea, which increased its parts exports to Korea from 1.3 to 5.2 percent (Table 4).

In 1992, Korea imported parts and components mostly from Japan, the United States, and Europe—a total of 82.1 percent—while importing only a miniscule amount—0.4 percent—from China. By 2004, however, imports from the former three sources decreased to 59.6 percent, while those from China increased to 12.2 percent (Table 3). The most dramatic change took place in computers and office products; radio, TV and communication equipment; and electrical machinery, their respective shares of imports from China increasing from 2.7 to 42.6 percent, 1.1 to 24.4 percent, and 0.5 to 30.5 percent. The fact that these increases took place while the share of parts imports in those groups from Japan, the United States and EU decreased is a sign of growing cross-border production networks between China and Korea and growing relative importance of China for Korea's manufacturing sector.

Table 3 Korea's parts trade and trade partners

		China		Japan		USA		EU 15	
		1992	2004	1992	2004	1992	2004	1992	2004
Total Trade	Export	3.5	19.6	15.1	8.5	23.7	16.9	12.8	13.3
	Import	4.6	13.2	23.8	20.6	22.4	12.9	12.8	10.5
Total parts trade	Export	0.9	26.9	10.5	9.2	31.4	13.4	12.7	9.8
	Import	0.4	12.2	40.3	27.3	29.8	20.1	12.0	12.2
Parts for computers & office products	Export	1.5	31.1	11.2	5.4	41.8	18.1	26.6	16.3
	Import	2.7	42.6	46.5	13.8	34.0	11.4	3.7	4.2
Parts for radio, TV, communication equip.	Export	1.0	39.0	17.4	5.8	22.1	6.3	16.9	10.2
	Import	1.1	24.4	65.4	40.6	12.2	9.1	9.6	7.6
Parts for precision, medical, optical instru.	Export	0.9	82.5	18.4	5.7	58.8	3.2	9.0	1.6
	Import	0.2	3.0	39.8	45.0	38.2	20.8	17.9	20.6
Parts for electrical machinery	Export	1.8	38.1	16.8	9.6	19.6	14.4	13.8	5.0
	Import	0.5	30.5	53.2	38.2	22.5	9.0	15.4	12.3
Parts for motor vehicles and trailers	Export	0.9	29.7	20.2	6.3	27.9	16.8	18.2	8.3
	Import	0.3	2.2	62.9	33.9	14.9	12.8	15.9	38.3
Parts for home appliance and machinery equip.	Export	1.9	23.9	15.7	13.9	26.5	13.7	16.0	10.6
	Import	0.4	7.5	39.4	33.7	30.7	21.8	22.9	28.1

Source: UN COMTRADE.

China's total parts imports from Korea also increased from 1.7 to 12.3 percent between 1992 and 2004, the most dramatic increase taking place in radio, TV and communication equipment (from 2.3 to 18.8 percent) and in motor vehicles and trailers (from 0.2 to 13.8 percent). These increases are not as large as the increases in Korea's parts imports from China, suggesting that by 2004 Korea had become much more dependent on China for parts and components in the manufacture of high- and medium-high technology products than China had on

Korea. This development is probably due to the fact that Korea has transferred some of its parts production to China through direct investment and that many of its parts imported from China are thus those manufactured by Korean affiliates in China. We investigate this possibility in the following section by looking into various possible linkages between foreign direct investment (FDI) and bilateral trade between Korea and China.

Table 4 China's major parts trade and trade partners

		Korea		Japan		HK		USA		EU 15	
		1992	2004	1992	2004	1992	2004	1992	2004	1992	2004
Total Trade	Export	2.8	4.7	13.7	12.4	44.2	17.0	10.1	21.1	9.4	16.8
	Import	3.3	11.1	17.0	16.8	25.5	2.1	11.0	8.0	13.5	12.2
Total parts trade	Export	1.3	5.2	7.2	11.3	54.7	25.9	8.8	16.3	5.5	13.4
	Import	1.7	12.3	22.3	21.2	33.8	2.5	10.2	6.1	19.1	11.6
Parts for computers and office products	Export	1.6	1.7	2.6	7.9	73.4	32.1	10.5	19.8	10.7	18.1
	Import	1.5	9.1	32.9	18.4	49.8	2.3	7.2	4.4	3.1	3.0
Parts for radio, TV, communication equip.	Export	2.1	9.5	13.2	14.1	73.7	27.7	2.3	11.1	1.8	12.3
	Import	2.3	18.8	15.2	20.9	53.9	3.8	4.2	3.2	14.9	11.0
Parts for precision, medical, optical instru.	Export	2.3	2.8	11.9	25.0	53.8	25.3	13.0	16.3	8.5	13.1
	Import	0.1	9.8	26.2	30.4	28.0	1.6	19.1	12.5	12.1	11.2
Parts for electrical machinery	Export	0.6	5.8	11.1	14.1	53.7	24.9	3.8	15.7	2.0	12.0
	Import	0.7	8.3	18.0	30.6	42.4	2.8	5.6	5.8	18.1	19.7
Parts for motor vehicles and trailers	Export	1.5	1.9	6.6	14.5	11.0	1.7	27.9	36.4	11.9	11.4
	Import	0.2	13.8	46.6	34.8	1.0	0.0	6.2	4.4	38.7	33.2
Parts for home appliance and machinery equip.	Export	1.7	4.2	6.2	15.4	30.7	5.4	17.0	21.2	7.9	18.4
	Import	1.1	5.9	23.4	24.8	14.8	0.9	13.8	12.3	34.3	39.4

Note: HK=Hong Kong.
Source: UN COMTRADE.

5 KOREA'S INVESTMENT IN CHINA AND KOREA-CHINA BILATERAL TRADE

In this section we examine how Korea's direct investment in China has led to an expansion in parts trade between the two countries and in bilateral trade as FDI generally precedes international fragmentation of production processes or production sharing (Arndt 2004; Jones 2001). As discussed above, one notable development in economic relations between the two countries has been the growth of parts trade between Korea and China and especially the rapid growth of parts exports from Korea to China, which has replaced the advanced industrialized countries such as the United States as the largest destination for Korea's parts exports.

Here we examine the procurement and sales patterns of affiliates, as reported in the surveys carried out in 1996 and 2003 by the Korea Institute for Industrial Economics and Trade (KIET). The 1996 KIET survey (discussed in Ha and Hong 1998) was carried out on a sample of 615 Korean companies (216 large firms and 399 small and medium-sized firms and their 952 offshore affiliates). The 2003 survey was carried out on 748 companies all in manufacturing (89 large firms and 659 small and medium-sized firms and their 1050 offshore affiliates) (KIET and MOCIE 2004). In Table 5 we report the sources of procurement by Korean affiliates by region. We find that between 1996 and 2003 the share of parts and components imported by Korean manufacturing affiliates in China from Korea decreased from 64.7 to 36.9 percent, while the share of local procurement increased from 26.5 to 45.6 percent, suggesting an increasing localization of parts supplies.

The results of these two surveys indicate that Korean investment in China has had a positive effect on the two countries' bilateral trade, although the share of parts imported from Korea in total procurement by the affiliates in China has declined. They also point to the fact that FDI has created extensive backward local linkages in China.

Table 5 also reports the procurement patterns of Korean affiliates in China by manufacturing industries. Between 1996 and 2003 the share of imports from Korea in total procurement decreased for most industries except for food and beverage, paper and printing, basic metals, and motors and freight. Electronics and telecommunication equipment, in particular, decreased from 86.0 percent in 1996 to 36.3 percent in 2003. Except for machinery & equipment industry, the industries that experienced a decrease in the share of imports from Korea experienced at the same time an increase in the share of local procurement between 1996 and 2003. This indicates strong local backward linkages created by Korean affiliates.

Table 5 Sources of procurement by Korean affiliates in China by industry (Unit: percent of total procurement)

| | Local procurement | | Imports from | | | |
| | | | Korea | | Third countries | |
	1996	2003	1996	2003	1996	2003
Manufacturing	26.5	45.6	64.7	36.9	8.8	17.5
Food and beverage	78.3	59.6	19.2	21.9	2.6	18.4
Textiles and apparel	46.0	63.3	53.8	25.7	0.2	11.0
Footwear and leather	2.6	18.2	94.9	65.6	2.5	16.1
Paper and printing	91.8	51.5	8.2	31.7	0.0	16.8
Petroleum and chemical prod.	1.0	37.1	62.9	47.3	36.1	15.6
Non-metallic minerals	49.0	93.0	51.0	3.2	0.0	3.8
Basic metals	88.6	9.0	11.4	90.8	0.0	0.2
Fabricated metals	0.5	41.7	99.5	56.9	0.0	1.4
Machinery and equipment	40.9	28.9	49.4	8.9	9.8	62.2
Electronics and telecommunications equip.	13.9	56.5	86.0	36.3	0.1	7.2
Motors and freight	78.8	40.8	21.2	59.2	0.0	0.0

Source: Ha and Hong (1998); KIET and MOCIE (2004).

Sales destinations for the output of Korean affiliates in China vary widely from industry to industry (Table 6). According to the 2003 KIET survey, in paper and printing, the petroleum and chemical sector, basic metals, and motors and freight, more than one-half of the affiliate output was destined for local markets. In contrast, in textiles and apparel, footwear and leather, fabricated metals, machinery and equipment, and electronics and telecommunication equipment, more than 60 percent of output was exported. Reverse imports—exports back to Korea—accounted for 17.8 percent of the entire manufacturing output and formed an especially big element in footwear and leather and in both non-metallic minerals and basic metals. Exports to third markets were especially large—at least as much as one-half of total output—in textiles and apparel, footwear and leather, machinery and equipment, and electronics and telecommunication equipment. These are industries that are either labour-intensive or assemblers of parts imported from Korea.

Table 6 Sales destination of Korean affiliates in China by industry (Unit: percent of total sales)

| | Local Sales | | Exports to | | | |
| | | | Korea | | Third countries | |
	1996	2003	1996	2003	1996	2003
Manufacturing	22.6	34.2	25.8	17.8	51.6	48.1
Food and beverage	51.2	43.4	27.4	35.3	21.5	21.2
Textiles and apparel	47.5	22.4	8.2	28.4	44.4	49.2
Footwear and leather	1.2	8.7	29.5	31.5	69.3	59.8
Paper and printing	13.1	97.3	51.2	0.0	35.7	2.7
Petroleum, chemical prod.	0.6	78.4	46.6	10.4	52.8	11.3
Non-metallic minerals	40.0	49.6	57.8	46.4	2.2	4.0
Basic metals	51.3	62.8	23.1	35.3	25.6	1.9
Fabricated metals	3.5	36.6	25.7	17.4	70.7	46.0
Machinery and equipment	51.6	16.1	47.0	6.4	1.4	77.5
Electronics & telecommun. equip.	30.5	32.1	60.7	12.8	8.9	55.1
Motors and freight	0.5	93.4	3.7	6.4	95.8	0.3

Source: Ha and Hong (1998), KIET and MOCIE (2004).

6 EFFECTS ON KOREA'S MANUFACTURING INDUSTRIES

How has China's convergence to Korea affected Korea's manufacturing industries? We noted at the beginning of the paper that the convergence had raised worrisome concerns about the future of the Korean economy, expressed in such phrases as 'a nutcracker situation' and 'between two neighbouring whales', as it has put Korea between price-competitive China and technologically advanced countries such as Japan. To see whether this in fact is the case we examine the profitability of firms in various industries: a generally declining or negative profitability of firms in labour-intensive, low-skill industries can be taken as a sign that those industries have received a negative impact from China's emergence, while a high profitability of firms in high-tech industries can be taken as a sign that Korea is making progress in acquiring a comparative advantage in new industries, thus avoiding a nutcracker situation.

Here we examine the profitability of 3,470 externally-audited firms, whose financial data are available for the past several years, by first classifying them into the four industry groups introduced earlier—low-technology, medium-low-technology, medium-high-technology, and high-technology industries. We further group them into large firms and small and medium-sized firms (SMEs) to see whether the two groups of firms have responded differently to the emergence of China.

In Figures 4 and 5 we report the operating profitability (the ratio of operating profits to total assets) of large firms and SMEs respectively, in the four industrial groups for ten years between 1996 and 2005. We find that large firms exhibit volatility in profitability in the high-tech industries, which we may attribute to a rapidly changing external demand in the information and communication technology (ICT) sector. If we exclude Samsung Electronics from the sample of firms in the high-tech industries, the large firms did not do so well as a group: in fact their profitability in 2005 was less than that for all other industries. This is a clear indication of the singularity of Samsung Electronics as a high performer in that industry group.

Figure 4 Operating profits/total assets by industry group: large firms (percent)

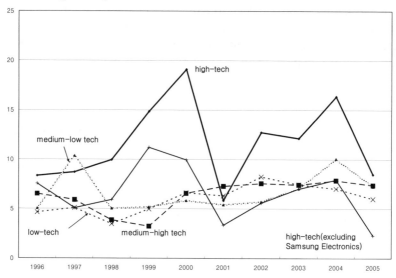

Source: Korea Information Service (KIS).

Figure 5 Operating profits/total assets by industry group: SMEs (percent)

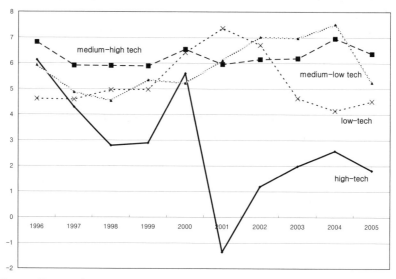

Source: Korea Information Service (KIS).

SMEs performed worse particularly in the high-technology industries, their profitability being much less than that of large firms. It fell sharply into a negative zone in 2001 largely as the consequence of a boom-bust cycle in the information technology (IT) industry. It then improved slightly but has remained low. The picture for SMEs in the low-technology group is slightly better: their operating profitability increased, decreased but remained at 4.5 percent in 2005, a level slightly lower than in 1996.

As a group, Korea's high-tech industry has done quite well in maintaining its profitability, although not so well, as noted above, if Samsung Electronics is excluded from the group. In comparison, the profitability of SMEs in general and especially of those in the high-tech group was less than that of the large firms in the same industry group. To illustrate this point further we examine changes in the distribution of profitability over time.

Figures 6 through 10 show the distributions of operating profitability for total manufacturing and the four industry groups (and also by firm size) for three separate years in the period 1996-2005. We see that the mean for operating profitability for all manufacturing firms shifted to the left during that period, a sign of a decreasing average profitability for the entire group, while both tails of the distribution were extended, a sign of greater dispersion in profitability and an increasing differential in the competitiveness of firms. The left-side tail, in particular, extended more than the right-side tail—an indication that an increasing proportion of firms are earning negative operating profits and thus becoming vulnerable to bankruptcy. This pattern of change is more pronounced among SMEs than among large firms and, especially, among SMEs in the high- and medium-high-technology industries. (In fact, there seems to be no change among large firms in the medium-high-technology industries.) This seems to reflect a 'polarization' trend among Korean manufacturing firms in the high-tech industries, resulting partly from government policies promoting venture businesses in the IT industry, which encouraged the entry of a number of small venture businesses into the industry, and partly from the greater ability of large firms to become competitive in the high-tech industries. Clearly, some small firms in the high-tech and medium-high-tech industries have done well in terms of profitability while many others seem to be failing. This is as to be expected in any new emerging industry and should be taken as a sign that Korea is successfully meeting the challenge of China and is not likely to be pushed into a nutcracker situation.

In the low-tech industries we find a clear downward shift in profitability for SMEs as well as for large firms. These are the industries in which Korea has been losing a comparative advantage, and the size of firm does not seem to make any difference in profitability when the firms are in declining industries.

Figure 6 Distribution of operating profitability for all manufacturing firms

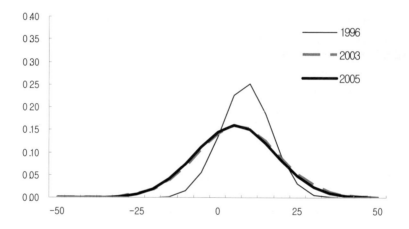

Source: Korea Information Service (KIS).

Figure 7 Distribution of operating profitability for high-tech industries

Large firms

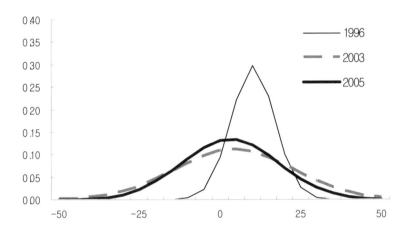

SMEs

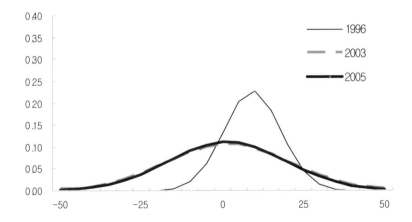

Source: Calculated from the KIS database.

Figure 8 Distribution of operating profitability for medium-high tech industries

Large firms

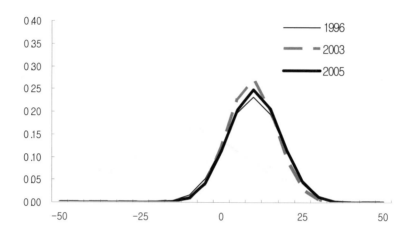

SMEs

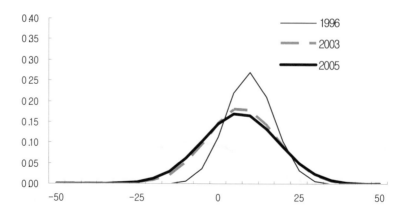

Source: Calculated from the KIS database.

Figure 9 Distribution of operating profitability for medium-low tech industries

Large firms

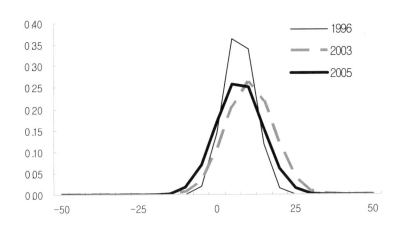

SMEs

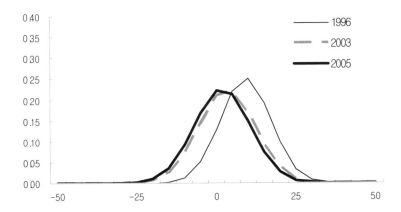

Source: Calculated from the KIS database.

Figure 10 Distribution of operating profitability for low-tech industries

Large firms

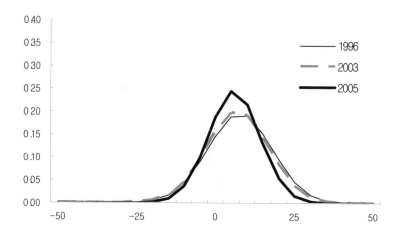

SMEs

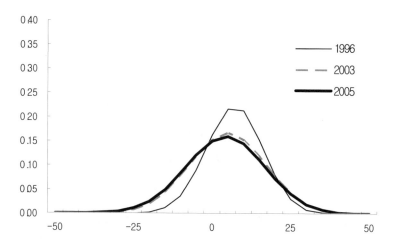

Source: Calculated from the KIS database.

7 CONCLUDING REMARKS

China's emergence clearly has had a significant impact on the Korean economy. It has become Korea's major competitor in world markets for manufacturing exports. At the same time, however, China has become Korea's major trade partner, importing many intermediate products from Korea for its own exports to the rest of the world and supplying Korea with inexpensive consumer goods. Furthermore, numerous production networks now span the two countries, bringing their economies closer together.

There is little doubt that China will continue to catch up with Korea, and how this catching-up will affect the Korean economy in the long run will depend on how Korea responds to this challenge. Korea will have to keep developing new areas of comparative advantage that will help it sustain economic growth and benefit from China's economic development.

In Korea, the government has selected a number of industries such as digital TV and next-generation mobile phones as the new industries that will lead the country's economic growth (Chun 2003). It is not clear, however, what specific measures the government can provide to promote those industries. Industrial policies such as those used to promote the heavy and chemical industries during the 1970s will be, we suspect, no longer appropriate for the Korean economy, which has become too big and too complex for such policies to be effective. Barring such policies, the government's role will be limited to improving the provision of public goods and social infrastructure, especially to keeping the capital and labour markets flexible and efficient and to improving its human capital.

The history of world economic primacy shows that economies that once held the position of economic primacy subsequently declined for reasons that were generally unique to each case. In the instance of Venice, for example, which held a world commercial leadership in 1550 but declined to insignificance some years before 1700, the factors that led to its decline included competition from Portugal in spices, from Britain in woollens, and from the Netherlands and Britain in shipping; the rigid attitude of guilds and workers; and a levelling-off of productivity (Kindleberger 1996: 65). Spain and the Low Countries, whose economic growth followed that of Venice, also had a similar fate, but for reasons of their own. Although what brought about the fall from the position of world economic primacy differed from case to case, there appears to have been one factor common to all: in each of those cases rigidity eventually overtook the vitality and flexibility that it had once had (Kindleberger 1996: 36). What actually triggered the downfall of each may have been some uncontrollable external events, but it was the inability to adapt to and successfully deal with those external events that ultimately brought about the downfall. That is a lesson that China's neighbours must learn from the history of world economic primacy: if their economic growth ever falters it will be not because of rapid economic development in China, which is beyond their control anyway, but because of the loss of vitality and flexibility in their economies. This does not mean, however, that China does not have the responsibility to help them facilitate structural changes by keeping its doors open for their exports.

In sum, China is a new major player in world markets, especially in East Asia, and is likely to continue to present a formidable challenge to Korea. It will at the same time offer Korea a myriad of economic opportunities both as a rapidly growing market and as a potential economic partner. Hence, the challenge for Korea is to respond to the 'Chinese threat' with flexibility and resilience by making the necessary domestic structural adjustments and enhancing competitiveness at home as it integrates into an increasingly borderless international economy.

REFERENCES

Ando, Mitsuyo and Kimura, Fukinari (2003), 'The Formation of International Production and Distribution Networks in East Asia', National Bureau of Economic Research (NBER) Working Paper No. 10167, Cambridge MA: National Bureau of Economic Research

Arndt, Sven W. (2004), 'Global Production Networks and Regional Integration', in: Michael Plummer (ed.), *Empirical Methods in International Trade: Essays in Honor of Mordechai Kreinin*, Cheltenham: Edward Elgar, pp. 129-142

Booz-Allen and Hamilton (1997), *Revitalizing the Korean Economy toward the 21st Century*, Seoul: Maeil Business Newspaper

Chun, Soo Bong (2003), 'Kukka Kyungjaengryuk Hyangsangeul Wihan Shinsanop Kaebal' [Developing new industries to improve the nation's economic competitiveness], in: *ITBI Review*, 19 (2), pp. 33-50 [International Trade and Business Institute]

Gaulier, Guillaume, François Lemoine and Deniz Ünal-Kensenci (2005), 'China's Integration in East Asia: Production Sharing, FDI & High-Tech Trade', CEPII Working Paper, No. 2005-09, Paris: Centre d'Etudes Prospectives et d'Informations Internationales

Ha, Byung-Ki and Hong, Seock-Il (1998), *Hankuk Kiopeui Haeoe Jikjup Tuja Kyungyung Siltae Boonsuk* [Analysis of the actual management conditions of Korean investors overseas], Seoul: Korea Institute for Industrial Economics and Trade

Howe, Christopher (1996), 'Introduction: The Changing Political Economy of Sino-Japanese Relations: A Long Term View', in: Christopher Howe (ed.), *China and Japan: History, Trends, and Prospects*, Oxford: Clarendon Press, pp. 1-22

Jones, Ronald W. (2001), 'Globalization and the Fragmentation of Production', in: *Seoul Journal of Economics*, 14 (1), pp.1-13

KIET (Korea Institute for Industrial Economics and Trade) and MOCIE (Ministry of Commerce, Industry and Energy) (2004), *2003-nyun Haeoe Tuja Kiop Siltae Josa* [2003 survey of business activities of Korea's overseas affiliates], Seoul: KIET and MOCIE

Kim, Joon-Kyung and Chung H. Lee (2003), 'Korea's Direct Investment in China and Its Implications for Economic Integration in Northeast Asia', in: *Korea Development Institute Journal of Economic Policy*, 25, pp.173-206

Kim, Joon-Kyung, Yangseon Kim and Chung H Lee. (2006), 'Trade, Investment and Economic Interdependence between South Korea and China', in: *Asian Economic Journal*, 20 (4), pp. 379-92

Kindleberger, Charles P. (1996), *World Economic Primacy: 1500 to 1990*, New York: Oxford University Press

Nam, Young-Sook (2004), 'Facing the Challenges of China's Industrial Rise: The Korean Case', in: Korea Institute for International Economic Policy, *Rising China and the East Asian Economy*, Seoul: Korea Institute for International Economic Policy, pp. 1-26 [Proceedings of conference held March 2004]

Ravenhill, John (2006), 'Is China an Economic Threat to Southeast Asia?', in: *Asian Survey*, 46 (5), pp. 653-74

Song, Ligang (2000), 'Trade Liberalization and Development of China's Foreign Trade', in Peter Drysdale and Ligang Song (eds.), *China's Entry to the WTO: Strategic Issues and Quantitative Assessments*, London and New York: Routledge, pp. 66-85

KOREAN MODERNISM, MODERN KOREAN CITYSCAPES, AND MASS HOUSING DEVELOPMENT: CHARTING THE RISE OF *AP'AT'Ŭ TANJI* SINCE THE 1960S[1]

Valérie Gelézeau

ABSTRACT

Completely unknown to Korean city-dwellers before the 1960s, large apartment complexes (*ap'at'ŭ tanji*) dominate South Korean cityscapes today. How did Western-style housing blocks migrate to Korea on such a large scale? These are issues in the relationships between the development of *ap'at'ŭ tanji* and South Korean modernisation. The paper will examine these issues in a Korea context, through an analysis centred on a macro-geographic approach allowing the interpretation of the cityscape.

The paper will first discuss the origin of the *ap'at'ŭ tanji* model, which takes its roots in intertwined modernist Western theories filtered through Japanese mediation during the colonial period and then processed by local post-colonial power structures; the paper will then show how the 'Koreanised' apartment complex was a central element of fashioning the modern Korean cityscape and urban society during the 1970s and 1980s. Finally, the paper attempts to reconsider the usually Eurocentric concepts of 'modernism' and 'modernity'.

1 INTRODUCTION

South Korean cities today are visually dominated by *ap'at'ŭ tanji*, or 'apartment complexes'. While single-family homes made up nearly 90 percent of Seoul's housing stock in 1970, their share had diminished to only 25 percent by 2000. During this same period, the share of apartment houses in the housing stock jumped from 4 percent to more

---

[1] This article is a revised and amended version of the paper presented at the annual meeting of the Association for Asian Studies in San Francisco in April 2006, under the title: 'Korean Modernism, the Visual City and Mass Housing Production: Charting the Cycle of *Ap'at'ŭ tanji* (1950-1980)'. The author would like to thank Frank Hoffmann for inspiring the subject, and Kim Kwangok for all his comments.

than 50 percent. This overall increase of apartments was coupled with the emergence of giga-sized apartment complexes in most South Korean metropolises, especially in Seoul. With fewer than 50,000 residents, the apartment complex (*grand ensemble*) of Sarcelles, north of Paris, is considered a very large housing estate, but some Korean *ap'at'ŭ tanji* today house more than 100,000 (Chamsil, Seoul), or even 200,000 people (Haeundae, Pusan).

This phenomenon is particularly striking when one considers that, whereas apartment complexes are at the core of Korean urban architecture today, they were almost completely unknown to Korean city-dwellers in the early 1960s. At that time, cities, with their low skylines, presented in many residential areas an urban fabric of individual houses connected by a maze of narrow pedestrian alleys. These large apartment complexes—*ap'at'ŭ tanji*—thus gave rise to urban environments completely alien to traditional landscapes, while being key elements in the constitution of the modern Korean city.

What is the connection between these collective housing forms and modernist theories of the city formulated in Western countries during the first part of the 20th century? How has the *tanji* model progressively become one of the main normative visual traits of South Korean cities? How did Western-style housing blocks migrate to Korea on such a large scale and achieve such wide success among local populations? These questions are at the heart of the research I have undertaken in Seoul since the mid-1990s, on the transformation of the urban landscape and the city residential environment (Gelézeau 2003, 2007).

While my analysis refers to a Korean context and is limited in this paper to macro-geographical facts[2] (the relationships between *ap'at'ŭ tanji* and urban construction), my approach is based on the theory of landscape interpretation, which considers the landscape an 'outside layer of geographical reality'[3] (Pitte 1983: 23) and thus a possible mediation in the understanding of the society connected to that particular landscape. In this perspective, a 'landscape', which can first be taken simply as the visual dimension of space seen by an observer, is more precisely defined as 'a mass of signs characterizing a geographical

---

[2] Thus leaving aside in this paper the micro-geographical consequences of apartment development on the city-dwellers' way of life. These aspects are otherwise developed in the third sections of both of the following books: *Séoul, ville géante, cités radieuses* (Gelézeau 2003) and *Ap'at'ŭ konghwaguk* (Gelézeau 2007).

[3] The original French wording is: 'une pellicule de la réalité géographique' (Pitte 1983: 23).

unit in both its physical and human traits'[4] (George 1990: 346). As recent works in geography show (Augustin Berque in France, Denis Cosgrove, James Duncan and Peter Jackson in the United States[5]), the landscape is not only an empirical object (which can be used as a research tool), but also an 'essential element of the social, cultural and political system' (Duncan 1994).

Acknowledging the considerable visual impact of the *ap'at'ŭ tanji* in contemporary Korean cities, I have taken them as the main research tools to engage in a landscape interpretation that attempts to weave a fabric of meaning in the relations between Korean society and its space. While carrying out this landscape interpretation,[6] I have based all my analyses on field research conducted in seven *ap'at'ŭ tanji* in Seoul that I had selected as case studies.[7]

This article focuses on the relationship among the development of *ap'at'ŭ tanji* in South Korea, modernism in urban and housing development, and the modernisation of the material and social city. For now, I take the meaningful and polysemic concepts of the 'modern' paradigm (modernisation and modernity) in their simple sense, and as they are used commonly in the field of space analysis (geography, space anthropology) and architecture. In geographical analysis, the 'modern' paradigm may first apply to the means used by a society to manage and control its environment (its *milieu*); in this respect, 'modern society' and 'modern space' designate industrial societies and the space they create, characterised among other things by a high level of urbanisation (over 75 percent of the total population). This sense is quite loose and encompasses an extremely large range of social reali-

---

[4] The original French phrase is: 'ensemble de signes caractérisant une unité géographique sur le plan physique ou humain'. Definition of 'landscape' in the dictionary of geography by Pierre George (George 1990: 346).
[5] See Anderson 2003; Duncan 1994; Cosgrove 1998.
[6] The interpretation of landscape encompasses several combined steps, among which the most important are: 1. to decompose the landscape into simple units, for example, a specific housing type or residential neighbourhood; 2. to analyse the morphogenesis of the landscape, i.e. the production mecanisms of that particular landscape; 3. to analyse the use of the landscape and the discourse about it emanating from the society connected to it.
[7] Two of them, Chamsil 2 *tanji* and Ku Panp'o Apt, are mass apartment-complexes (more than 4,000 housing units) developed by the public sector in the mid-1970s. Two other (Apkujŏng Ku Hyŏndae Apt, Pangbae Samik Apt) were developed by the private sector at the end of the 1970s-beginning of the 1980s; they differ by size (over 3,000 housing units for Apkujŏng Ku Hyŏndae Apt, but only 308 in Samik). The last three case studies are urban renewal *apat'ŭ tanji*, all constructed after the 1990s and comparable in size (about 1,000 units).

ties, from the rationalisation of, say, industrial production systems to the emergence of nuclear families or a 'disenchanted world' (Gaucher 1985).

As for the words 'modernist' and 'modernism', I will first take them as referring to a more specific paradigm framed by the rationalisation of society and space, and shaped by a belief in permanent progress for the human being, which first emerged as a real movement driving various field of social and cultural life in Europe at the end of the 19th century. In the fields of architecture, modernism is closely linked to the movement organised by leading architects such a Gropius, Mies van der Rohe and Le Corbusier around the Congrès Internationaux d'Architecture Moderne (CIAM) in the 1920s and 1930s, although it is far from restricted to it.

These definitions established, the paper will address the question of the various origins of the *ap'at'ŭ tanji* model, which has its roots in intertwined modernist Western theories filtered through Japanese mediation during the colonial period and then processed by local postcolonial power structures; the paper will thus show the crucial role of the 1970s and 1980s in making the 'Koreanised' apartment complex a central element of the modern Korean cityscape and urban society. Finally, the paper attempts both to place the shift from 'modernism' to 'modernity' into a Korean context and to study these concepts outside the European concepts they are usually associated with.

2 THE MODEL OF THE APAT'Ŭ TANJI: HYBRID MODERNISM AT THE SOURCE OF MODERN KOREAN URBAN NEIGHBOURHOODS

2.1 *The* ap'at'ŭ tanji: *standard of modern urban neighbourhoods*

The definition of *ap'at'ŭ tanji*, which I translate as 'apartment complex', corresponds to the definition that the urbanist Paul Clerk, the geographer Yves Lacoste and the sociologist René Kaës have used in France for the *grands ensembles* (Clerk 1967; Lacoste 1963; Kaës 1963) and which still is accurate today (Dufau and Fourcaut 2004).

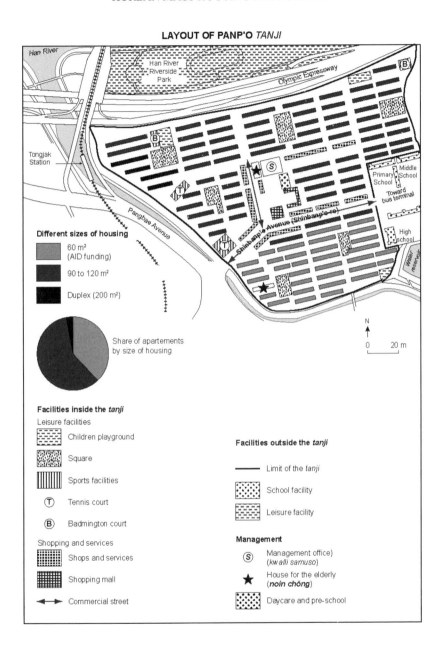

Figure 1 Layout of a *tanji*: the example chosen is the Panp'o *tanji* in Seoul, 1973-78, 4,053 apartments

Figure 2 Apartment complex in Ilsan, showing a standard living environment in South Korea today (Photo: Valérie Gelézeau 2004)

First, a *tanji* should include a group of apartment buildings built in a short period of time (two years on average). Second, a *tanji* is to be constructed according to a master plan that provides a certain level of functional autonomy, by including collective structures and facilities. Finally, a *tanji* should offer a large number of apartments, at least 300 units in the Korean case, as this limit was originally specified by the legal constraints on the management of *ap'at'ŭ tanji*.[8]

The term '*ap'at'ŭ*', which originates from the contraction and transcription of the English-language expression 'apartment house' in *hangŭl*, corresponds to the original definition, more common in the United States, of an 'apartment house': a collectively-used residential building of at least five floors or stories (5 *ch'ŭng*) the *tanji* to function as an autonomous unit.

As a matter of fact, in addition to the management office or *kwalliso* (sometimes located in one of the apartment buildings), all Korean *ap'at'ŭ tanji* are equipped with a minimum of shared facilities to as-

---

[8] Any apartment complex of more than 300 units must be managed by a specially licensed agent. In line with the development of collective housing, this limit changed over time.

sure this autonomy. For residents outside of school or working ages, a nursery and a house for the elderly (*noin chŏng*) are always provided. Also found in every *tanji* is a small shopping centre offering basic shops and services. Lastly, each *tanji* offers children's playgrounds and pedestrian squares, and often tennis courts as well. Some more luxurious *tanji* benefit from additional amenities, such as swimming pools or other sports facilities (for example, basketball or badminton courts).

2.2 *The* ap'at'ŭ tanji: *a hybrid product of modernist urban theories*

As their 'Konglish' name suggests, the *ap'at'ŭ tanji* are structures imported from the West. Their morphology shows a direct heritage from the modern movement in architecture, fashioned between the two wars by architects rallied around the CIAM (see Benevolo 1988).

Although the first apartment-like homes appeared during colonial times, the *ap'at'ŭ tanji* model *per se* was progressively elaborated and developed during the 1950s and 1960s. Two founding projects, both in Seoul, are worth mentioning.

The first is the Chongam apartments (Chongam *Ap'at'ŭ*) project: three buildings of four and five floors (152 housing units), built in Chongam-dong by the Korean Housing Office (*Chosŏn Chut'aek Yŏngdan*), on a piece of land belonging to the city of Seoul, which had commissioned the project. A German firm drafted the plans, and engineers from other foreign countries participated in the construction. These workers introduced the previously unknown term 'apartment house', the root of the neologism 'ap'atŭ' (Gelézeau 2003: 101-02; Kang Surim 1991). The second founding project is that of the Map'o apartments (Map'o *Ap'at'ŭ*, 642 units), built between 1962 and 1964 by the Korean National Housing Corporation (KNHC), a nationalised company created in 1962 after the reorganisation of the Korean Housing Office. Although the rules were formalised by law later on, the Map'o apartment complex instituted the planning principles for the layout of *tanji*: collective housing, at least 300 units, autonomy, and shared facilities.

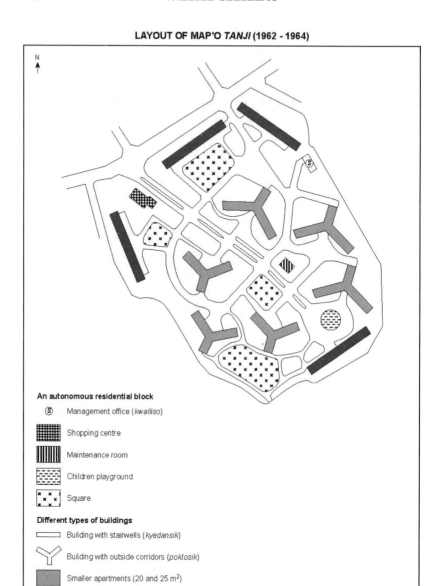

Figure 3 Layout of Map'o *Ap'at'ŭ*, 1964

As models go, the Map'o *Ap'at'ŭ* first refers to the modernist theoretical notion of the neighbourhood unit which, in most Korean sources related to this issue, officially shaped the model of the Korean *tanji*.[9] Conceived in 1929 by the American urbanist Clarence Perry, the neighbourhood unit consists of an urban residential block delimited by transportation arteries. This residential block should be functionally autonomous and include all the shops, services and facilities necessary to the life of its residents. The population living in the neighbourhood unit should range between 3,000 and 9,000 residents, which corresponds to the capacity of a primary school of some 1,000 to 1,600 students.

It is significant to note here that the neighbourhood unit theory, closely linked to that of the Garden City, originally envisioned housing forms that were both individual, and rather low rise. However, the choice of collective and high-rise housing for the Map'o project (ten six-floor apartment buildings were constructed) shows that the Korean intellectual context was also influenced by the Swiss architect Le Corbusier, whose ideas represented a very different current of modernism in architecture. Le Corbusier's ideas favoured collective and high-rise buildings, as erecting taller residential structures could then leave more land available for open spaces and green areas devoted to leisure and recreation. Famous figures such as the Korean architect Kim Chungŏp, who worked in Le Corbusier's studio between 1952 and 1956, played an important role in the introduction of these theories to Korea.

Thus the Korean *tanji* appear to be the result of a combination of two different foreign theoretical models. As Françoise Choay recalls in *L'urbanisme, utopies et réalités,* the universal aim of international urbanism has not kept members of the modernist movement from offering two housing options for the 'new man' of the modern era (Choay 1965: 39-41). The first, studied mostly by the Anglo-Saxons and the Dutch, tended to promote low, single-family homes (Garden City, neighbourhood unit). The second option is the very large, multi-family building, of which Le Corbusier's 'housing units of standard size'[10] built in France between 1952 (Marseille) and 1959 (Briey) are concrete examples. Contrary to these French products, the Korean

---

[9] Geléezau 2003: 185; O and Mun 2000. On the early development of apartments in Korea, see Yim 1996, Kang Pusông 1993, Zchang 1994, Kang Surim 1991.
[10] 'Unité d'Habitation Grandeur Conforme'.

tanji is not a simple creation, since it associates the concept of the Garden City with that of the Le Corbusian giant collective building—concepts considered irreconcilable in Western cities themselves ...

The result of a hybrid modernism theorised in city planning and housing development, the Korean apartment complex thus testifies to the diversity of models that have intermingled across Asia, Europe and the Americas (via the writings and travels of architects, city planners and university professors), and have contributed to the standardisation of the Korean cityscape.

2.3 Trajectories of modernism: reconsidering the Japanese mediation

The relationship between the sources (Western modernist architectural theories) and the result (South Korean mass housing in *ap'at'ŭ tanji*) is quite complex, and the journey from the Western world to Korea has not always been the most direct.

In this complicated network where ideas and models are transferred, Japan occupies, as expected, an important position, for well-known historical reasons (the colonial era) and for its geographical proximity. For example, the use of the word *tanji* for 'complex' was first introduced to the Korean economic and social landscape by the construction of industrial complexes (*kongŏp tanji*) by the Japanese during the 1920s and 1930s. As for daily and residential environments, we know that the first apartment-like homes were of Japanese origin as well. In 1932, the colonial authorities built the five-floor Yurim building, on Ch'ungjŏng avenue in Seoul, for the employees of the colonial government. A few residential apartment buildings, of four or five floors, were also built at the end of the 1930s in the heart of the downtown area or in other Japanese neighbourhoods of the capital city—buildings that have all disappeared today (Gelézeau 2003: 188; Kang Pusŏng 1993).

The important role played by the Korean Housing Office, furthermore, merits mention. It was created in 1941, shortly after its Japanese counterpart (*Nihon Jūtaku Eidan*). It had more of a theoretical influence on urban and housing development than a practical impact on Seoul's emerging housing problem (*chut'aek munje*)—it built fewer than 5,000 housing units in Seoul between 1941 and 1945, when there was a need at the time for about twenty times that number. As a matter of fact, the housing projects that it did administer contributed to the spread throughout Korea of new housing models, developed in Japan by a group of architects steeped in the international current of modernist urban theories (Garden City/Le Corbusian city), disseminated throughout Europe and the United States between the two wars (Delissen 1997).

But we should not here see the Japanese mediation as a one-sided process: the issue of housing models is a good example to demonstrate that travel and contacts of professionals, of workers and persons, were happening in both directions. While working in Japan on the Tokyo Imperial Hotel (1922), American architect Frank Lloyd Wright discovered the floor heating system (*ondŏl*) in a Korean inn and used it in further housing projects created in the United States. Much later, this heating system would be found in many European housing projects of the 1960s and 1970s, such as the well-known apartment complex of Parly II, built near Versailles in 1967 (Delissen 1994: 224).

3 THE *AP'AT'Ŭ TANJI* AT THE CORE OF THE MODERN KOREAN CITYSCAPE AND URBAN SOCIETY: TRAJECTORIES AND OUTCOMES OF A MODERNIST PRODUCT

3.1 *The backdrop: hectic urban growth and drastic housing problems of the 1970s and 1980s*

In the 1960s and 1970s, South Korea was developing its economic and industrial systems at a very rapid pace. In this period of fast modernisation, made possible by the industrialisation of the construction industry (use of new techniques, new materials, etc.), the building of *ap'at'ŭ tanji* was at the core of urban expansion in South Korean cities. As a matter of fact, this type of dense and standardised collective housing form is very well adapted to the Fordist production system on which a growing economy, such as the Korean economy from the 1960s to the late 1980s, is usually based. So, not only were the *ap'at'ŭ tanji* mere productions of the modernising economic environment, but they also responded extremely well to the imperatives of rapid urban expansion by providing the large-scale estates to house the fast-growing city population.

In that respect, the rise of Korean apartment complexes came against a backdrop of exponential urban growth, of which the main aspects are here recalled.[11] Between 1965 and 1985, fuelled by a massive rural exodus, the population of large Korean cities rose by an average 5 percent per annum. Seoul, with only 2.5 million inhabitants in 1960, would house more than five million people in 1970, rising to eight million in 1980. This context of brutal urban transition exacerbated the housing crisis in the cities, unsolved since the Korean War (1950-53), the problem being the quality of housing as much as the quantity. In Seoul, for example, the housing ratio (number of households/number of housing units: *chut'aek pogŭmyul*) deteriorated consistently throughout the 1960s and 1970s, settling as low as 53 percent in the mid-1980s. In the late 1970s, the level of housing amenities in Seoulite residences was one of the elements contributing to Seoul's image as a 'third world' city: only 55 percent of housing units were equipped with flush toilets, and 40 percent had no bathrooms whatsoever; 60 percent were coal-heated (by *yŏnt'an*, both impractical and dangerous[12]), while only 10 percent were equipped with central heating.[13]

3.2 *A mass housing policy changing the Seoul cityscape*

Measures were taken in the early 1970s to solve the housing problem. The Korean government launched a mass housing policy, supported by the Housing Construction Promotion Act (*Chut'aek Kŏnsŏl Chokchin Pŏp*) of 1972, which encouraged housing construction and established norms and procedures for the development of *ap'at'ŭ tanji*. Amended and strengthened in the early 1980s, the law, still in force today, facilitates collective residential development by creating within cities 'apartment zones' (*ap'at'ŭ chigu*), where the maximum allowable floorspace ratio is 300 percent with no limits on building height.[14] The application of this law thus permitted the creation of residential areas with greater density by encouraging the construction of collective housing and high-rise buildings.

---

[11] For a general overview of Seoul's development until the mid-1990s, see Kim and Choe 1997. See also Lee and Kim 1995 for the national context of urban development and city planning.

[12] *Yŏnt'an* or coal briquets, used as a combustible in the floor-heating system (*ondŏl*).

[13] *In'gu mit chut'aek sensŏsŭ* [Census of population and housing] 1980.

[14] The maximum allowable floorspace ratio in residential areas was 150 percent until 1983, then 220 percent.

Likewise, the Ministry of Construction and Transportation set high targets for housing construction: 800,000 units during the third five-year plan for economic development (1972-76), then 1.2 million during the fourth plan (1977-81). Beginning in 1981, a long-term target of five million housing units was fixed for the next fifteen years (1981-95), a target which was accelerated by the 1988 Housing Construction Programme, which planned the construction of two million units over five years (1988-92). From the 1990s through the beginning of the new millennium, the target for the construction of new homes would remain around 500,000 housing units per annum. Even though these goals were never achieved, they nonetheless pushed the Korean housing production system towards mass production, which favours the construction of *ap'at'ŭ*: from 58,000 apartment units in 1978, total construction in Korea would rise to more than 90,000 in the mid-1990s, passing 200,000 units per annum in 1990, and oscillating between 300,000 and 450,000 units per annum since.

From the early 1970s, the development of the Kangnam—'south of the river'—area in Seoul thus involved the large-scale application of the model elaborated with the Map'o *Ap'at'ŭ* a decade earlier, through land readjustment procedures undertaken by public authorities (Doebele 1989; Park 1991). The land to be urbanised was structured by a grid of large avenues devoted to motorised traffic, and various infrastructure networks (water, sewage, electricity) were constructed. The *ap'at'ŭ tanji* were then erected in these macro-blocks, of some 500 to 800 metres per side. In Seoul, major urban development projects in the 1970s and 1980s were concentrated in this area south of the Han, first by the creation on the river banks of a 'Great Wall' of *tanji*, of which many were large-scale operations undertaken by the public sector (Chamsil, Panp'o) or the private sector (Apkujŏng). Beginning in the late 1980s, the pioneering front of *tanji*, which continued to progress towards the city periphery as part of new urban developments or renewal of large squatter settlements (Thomas 1993), also began to spring up all over the city, as part of smaller urban renewal projects. The application of urban land readjustment procedures in Cooperative Redevelopment Projects (CRP: *Haptong Chae Kaebal*) even allowed the private sector to contribute to the urban renewal movement, while profiting from its investments (Gelézeau 2003: 124-8). The CRP procedures thus promoted the replacement of run-down neighbourhoods and squatter settlements near the city centre by mini-*tanji* of 500 to 2,000 or 3,000 units built by private companies.

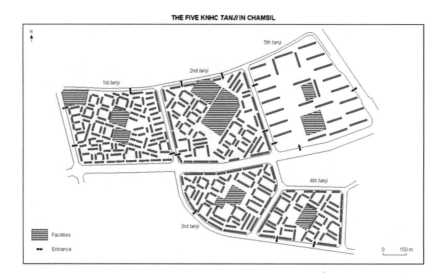

Figure 4 Master plan of the five KNHC *tanji* in Chamsil, 1975-77

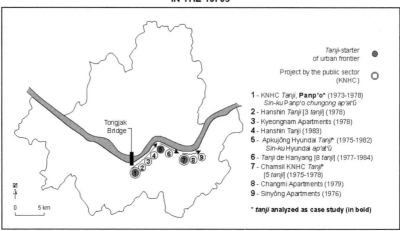

Figure 5 Progression of the 'Great Wall' of *tanji* along the south bank of the Han river, 1970-80

Figure 6 An urban renewal *tanji* near the historic centre of Seoul (Photo: Valérie Gelézeau 2003)

Overall, the *ap'at'ŭ tanji* have become an ultra-dominant form of urban extension in Korea, both on newly urbanised land or in urban renewal neighbourhoods. Driven by the strength of urban growth and its related housing problems, the trajectory of both Perry's neighbourhood units and Le Corbusier's giant collective buildings combined in the Korean *tanji* and applied to large-scale housing developments stood at the core of the Korean urbanisation process.

In the general frame of landscape interpretation shaping my analyses, the impact of *ap'at'ŭ tanji* on the cityscape, i.e. the visual dimension of cities, is to be taken as a sign of many existing connections between this housing form and the social dimensions of the city.

3.3 *The* ap'at'ŭ tanji*: an 'urban middle-class production factory'?*

How has the *ap'at'ŭ tanji* helped shape modern Korean urban society? First consideration must be given to the property acquisition process, which is central in explaining how the *ap'at'ŭ tanji* has acted as a very efficient 'urban middle-class production factory'.

In Korea, the rise of *ap'at'ŭ tanji* has been based on a policy of home ownership, differing radically from the 1950s and 1960s housing policies that surrounded the development of apartment complexes in Europe, which were connected there with 'social housing', defined as 'housing created by means of government support and finance in order to provide normal living conditions for the most disadvantaged segments of the population' (Flamand 1989: 9, also 288-93). Korean housing policy, on the contrary, has been driven more by the promotion of an omnipresent discourse on 'public housing' (*konggong chut'aek*[15]), providing either small housing units (under 60 sq m) built with construction subsidies from the government or other funds, or housing units built by the KNHC.[16] Yet, while the number of subsidised small units under 60 sq m has always represented a minority of apartments built in Korean complexes, surface areas of 100 sq m to 140 sq m, better adapted to the means of the middle, or even upper classes, have consistently been much more numerous. And as for the apartments built by the public sector (in particular by the KNHC), their numbers have been decreasing since the mid-1970s, dropping from 51 percent of units built in 1976 to less than 15 percent in 2002 (Gelézeau 2003: 143).

Lastly and most important, this 'public housing' (apartments of less than 60 sq m or those built by the KNHC) has always been directed to home ownership. Of course, public rental housing of different kinds comparable to the French HLM[17] or British council housing has existed in Korea, especially since the late 1980s. However, the rental apartments are only a small fraction of the housing stock in Korea, as shown by the fact that, for example, less than 10 percent of all new housing built between 1988 and 1992 was designed as rental housing. By the late 1990s, public rentals made up only 2 percent of the total housing stock in Korea (Yoon 2002).

---

[15] The terms 'social housing' and 'public housing' are not to be confused with each other. The translation of *konggong chut'aek* by 'social housing', which is often made in both directions (English to Korean and Korean to English) is thus not accurate.

[16] Korea National Housing Corporation or *Taehan chut'aek kongsa*, created in 1962. Directly under the Ministry of Construction and Transportation (Ministry of Construction at the time of its creation), this national agency supervises the construction and renovation of state-subsidised housing, produces and sells construction materials, administers the distribution of land to be developed (specifically by land regrouping activities) and fulfils an urban planning role.

[17] Habitation à Loyer Modéré, literally 'low-cost rental housing', which is managed by public authorities.

The Korean policy of home ownership that triggered the rise of *ap'at'ŭ tanji* was facilitated by the control of new housing prices.[18] The 1972 Housing Construction Promotion Act stipulated the creation of a price ceiling fixed below the market price for new housing units sold in projects of more than twenty units. In 1977, prompted by the success of the first sales, a complex lottery system was launched to select prospective buyers.[19] It should be emphasised that the enormous success of this policy, while clearly the result of its price control principles, is also an outcome of the particularly good fit between these principles and the characteristics of the Korean private rental market dominated by the *chŏnse* system. In this system, the tenant does not pay a monthly rent to the owner, but rather entrusts the owner with a deposit equivalent to 35 percent to 50 percent of the apartment's value, which is returned to the tenant when the apartment is vacated. So, while the price controls reduced the economic incentive to rent rather than to buy, home ownership was made economically possible for the middle and upper classes, who were living on *chŏnse* rentals, had accumulated capital, and were capable of increasing their savings.[20] Thus, contrary to European experiences, the rise of Korean apartment complexes was related less to a social housing policy for the poor than to the provision of housing units to the more solvent sectors of the population. In a context of social and economic modernisation, the development of *ap'at'ŭ tanji* increased access to home ownership for the ever-growing urban middle classes, while the price control system reaffirmed their very socio-economic status (families selected by lottery to receive an apartment quickly increased and consolidated their wealth).

The peculiarities of the housing policy are central to the phenomenal rise of apartments in Korea. But the ideological dimensions of *ap'at'ŭ tanji* developments, which may be less apparent, are nonethe-

---

[18] On the property market and land policy, see also Aveline and Li 2004.

[19] Price controls were progressively waived from 1995, staying in place only in the Seoul region (capital region) until 1998. Between 1998 and 2006, the system was totally liberalised, and the prices of new housing were adjusted to the market, although the distribution lotteries were still functioning. In November 2006, due to soaring apartment prices and uncontrollable housing price speculation in the capital region, price control was re-established, after several sets of measures to curb the rise of apartment prices had been implemented in August 2005 (especially raising of the capital gains taxes on people owning more than one house).

[20] Although this system is presently undergoing a transformation, it was dominant in the rental housing market through to the end of the 1990s.

less extremely important to the increasing popular success of the *ap'at'ŭ tanji*, which made them symbols of wealth and modernity.

4 FROM A MODERNIST IDEOLOGY TO A GENUINE KOREAN MODERNITY?

4.1 Ap'at'ŭ tanji, *modernist ideology and control of the population*

Today, recent opinion polls as well as my own surveys in the field[21] show that many families with the means to inhabit a comfortably appointed, modern individual house still prefer to live in a *tanji* apartment. But this attitude is the result of a past change in public opinion, as one tends to forget now that, in the early 1970s, most Koreans considered that living in an apartment was a sign of low social status. At that time, most of the few apartment building sites developed by public authorities for the renewal of squatter settlements in downtown Seoul were designed to provide 'social housing' in small units (less than 60 sq m). The collapse of the Wau Ap'at'ŭ in April 1970 added 'dangerous' to all the negative images of the apartment.

The government therefore used Seoul as an experimental laboratory where techniques were developed to warm up the great majority of Korean society to apartment life; this process was coupled with a large-scale and multifaceted campaign to encourage the move to the south bank of the Han river and the urban development of the Kangnam area.

In the first place, luxury *tanji* advertised their large apartments adapted to the needs of the leisure classes, who at the time had been suffering from a general lack of comfortable living spaces. Completed in 1971, the Tongbu Inch'ŏn-dong *tanji* of 3,260 units offered 700 units of some 100–240 sq m, as well as 1,312 units officially reserved for civil servants (*kongmuwŏn ap'at'ŭ*), a social category that garners much prestige in the Korean system of social values. Between 1973 and 1978, near the Tongjak bridge, the KNHC developed the Panp'o *tanji*, which accounted for 4,053 apartments, ranging from tiny 55 sq m units to vast duplexes of 190 sq m. Here again, a certain number

---

[21] In order to evaluate the consequences of the Korean crisis and of globalisation to the urban environment and quality of life, I conducted new surveys in 2004 and 2005 within the seven *tanji* that had formed my first case studies from the mid-1990s.

of spaces were reserved for sale only to civil servants and university professors.

Directed towards the wealthier and/or more respected segments of Korean society, the active promotion of some *tanji* was accompanied by other planning changes—such as the redesigning of public school districts—meant to make the Kangnam zone seem more attractive. In Korean society, which attributes great importance to the education of its children, the transplanting of the best high schools to this part of the city resulted *de facto* in the elite and the leisure classes migrating there too. In addition to this policy, specially designed to drag the elite and upper classes into the *ap'at'ŭ tanji* that were blooming in the Kangnam area, the government supported the construction of mega-estates (such as the five Chamsil KNHC *tanji* built between 1975 and 1977, about 20,000 apartment units), which provided small- or mid-sized apartments for the less affluent. But since all these apartments were privately owned, instead of being rental housing managed by public authorities, as had been the case in France for most of the apartments built in the grands ensembles in the 1950s and 1960s, the Chamsil *tanji* did not undergo the degradation that affected the French complexes after the mid-1970s.

Lastly, Korean housing policy and all the effective actions taken to promote the *tanji* model have been associated with a form of government propaganda that drove home the links between apartments, development and modernity. As a symbol of modern and urban life, the *ap'at'ŭ tanji* was presented, or rather imposed, as a development tool to be used for Korea to free itself from its archaic rural past. In this respect, Park Chung-hee spoke at the inauguration of the Map'o apartments (the *tanji* whose founding role I have already underlined):

> Korea is now emancipated from the feudal lifestyle which has passed down its customs since Antiquity; today I am certain that by adopting collective housing, Koreans will save considerable time and money, which will contribute to the improvement of the living conditions and the culture of our people.[22]

Although the word 'modern' is not mentioned here, this speech expresses the same belief in permanent progress, together with the devaluation of the 'past' (be it pre-industrial society or even, as here, distant Antiquity), which characterises a modernist ideology (Maffesoli and Rivière 1985). More than twenty years later, this image of

---

[22] Cited in Kang Hongbin 1985: 190.

collective housing, and by extension this vision of apartments, is still strongly embedded in the Korean mentality.

4.2 *Beyond the housing problem and land pressure:* ap'at'ŭ tanji *as products, vectors and symbols of Korean modernity*

The development of *tanji* provided an effective solution to the housing problem, as shown by both the considerable improvement of the housing ratio and the level of amenities in housing from the 1990s. Indeed, most of the indicators assessing the quality of housing are now close to those found in other industrialised countries of Western Europe or in North America. In 2000, 94 percent of Korean homes had hot water, 87 percent had flush toilets and 94 percent had a modern kitchen. The housing supply ratio stood at more than 96 percent in 2000, and reached 100 percent in 2002. According to Koh Chul, president of the Korea Housing Institute, housing in Korea has met EU standards since 1990 (Koh 2004).

In the effective solution provided to the housing problem, at least partially,[23] the constraint of land pressure has been a very powerful argument in explaining the choice for apartments made by decision-makers and city planners: apartment complexes are particularly well adapted to provide high-density housing settlements. However, as most of the theoretical and applied research in geography and city planning shows, 'density' is a very complex concept that is not to be reduced to the simple ratio of population numbers to an available surface of land (Fouchier and Merlin 1994). And even if we consider only this ratio, Seoul, designated a Special City (*T'ŭkpyŏlsi*), with all its apartment complexes is less dense than the comparable part of Paris (Paris *intra muros*).[24] In Seoul itself, Kangnam, where apartments are ubiquitous, is actually less dense than Kangbuk, north of the river. Last but not least, the construction of urban renewal apartment complexes in Kangbuk has not resulted in significant increase of population in the neighbourhoods targeted for urban renewal. I have analysed this phenomenon by studying Singongdŏk-tong, an urban

---

[23] In fact, the general improvement in housing hides persistent inequities in housing access and consumption within Korean society. These inequities have worsened in Seoul since the financial crisis (Gelézeau 2006).

[24] Seoul = around 16,500 residents/sq km (10 million to 600 sq km) / Paris = around 22,000 residents/sq km (2.3 million to 100 sq km).

renewal area in Map'o-gu, from the mid-1990s to the mid-2000s. The construction of the apartment complex went together with an increase in the size of the average dwelling, coupled with the gentrification of the area and a reduction in the average size of households. All together, the population of this area went from around 3,050 inhabitants in 1996 before renewal to 3,400 today in the *tanji*.[25] Well-known research on urban density shows that the construction of eleven high-rise buildings is not the only way to achieve this mere 10 percent increase in population density (Fouchier and Merlin 1994). Of course, pressure on land, and the supposedly pragmatic choice made by the Korean decision-makers account for the choice for apartments as the standard housing style. But it seems quite clear that the inexorable demands of land pressure are far from all there is to apartment development in Korea. In fact, as has been pointed out for the Japanese case (Pelletier 1994), one may wonder if decision-makers have not invoked demographic pressure to serve as a pretext for choices in fact made for far more complex reasons.

As a matter of fact, the crucial role of apartment complexes in shaping the modern Korean city is not to be reduced to the practical one of achieving modern housing standards, nor it is to be reduced to a necessary response to land scarcity. Against the backdrop of mass housing production decided upon by the Korean state from the early 1970s to solve the housing problem, *ap'at'ŭ tanji* have also been the most obvious outcome as well as the most efficient vectors of the 'miracle on the Han', as is argued here.

The construction of *ap'at'ŭ tanji* created a large market for the construction industry, itself central to Korea's industrial system, and, at the same time, this fundamental industrial sector and the connected services (architecture, urbanism and city planning—*kŏnch'uk, tosi kyehoek, tosi kaebal*) provided the growing middle class and upper-middle class (*chunggan kyegŭp, chungsan ch'ŭng*) with many jobs, as well as homes, in the form of apartments in the *tanji*. As was demonstrated previously, the price controls associated with the lottery system as late as 1995-98 enabled the more solvent segments of the population to increase their wealth: the apartments seemed to manufacture members of the middle and upper-middle classes. Finally, as is shown by works such as Denise Lett's book on the making of the South Korean 'new' urban middle class (Lett 1998), the *ap'at'ŭ tanji* pro-

---

[25] Field research data.

vided this social group with symbols by which to recognise their social status, exactly at the moment when the rural exodus was disturbing, if not destroying, traditional identity referents; for example, the importance of the birth village (*kohyang*).

Overall, the *tanji* became a very powerful tool for guiding and managing the social groups that have been at the core of South Korea's economic development. Indeed, from Michel Foucault's analytic framework, one could indeed state that the promotion of *tanji* permitted the state to directly or indirectly control a large number of those whose work fuelled the economic growth of the country (Foucault 1975).

5 Conclusion: Re-thinking Korean and Western in Modern Korean Cityscapes

Faced with many possible responses to drastic urban growth, Korean decision-makers have systematically chosen collective high-rise housing. This choice is to be connected to a mixture of pragmatic responses to the constraint of land pressure and to urban growth, and is at once both an outcome and a vector of the South Korean socio-economic system of the developmental period. This dual role distinguishes the Korean from the French case, where the construction of the '*grands ensembles*' was above all a very strong ideological adhesion to Le Corbusier's Athens Charter, at the time Sarcelles was built in 1954. On the contrary, the choice for apartments in Korea seems more to be the adaptation to the Korean context of a variety of urban theories developed in the Western world at the turn of the 20th century. In this respect, Western modernism, through the combination of theories and models that had emerged in that era, was at the origin of the Korean *ap'at'ŭ tanji*. But the dominant visual trait of the Korean cityscape, far being from the simple result of imported modernism during the colonial era or just after the wars, is instead the result of the political, economic and social mechanisms which characterised postcolonial Korean power structures. In the complex interplay of these power structures, the housing production system of the 1970s and 1980s played a crucial role in giving a formidable momentum to the development of apartment complexes, a phenomenon probably linked to the intensity of land and housing speculation in South Korea today.

Moreover, by extending the Korean case to Asia more generally and considering, for example, the new urban developments in Shanghai (Pudong) or Beijing, one could even wonder to what extent the *tanji* model is related to a very specific type of city: those emerging from a context of high-density human populations and high land pressure, and in countries where fast growth is driven by a power structure promoting an authoritarian capitalism. Could *tanji* then be one of the most significant objects of Asian development? At least in South Korea, far from being the mere effects of a Westernisation process, the *ap'at'ŭ tanji* have instead been the vectors and symbols of a genuine Korean urban modernity.

As such, the *ap'at'ŭ tanji* give a very false impression of 'Westernised', if not 'Americanised', cityscapes which indeed do not belong to the Western world, as the very specific patterns of urban extension in Korea testify to this day. Where is the Western modernity in the clash of paddy field and *tanji* on the outskirts of cities?

These reflections are further acknowledgment of the fact that, while the connection between modernity/modernisation and Westernisation refers mostly to the geographical world order of the end of the 19th century to the first part of the 20th century, modernity can indeed be considered, as the anthropologist Georges Balandier puts it, 'a drive, a movement' (Balandier 1985).[26] Not only has a genuine Asian modernity emerged in the past few decades, indeed, it is spreading throughout the entire region by the transmission of various models in many fields of social and cultural life—be they manga-type cartoons, neon cityscapes, or hyper-connected digital lifestyles. In the area of urban space and architecture, Korean urban modernity is already recognised as a movement and a drive, as is shown, for example, by the work and discourse of Dutch architect Rem Koolhas to whom the Asian cities, and Seoul in particular, embody the concept of 'generic city'[27]. The

---

[26] Arguing in his book entitled *Le Détour: pouvoir et modernité* that definitions of modernisation and modernity suffer from the two major inconsistencies of being vague, evolutionist and Eurocentric—thus carrying ideological implications—, the anthropologist Georges Balandier ends up with an almost poetic anthropological definition of modernity: 'The term "modernity" is polymorphous and polysemic, but it does nonetheless express "a drive, a movement" ' (Balandier 1985: 133).

[27] For Koolhaas, the urban is so pervasive, that the architecture, as well as the concepts and the way we used for the cities until now are not relevant any more and new forms and concepts have to be created. The 'generic city' designates this general and pervasive urbanization transforming the nature itself of human settlement. Asian cities seem to embody the 'generic city' (Koolhaas et al. 1994).

trajectory of the *ap'at'ŭ tanji* model is unlikely to come to an end at the gates of the peninsula.

In conclusion, I will return to Korea and bring up the issue of the future of *tanji*.

As one can imagine, *ap'at'ŭ tanji* will soon become (if they are not already) high-stake issues in the management of Korean cities. The buildings were constructed to have life spans of twenty to thirty years. As most of the apartments dated from the 1960s have already been replaced by newer ones, the reconstruction of some mega-*tanji* of the 1970s (Chamsil) is now booming in Seoul, and the problem of remodelling the apartments from the 1980s is already appearing. In fifteen or twenty years, the major construction programmes of the 1980s and 1990s will start to degrade. How will the maintenance and rehabilitation, or even reconstruction, of all these buildings be guaranteed and undertaken?

The problem is all the more urgent in the light of recent housing trends: the elite have for some time left the *tanji* for luxurious individual homes (*pilla*), and the urban bourgeoisie will abandon their apartments as soon as this housing type no longer permits them to affirm their 'distinction' (Bourdieu 1979). The deregulation of housing prices in 1998 has already given rise to new housing types, closer to the Singaporean condominium model, in luxury complexes such as the Acrotown complex (where the notorious Tower Palace apartments are located) in Togok-tong (Gelézeau 2006). A process of sub-urbanisation is also beginning, in which members of the urban bourgeoisie seek a more country style of living (*chŏnwŏn chut'aek*), within 30 to 60 km of large cities (Koo 1998). At the same time, in the urban periphery, recent years have seen many *ap'at'ŭ tanji* where 80 percent of their housing units smaller than 50 sq m are destined to more modest social classes. The expulsion of *tanji* to the outskirts may sow the seed for future urban problems, of which the French *banlieues* are an example. While the Korean-style *ap'at'ŭ tanji* model is spreading in other Asian countries, is this model on the slow road to failure in the peninsula? How will city managers respond to this challenge? A shift of public opinion and image comparable to that which affected French apartment complexes would certainly suggest a very gloomy future for Korean *tanji*, or at least for those handicapped by a difficult location and poor facilities. While geography-fiction is to be avoided, it nonetheless seems clear that the success of a sustainable development policy for Korean cities must be closely bound to the management of all these *tanji* built since the 1970s, which are today part of the urban heritage.

This major challenge for Korean city government and administrations will be a test for the Korean modern (and post-modern?) city.

References

Anderson, Kay (2003), *Handbook of Cultural Geography*, London: Sage Publications
Aveline, Natacha and Ling-hin Li (eds.) (2004), *Property Markets and Land Policies in Northeast Asia: The Case of Five Cities, Tokyo, Seoul, Shanghai, Taipei and Hong Kong*, Hong Kong: Maison Franco-Japonaise-Tokyo and Centre for Real Estate and Urban Economics, University of Hong Kong
Balandier, Georges (1985), *Le détour: Pouvoir et modernité*, Paris: Fayard
Benevolo, Leonardo (1988), *Histoire de l'architecture moderne: L'inévitable éclectisme 1960-1980*, Paris: Dunod
Bourdieu, Pierre (1979), *La Distinction: critique sociale du jugement*, Paris: Editions de Minuit
Choay, Françoise (1965), *L'urbanisme, utopies et réalité: Une anthologie*, Paris: Seuil
Cosgrove, Denis E. (1998) (1st edition 1984), *Social Formation and Symbolic Landscape*, Madison WI: University of Wisconsin Press
Clerk, Paul (1967), *Grands ensembles, banlieues nouvelles* (Travaux et documents de l'INED n°49), Paris: CRU
Delissen, Alain (1994), *Séoul, Kim Sugŭn et le Groupe Espace (Konggan): 1960-1990. Identité nationale et paysages urbains*, Ph.D. dissertation, Ecole des Hautes Etudes en Sciences Sociales, Paris
Delissen, Alain (1997), 'Kyŏngsŏng chut'aek munje: crise de la maison coréenne ou crise du logement colonial dans le Séoul des années 20 et 30?', in: *Revue de Corée*, 29 (2), pp. 197-229
Doebele, William A. (1989), *Land Readjustment*, Lexington KY: Lexington Books
Dufau, Frédéric and Annie Fourcaut (eds.) (2004), *Le monde des grands ensembles*, Paris: Créaphis
Duncan, James (1994), 'Landscape', in: Ron Johnston, Derek Gregory and David M. Smith (eds.), *Dictionary of Human Geography*, 3rd ed., Oxford: Blackwell, pp. 316-17
Flamand, Jean-Paul (1989), *Loger le peuple: Essai sur l'histoire du logement social*, Paris: La Découverte
Foucault, Michel (1975), *Surveiller et punir*, Paris: Gallimard
Fouchier, Vincent and Pierre Merlin (eds.) (1994), *Les fortes densités urbaines: une solution pour nos villes?*, Hong Kong: Institut Français d'Urbanisme/International Urban Development Association
Gaucher, Marcel (1985), *Le désenchantement du monde*, Paris: Gallimard
Gelézeau, Valérie (2003), *Séoul, ville géante, cités radieuses*, Paris: CNRS Editions
Gelézeau, Valérie (2006), 'Segyehwa, chut'aek munhwa, kŭrigo sŏul saeroun chugŏ pulli' [Globalisation, housing culture and new residential segregations in Seoul], in: *Asea Yŏn'gu* (Korea University), 49 (4), pp. 7-36
Gelézeau, Valérie (2007), *Ap'at'ŭ Konghwaguk. P'ŭlangsŭ chirihakchaga pon han'gukŭi ap'at'ŭ* [The Republic of Apartments: South Korean Apartments seen by a French Geographer], Seoul: Humanitas
George, Pierre (1990/1970), *Dictionnaire de la géographie*, Paris: PUF
Jackson, Peter (1994), *Maps of Meaning: An Introduction to Cultural Geography*, New York: Routledge
Kaës, René (1963), *Vivre dans les grands ensembles*, Paris: Editions ouvrières
Kang, Hongbin (1985) 'Tosiŭi skyline' [The urban skyline], in: *Saramŭi tosi* [A city for people], Seoul: Simsŏldang, pp. 118-247
Kang, Pusŏng (ed.) (1993), *Tosi chiphap chut'aegŭi kyehoek* [Planning in urban collective housing], Seoul: Parŏn

Kang, Surim (1991), 'Urinara chut'aek saŏpŭi kwejŏk: Kongdong chut'aek chungsimŭro', in: *Han'gukŭi ap'at'ŭ* [South Korean apartments], Seoul: Hanguk Chut'aek Saŏp Hyŏphoe, pp. 9-26
Kim, Joochul and Choe, Sangchuel (1997), *Seoul: The Making of a Metropolis*, Chichester, UK: John Wiley & Sons
Koh, Chul (2004), *Overview of Housing Policies and Programs in Korea*, Seoul: Housing Institute Report
Koo, Donghoe [Ku Tonghoe] (1998), *Tae tosi chuminŭi chŏnwŏn chihyang ijugwa chŏnggwa saenghwal yangshik: Sudokwŏn chŏnwŏn chut'aek chungsimŭro* [The exurbanisation of the inhabitants of large cities: a study centred on 'garden houses' in the capital region], Ph.D. dissertation, Seoul National University, Department of Geography
Koolhaas, Rem, Hans Werlemann and Bruce Mau (1994) (2nd edition 1997), *S,M,L,XL*, New York: The Monacelli Press
Lacoste, Yves (1963), 'Un problème complexe et débattu: les grands ensembles', in: *Bulletin de l'Association des Géographes français*, re-published in: Marcel Roncayolo and Thierry Paquot (eds.) (1992), *Villes et civilisation urbaine XVIIIe-XXe siècle*, Paris: Larousse, pp. 497-502
Lee, Gunyoung and Kim, Hyunsik (1995), *Cities and Nations: Planning Issues and Policies of Korea*, Seoul: Nanam
Lett, Denise (1998), *In Pursuit of Status: The Making of South Korea's 'New' Urban Middle Class*, Cambridge MA: Harvard University Press
Maffesoli, Michel and Claude Rivière (eds.) (1985), *Une anthropologie des turbulences*, Paris: Berg international
O, Tŏksŏng and Mun Honggil (2000), *Tosi sŏlgye* [City planning], Seoul: Kimundang
Park, Heon-Joo (1991), *Housing Land in Government Intervention*, Stockholm: Akademitryck
Pelletier, Philippe (1994), 'Japon', in: Roger Brunet (ed.), *Géographie universelle*, volume 5, *Chine, Japon, Corée*, Montpellier: GIP Reclus, pp. 219-427
Pitte, Jean-Robert (1983), *Histoire du paysage français*, Paris: Tallandier
Thomas, James Philip (1993), *Contested from Within and Without: Squatters, the State, the Minjung Movement and the Limits of Resistance in a Seoul Shanty Town Targeted for Urban Renewal*, Ph.D. dissertation, Rochester University NJ, Department of Anthropology
Yim, Changbok [Im Ch'angbok] (1996), 'Tosi chut'aekŭi pyŏnch'ŏn' [The transformation of urban housing], in: *Hanguk hyŏndae kŏnch'uk* [Contemporary Korean architecture], Seoul: Han'guk Chut'aek Hyŏphoe, pp. 199-216
Yoon, Juhyun (2002), *Hanguk chut'aek* [Korean housing], Seoul: Korea National Statistical Office
Zchang Sungsoo [Chang Sŏngsu] (1994), *1960-1970 nyŏndae hanguk ap'at'ŭŭi pyŏnch'ŏne kwanhan yŏn'gu* [The transition towards apartments in Korea, 1960s-1970s], Ph.D. dissertation, Seoul National University, Department of Architecture

NEW ANCESTRAL SHRINES IN SOUTH KOREA[1]

Heonik Kwon

ABSTRACT

Since the collapse of the cold war's geopolitical order in the early 1990s and the related decline of communism or anti-communism as viable political ideologies, there have been several important changes in the political life of South Koreans. One notable change is found in the domain of ancestor worship. Many communities are now reshaping their ancestral rites into a more inclusive form, introducing demonstratively into them the memories of the dead who, previously labelled as supporters of communism, had been invisible in public memory. In places where people experienced the global cold war as a violent communal conflict, the above development involves difficult negotiations between the community's politically bifurcated ancestral heritages. This article examines a set of new ancestral shrines erected as part of this communal effort to repair the broken genealogical condition, and enters into critical dialogue with an influential idea in contemporary scholarship about social development beyond the cold war.

1 INTRODUCTION

Since the decades of authoritarian anti-Communist rule ended in the late 1980s, and the cold war's geopolitical order collapsed in the wider world shortly thereafter, there have been several important changes in the political life of South Koreans. One notable change is found in the

---

[1] The research for this article was conducted on several occasions in 2003-2006, supported by a fellowship grant from the Economic and Social Research Council (RES-000-27-0022). In Cheju, it benefited enormously from the guidance and assistance provided by the library of Cheju National University, Institute of the Cheju 4.3. Incident Studies, Association for the Families of the Cheju 4.3 Incident Victims, and members of the Hagui Village Development Committee. I thank them all for their kind support. Special thanks to Hyun Kil-on, Han Lim-Hwa, Kim Seong-Nae and An Mi-Jeong, who generously shared with me their immense knowledge of the island's history and culture, and to Park Jun-Hwan for sharing with me his knowledge of shamanic rituals.

domain of ritual life or, more specifically, in the activity of death commemoration and ancestor worship. In an increasing number of communities across the Republic of Korea (ROK), people are now actively reshaping their ancestral rites into a more inclusive form, introducing demonstratively into the ritual domain the politically troubled memories of the dead, which were excluded from the public sphere under the state's militant anti-Communist policies.

Some argue that, for South Koreans, the prospect of genuine political democracy is inseparable from imagining an alternative public culture, free from the hegemony of anti-communism as an all-encompassing state ideology (Cho-Han 2000: 317; Kwon Hyuk-bum 2000: 30; see also Whitfield 1996). In this context, overcoming the legacy of anti-communism is considered a necessary condition for the political community's progress towards a post-cold war era, and thereby for joining the outside world, which, it is believed, has moved away from the grid of bipolar politics. Because the experience of the global cold war was an exceptionally violent one for Koreans, involving a catastrophic civil war, the above conceptualisation of historical transition has involved myriad reflections and disputes about the nation's violent past and its enduring effects.[2] This has been the case at the community level as well as nationally. The changes in ancestral rituals mentioned earlier should be considered in this broad contemporary historical context, and as efforts to repair the broken communal identity by restoring the normative aspect of its hidden genealogical heritage, which was outlawed by the state and stigmatised as a dangerous 'red' (i.e. Communist) element in public consciousness (Yun 2003: 148-52).

---

[2] In this article the idea of 'global cold war' is used deliberately, in distinction to that of the 'cold war'. The term 'cold war' refers to the prevailing condition of the world in the second half of the 20th century, divided as it was into two separate paths of political modernity and economic development. In a narrower sense it means the contest of power and will between the two dominant states, the United States and the Soviet Union, which (according to George Orwell, who coined the term in 1945) set out to rule the world between them under an undeclared state of war, being unable to conquer one another. In a wide definition, however, the global cold war also entails the unequal relations of power among the political communities, which pursued or were driven to pursue a specific path of progress within the binary structure of the global order. The cold war's dimension of a contest of power has been an explicit and central element in cold war historiography; the aspect of a relation of domination is a relatively marginal and implicit element. Following Westad (2005), I use the term 'global cold war' as a reference that incorporates both of these analytical dimensions.

Existing literature on South Korea's democratic transition tends to focus on organised mass mobilisation in the public sphere, notably the activism of dissident political leaders, intellectuals, students and the labour force. Although this focus is justified for a society where influential political discourses typically take on the scale of the national community, it is also problematic through its lack of analytical attention to the organised actions and social developments taking place in less centralised, more intimate spheres of life.[3] In this respect, this article seeks to bring to attention the process of democratic transition at community level. It shows how communities, once devastated by violently bipolarising political forces in the midst of the global cold war, are now struggling to overcome the wounds of past conflicts and violence, and how people in these communities are advancing forceful initiatives for political justice and moral reconciliation.

My discussion will focus mainly on Cheju island at the southern maritime edge of the Korean peninsula, and will examine new ancestral shrines arising in parts of this island and the process of family and community repairs associated with these sites of memory. Although this process is not restricted to this region, the experience of Cheju nevertheless provides an exemplary case in this matter (Park 1999). The claims for justice and related activities of community repair developed in Cheju earlier than in most other parts of South Korea and have been particularly strong. I argue that the islanders' new ancestral shrines not only demonstrate a process of genealogical reconstitution, but also constitute politically mixed religious shrines whose presence in the community testifies to both an enduring legacy of damaging bipolar politics and a vigorous communal will to overcome this violent legacy. These developments interact with recent changes in South Korea's domestic politics but also, more broadly, with the end of the cold war as a prevailing geopolitical paradigm of last century. Therefore I will situate the islanders' commemorative activities also in a critical dialogue with an existing idea about social democracy after the cold war, and will show how this influential idea is based on a prob-

---

[3] Despite South Korea's appearance of being a highly industrialised and urbanised modern society, as observers note, political relations actually have strong elements of a traditional agrarian society, where public life and political association rely heavily on existing solidary relations based on a common place of origin or lineage identity, including close interpersonal ties traced to common educational backgrounds (see Kim Kwang-Ok 2000). Traditional social identities continue to matter in Korean public culture, and this applies to the process of democratisation.

lematic understanding of bipolar political history, ignoring its violent realities such as those endured by the Cheju islanders.

2 BEYOND LEFT AND RIGHT

The democratic family, it has been argued, is the backbone of a successful 'third way' political development beyond conventional left and right oppositions. Painting an outline of social democracy in the post-cold war world, Giddens (1998) repudiates both what he calls the 'rightist' idealisation of the traditional, patriarchal familial order and the 'leftist' view of the family as a microcosm of an undemocratic political order. In their stead he proposes a new model of family relations, which can synthesise the imperative of communal moral solidarity with the freedom of individual choice, as a unity based on contractual commitment among individual members. This social form of democratic family relations, according to Giddens (1998: 90-93), will respect the norms of 'equality, mutual respect, autonomy, decision-making through communication and freedom from violence.'

Giddens (1998: 89) writes about family and kinship relations at length in a work devoted to the political history of bipolar ideologies, because he believes that families are a basic institution of civil society and that a strong civil society is central to a successful social development beyond the legacy of left and right oppositions. His third way agenda is based on the notion that new sociological thinking is demanded after the end of the cold war. According to him, political development after the cold war depends on how societies creatively inherit positive elements from both right and left ideological legacies, and its main constituents will be 'states without enemies' (as opposed to states organised along the frontline of bipolar enmity), 'cosmopolitan nations' (as opposed to the old nations pursuing nationalism), a 'mixed economy' (between capitalism and socialism) and 'active civil societies'. At the core of this creative process of grafting, Giddens argues, are the 'post-traditional' conditions of individual and collective life, an understanding of which requires transcending the traditional sociological imagination that sets individual freedom and communal solidarity as contrary values (Giddens 1994: 13). The 'post-traditional' society, according to him, is expressed most prominently in the social life of 'the democratic family'.

The merit of Giddens's approach is that his view of the political transition from the cold war does not privilege the changes taking place in state identities and interstate relations. Instead, he relates these changes to other general issues in social structure, including individual identity and the relationship between state and society. For Giddens, 'the new kinship'—based on mutual recognition of individual rights, active communal trust and tolerance of diversity—will be a key agent in making a general social break with the era of politically bifurcated modernity, which appropriated individual freedom and collective solidarity into falsely contradictory, mutually exclusive categories (Giddens 1994: 14; see also Laïdi 1998: 15-28).

Giddens's discussion of the social order after the cold war is based primarily on the specific historical context of Western Europe. In his accounts, the positions of 'left and right' appear mainly as those about visions of modernity and schemes of social ordering. According to the Italian philosopher Bobbio, left and right are correlative positions, like two sides of a coin, in which '[the] existence of one presupposes the existence of the other, the only way to invalidate the adversary is to invalidate oneself' (Bobbio 1996: 14). This privileged experience of left and right oppositions as both being integral parts of the body politic, however, may not extend to other historical realities of the cold war. In the latter, the left and right were mutually exclusive positions, rather than correlative ones, in the sense that taking the position of one side meant denying the other side a *raison d'être*, or even physically annihilating the latter from the political arena.

In the situation of an ideologically charged armed conflict or systemic state violence, left or right might not be merely about an antithetical political distinction, but rather a question that is directly relevant to the preservation of human life and the protection of basic civil and human rights. Against this historical background of the cold war experienced as the 'balance of terror' and 'balance of conformity' rather than 'balance of power' (Cumings 1991: 51), moreover, we may consider the relevance of family or kinship relations in the general social transition from the bipolar order differently from Giddens's discussion of the issue.

3 LAMENTATIONS OF THE TRAGIC DEAD

3.1 *Form of the ritual*

In April 2004, many places on Cheju island were bustling with people preparing for their annual commemoration of the 4.3 (April Third) incident. The 'incident' refers to the Communist-led uprising triggered on 3 April 1948 in protest against both the measures undertaken by the United States' occupying forces to root out radical nationalist forces from post-colonial Korea, and the policies of the US administration to establish an independent anti-Communist state in the southern half of the Korean peninsula (Cumings 1981; Park 1999; Suh 1999). But the reference also points to the numerous atrocities of civilian killings that devastated the island following the uprising, caused by brutal counter-insurgency military campaigns and counteractions from the Communist partisans. This violent period was, in many ways, a prelude to the Korean War (1950-53). The 4.3 incident has only recently become a publicly acknowledged historical reality among the islanders, in contrast to the past decades during which the subject remained strictly taboo in public discourse (Cheju 4.3 Yŏnguso 2003; Gwon 2006). Nowadays the islanders are free to hold death-anniversary rites for their relatives who were killed or who disappeared in the chaos of 1948. Every April, the whole island turns briefly into a gigantic ritual community consisting of thousands of separate but simultaneous family or community-based events of death commemoration.

It is now a familiar experience for visitors to the island during the month of April to step accidentally into a ritual occasion that the anthropologist Kim Seong-nae (1989, 1999) calls 'the lamentations of the dead'. Presided over by local specialists in ritual, these occasions invite the spirits of those who have suffered a tragic death, offer food and money to them, and later enact the clearing of obstacles from their pathways to the nether world. A key element in this long and complex ritual procedure is when the invited spirits of the dead publicly tell of their grievous feelings and unfulfilled wishes through the ritual specialists' speeches and songs.

In a family-based performance, the lamentations of the dead typically begin with tearful narration of the moments of death, the horrors of violence and the expression of indignation against the unjust killing. Later, the ritual performance moves on to the stage where the spirits, exhausted with lamentation and somewhat calmed down, engage with the surroundings and the participants. They express gratitude to their family for caring about their grievous feelings, and this phase is often accompanied by speculations about the family's health matters or financial prospects. When the spirits of the dead start to express concerns about their living family, this is understood to mean that they have become relatively free from the grid of sorrows, which the Koreans express as a successful 'disentanglement of grievous feelings' (Kwon Heonik 2004).

In a ritual on a wider scale that involves participants beyond the family circle, the lamentations may include the spirits' confused remarks about how they should relate to the strangers gathered for the occasion, which later typically develop into remarks of appreciation and gratitude. The spirits thank the participants for their demonstration of sympathy to the suffering of the dead, who have no blood ties to them and to whom, therefore, the participants have no ritual obligations. If the occasion is sponsored by an organisation that has a particular moral or political objective, moreover, some of the invited spirits may proceed to make gestures of support for the organisation. Thus, the spirit narration from the victims of a massacre may explicitly invoke concepts such as human rights if the ceremony is sponsored by a civil rights activist group, and other modern idioms such as gender equality if the occasion is supported by a network of feminist activists. The lamentations of the dead closely engage with the diverse aspirations of the living.

3.2 *Aesthetic dimensions*

Several observers of Korea's modern history have noted that South Korea's recent democratic transition, and the vigorous popular political mobilisation since the late 1980s that enabled this transition, are not to be considered separately from the aesthetic power of ritualised lamentations (Kim Kwang-ok 1994; Kim Seong-nae 1999). The country's civil rights activist groups disseminate the voices of the victims of state violence as a way of mobilising public awareness and support for their cause, and employ forms of popular shamanic mortuary processions to materialise the dead victims' messages. The lamentations of the dead are, according to Kim Kwang-ok (1994), a principal aesthetic instrument in Korea's 'rituals of resistance'. The voices of the dead are considered both as evidence of political violence and as an appeal for collective actions for justice. Political activism in South Korea is so intimately tied to the ritual aesthetics of lamenting spirits of the dead that even an academic forum may not do without the aesthetic form. When the annual conference of Korean anthropologists chose the cultural legacy of the Korean War as its main theme in 1999, the conference included a grand shamanic spirit consolation rite dedicated to all the spirits of the tragic dead from the war era. In these situations, the history of mass war death is not merely an object of academic debate or collective social actions, but takes on a vital agency of a particular kind that influences the course of communicative actions about the past. In *Beyond Good and Evil*, Nietzsche wrote, 'A thought comes when "it" wants to and not when "I" want; thus it is a falsification to say: the subject "I" is the condition for the predicate "think." It thinks: but there is ... no immediate certainty that this "it" is just that famous old "I"' (cited from Bettelheim 1985: 61). The remembering self's incomplete autonomy and the remembered other's incomplete passivity are perhaps implicit in any form of commemoration. The lamentation of the dead is a radical example of this intersubjective nature of remembrance.

The lamentations of the dead constitute an important aesthetic form in Korea's culture of political protests, and this should be considered against the nation's particular historical background; most notably, its experience of the cold war in the form of a violent civil war, and the related political history of anti-communism. The proliferation of the spirit narration of violent war death in the present time relates to the repression of the history of mass death in the past decades.

The rich literary tradition of Cheju testifies to this intimate relationship between the grievance-expressing spirits of the dead and the inability of the living to account for their memories. Hyun Kil-on's short story *Our Grandfather*, for instance, tells of a village drama caused by a domestic crisis when a family's dying grandfather is briefly possessed by the spirit of his dead son. The possessed grandfather suddenly recovers his physical strength and visits an old friend (of the son) in the village. The villager had taken part in accusing the son of being a Communist sympathiser during the 4.3 incident, thereby causing his summary execution at the hands of counter-insurgency forces. The grandfather demands that he publicly apologise for his wrongful accusation. The villager refuses to do so and instead gathers other villagers to help him in his plot to lynch the accuser. The return of the dead in this magical drama highlights the villagers' complicity with the dominant ideology of anti-communism and the related rule of silence about past grievances. The story's climax comes when the son's ghost realises the futility of his actions and turns silent, at which moment the family's grandfather passes away (cf. Hyun 1990).

Just as the silence of the dead was a prime motif in Cheju's resistance literature under the anti-Communist political regimes, so their publicly staged lamentations are now a principal element in the island's cultural activity after the democratic transition. Between the past and the present, a radical change has taken place in that the living are no longer obliged to play deaf to what the dead have to say about history and historical justice. What is continuous in time, however, is that the understanding of political reality at the grassroots level is expressed through the communicability of historical experience between the living and the dead.

3.3 *Rehabilitative initiatives*

The rituals displaying the lamenting spirits of the dead have become public events in Cheju since the end of 1980s and were part of the forceful nationwide civil activism in the 1990s. In Cheju, the activism was focused on the moral rehabilitation of the casualties from the 4.3 incident as innocent civilian victims, instead of their previous classification as Communist insurgents. The rehabilitative initiatives have since spread to other parts of the country and resulted in the legislation in 2000 of a special parliamentary inquiry into the 4.3 incident. This was followed by legislation passed in May 2005 on the investigation of incidents of Korean War civilian massacres in general. These initiatives led to forensic excavations on a national scale in subsequent years for suspected sites of mass burial. The 2005 legislation includes an investigation of the round-up and summary execution of alleged Communist sympathisers in the early days of the Korean War, an estimated two to three hundred thousand civilians.[4]

These dark chapters in modern Korean history were relegated to non-history under the previous military-ruled authoritarian regimes, which defined anti-communism as one of the state's prime guidelines. Since the early 1990s, in contrast, these hidden histories of mass death have become one of the most heated and contested issues of public

---

[4] See the material available online at www.genocide.or.kr.

debate, and their emergence into public discourse is, in fact, regarded by observers as a key feature of Korea's political democratisation (Kim Dong-chun 2000; Park 1999; Pyo et al. 2003). The province of Cheju is exemplary in terms of this development. It initiated an institutional basis for a sustained documentation programme for the victims of the 4.3 atrocities and province-wide memorial events. It has excavated several suspected mass burial sites and plans to preserve these sites as historical monuments. The provincial authority also hopes to develop these activities to promote the province's public image as 'an island of peace and human rights'.

These achievements of Cheju islanders were made possible by their sustained community-based grassroots mobilisation, activated through a network of non-governmental organisations and civil rights associations, including the association of the victims' families. For those active in the family association, the beginning of the 1990s was a time of sea change. Before 1990 the association was officially called the Anti-Communist Association of Families of the Cheju 4.3 Incident Victims (Chejudo 4.3 Sagŏn Minganin Hŭisaengja Bankong Yujokhoe) and, as such, it was dominated by families related to a particular category of victims—local civil servants and paramilitary personnel killed by the Communist militia (Cheju 4.3 Sakŏn Hŭisaengja Yujokhoe 2005: 262). This category of victims, in current estimation, amounts to 10 to 20 per cent of the total civilian casualties. The rest were the victims of the actions of government troops, police forces or the paramilitary groups, and previously were classified as Communist subversives or 'red elements'. Since 1990, the association gradually has been taken over by the families of the majority side, relegating the family representatives from the anti-Communist association era to minority status within the association. This was 'a quiet revolution', according to the association's current president, Kim Du-yon, a result of a long, heated negotiation between different groups of family representatives.[5] During the transition from a nominally anti-Communist organisation to one that intends to 'go beyond the blood-drenched division of left and right', the association faced several crises: some family representatives with anti-Communist family backgrounds left the association, and some new representatives with opposite backgrounds refused to sit with the former. Conflicts still exist not only within the provincial-level association, but also at the village level.

---

[5] Interview with Mr. Kim Du-Yon in Cheju city, South Korea, January 2007.

Nevertheless, the association's resolute stand that its objective is to account for all atrocities from all sides, Communist or anti-Communist, has been conducive to preventing the conflicts from reaching an implosive level. Equally important was the fact that many family representatives (particularly from the villages in the mountain region, which suffered both from the pacification activity of the government troops and from the retributive actions from the Communist partisan groups) had casualties on both sides of the conflict within their immediate circle of relatives. The democratisation of the family association was a liberating experience for the families on the majority side, including those who were members of it before the change. Under the old scheme, some of the victims of the state's anti-Communist terror were registered as victims of the terror perpetrated by Communist insurgents. This was partly a survival strategy of the victims' families and was partly caused by the prevailing notion that the 'red hunt' campaign would not have happened had there been no 'red menace'. The 'quiet revolution' of the 1990s meant that these families are now free to grieve for their dead relatives of 1948 publicly and in a way that does not falsify the history of their mass death.

4   New Ancestral Shrines

The above development has affected the islanders' ritual commemorative activities. As previously noted, earlier works on this issue emphasised the relevance of shamanic rituals in the politics of memory. It has been argued that the shamanic rituals are relatively open to the intrusive actions of politically troubled ancestral spirits, thus giving the latter an opportunity to express their grievances about their violent historical experience—an opportunity unavailable in family-based ancestral rites (Kim Seong-nae 1989; see also Janelli and Janelli 1982: 151-67). These works describe ancestral rituals as having been under the grip of the state's anti-Communist policies, whereas shamanic rituals are considered to have been relatively free from political forces. This changed in the 1990s. Many communities in Cheju have recently begun to introduce the previously outlawed 'red' ancestral identities into their communal ancestral rituals, thereby placing their memorabilia in demonstrative coexistence with the tablets of other 'ordinary' ancestors, including the memorabilia of patriotic 'anti-Communist' ancestors.

4.1 Example of Hagui village

The last process has resulted in the rise of diverse, highly inventive new ancestral shrines across communities in Cheju and elsewhere in South Korea. One of them is the monument in the village of Hagui, in the northern district of Cheju island, completed in the beginning of 2003 (see Figure 1 below). In the white stone at the centre of the picture is inscribed, in Chinese characters, 'Shrine of spirit consolation'. The two black stones on the left commemorate the patriotic ancestors from the colonial era, the patriotic fighters from the village during the Korean War and, later, from the military expedition to the Vietnam War. The two black stones on the right side commemorate the hundreds of villagers who fell victim to the protracted anti-Communist counter-insurgency campaigns waged in Cheju before and during the Korean War.

Figure 1 New ancestral shrine in Hagui, Cheju island

The completion of this village ancestral shrine has a complex historical background. An important factor was the division of the village into two separate administrative units in the 1920s, which the locals understand now to have been a divide-and-rule strategy of the Japanese colonial administration at the time, and the distortion of this division during the chaos following the 4.3 uprising. Hagui elders recall that the village's enforced administrative division developed into a perilous, painful situation at the height of the counter-insurgency military campaigns. The logic of these campaigns set people in one part of the village, labelled then as a 'red' hamlet, against those in the other, who then tried to dissociate themselves from the former. After these campaigns were over, Hagui was considered a politically impure, subversive place in Cheju (just as the whole island of Cheju was known as a 'red' island to mainland South Koreans). Villagers seeking employment outside the village experienced discrimination because of their place of origin, and this aggravated the existing grievances between the two administratively separate residential clusters. People of one side felt it unjust that they were blamed for what they believed the other side of the village was responsible for; and the latter found it hard to accept that they should endure accusations and discrimination even within a close community. It was against this background that some Hagui villagers petitioned the local court to give new, separate names to the two village units. Their intention was partly to bury the stigmatising name of Hagui, and also to eradicate signs of affinity between the two units. This was just after the end of the Korean War in 1953. Since then, the village of Hagui became separated in official documents into Dong-gui and Gui-il, two invented names that no one liked but which were, nevertheless, necessary.

The above historical trajectory resulted in a host of problems and conflicts in the villagers' everyday life. Not only did a number of them suffer from the extra-judicial system called *yŏnjwaje*, which prevented individuals with an allegedly politically impure family and genealogical background from taking employment in public sectors or from enjoying social mobility in general; but some of them also had to endure sharing the village's communal space with someone who was, in their belief, culpable for their predicament. This last point relates to the enduring wounds of the 4.3 history within the community, caused by the villagers' complex experience with the counter-insurgency actions. These included being coerced into accusing close neighbours of supporting the insurgents. These hidden histories are occasionally pried open to become an explosive issue in the community, as when, for instance, two young lovers protest against their families' and the village elders' fierce opposition to their relationship, without giving them any intelligible reason for doing so.

The details of these intimate histories of the 4.3 violence and their contemporary traces remain a taboo subject in Hagui. The most frequently recalled and excitedly recited episodes are instead related to festive occasions. Some time before the villagers began to discuss the idea of a communal shrine, the two units of Hagui joined in an inter-village sporting event and feast organised periodically by the district authority. They had done so on many previous occasions, but this time, the two football teams of Dong-gui and Gui-il both managed to reach the semi-final, each hoping to win the final. During the competition, the residents of Dong-gui cheered against the team representing Gui-il, supporting the team's opponent from another village instead, and the same happened with the residents of Gui-il in a match involving the team from Dong-gui. This experience was scandalous, according to the Hagui elders I spoke to, and they contrasted the divisive situation of the village with an opposite initiative taking place in the wider world. (At the time of the inter-village feast, the idea of joint national representation in international sporting events was under discussion between South and North Korea.) The village was going against the stream of history, according to the elders, and they said that the village's shameful collective representation on the district football ground formed the momentum for thinking about a communal project that would help to reunite the community of Hagui.

In 1990, the village assembly in Dong-gui and its counterpart in Gui-il agreed to revive their original common name and to shake off their nominal separation for the past four decades after the Korean War. They established an informal committee responsible for the rapprochement and reintegration of the two villages. In 2000, this committee proposed to the village assemblies the idea of erecting a new ancestral shrine based on donations from the villagers and from those living elsewhere. When the shrine was completed in 2003, the Hagui villagers held a grand opening ceremony in the presence of many visitors from elsewhere in the country and from overseas (many from Hagui live in Japan). The black memorial stones on the left (from the spectator's perspective) are inscribed with names of patriotic village ancestors, including one hundred names from colonial times, dozens of patriotic soldiers from the Korean War or the Vietnam War, and a dozen villagers killed by Communist partisans during the 4.3 chaos.[6]

---

[6] The twelve villagers killed by the insurgents belonged to the village's *minbodan*, the civil defence groups hastily organised by the South Korean counter-insurgency

The two stones on the right commemorate 303 village victims of the anti-Communist political terror during the 4.3 incident, and dedicate the following poetic message to the victims:

> When we were still enjoying the happiness of being freed from the colonial misery,
> When we were yet unaware of the pains to be brought by the Korean War,
> The dark clouds of history came to us, whose origin we still do not know after all these years.
> Then, many lives, so many lives, were broken and their bodies were discarded to the mountains, the fields and the sea.
> Who can identify in this mass of broken lives a death that was not tragic?
> Who can say in this mass of displaced souls some souls have more grievance than the others?
> What about those who could not even cry for the dead?
> Who will console their hearts that suffered all those years only for one reason that they belonged to the bodies who survived the destruction? ...
> For the past fifty years,
> The dead and the living alike led an unnatural life as wandering souls, without a place to anchor to.
> Only today,
> Being older than our fathers and aged more than our mothers,
> We are gathered together in this very place.
> Let the heavens deal with the question of fate.
> Let history deal with its own portion of culpability.
> Our intention is not to dig again into the troubled grave of pain.
> It is only to fulfill the obligation of the living to offer a shovel of fine soil to the grave.
> It is because we hope some day the bleeding wounds may start to heal and we may see some sign of new life on them ...
> Looking back, we see that we are all victims.
> Looking back, we see that we are all to forgive each other.

---

police forces. Most of them were not equipped with firearms and had been forcibly recruited to the role. Whether to place the names of these twelve individuals on the side of patriotic ancestors or that of tragic mass death was one of the most difficult, contested questions during the three-year preparation for the shrine. The one hundred patriotic ancestors from the colonial era include a few persons whose dedication to the cause of national liberation was combined with a commitment to socialist or Communist ideals. The merit of these so-called left-wing nationalists was not recognised before the 1990s, and the South Korean administration has recently begun to nominate some of them as national heroes. The rewriting of Korea's history of independence movements or nationalist movements in a more inclusive form that recognises the heritage of radical as well as moderate nationalist movements, which is quite active today among historians in South Korea, has had a positive influence on the development of local initiatives for political reconciliation, including those in Hagui.

In this spirit, we are all together erecting this stone.
For the dead, may this stone help them finally close their eyes.
For us the living, may this stone help us finally hold hands together.[7]

5 Democratic Kinship

The democratisation of kinship relations is at the heart of political development beyond the polarities of left and right. This is not merely because family and kinship are elementary constituents of civil society as Giddens describes it, but primarily because kinship has actually been a locus of radical, violent political conflicts in the past century, which, by extension, means that social actions taking place in this intimate sphere of life are important for shaping and envisioning the horizon beyond the politics of the cold war.

The end of the cold war as the dominant geopolitical paradigm of the past century has enabled people to publicly recount their lived experience of bipolar conflict without fearing the consequences of doing so, and it also has encouraged many scholars of cold war history to turn their attention from diplomatic history to social history (see Appy 2000; Whitfield 1996). These two developments are interconnected and together constitute the now emerging field of social and cultural histories of the cold war. In societies that experienced the cold war in the form of a vicious civil war, recent research shows how the violently divisive historical experience continues to influence interpersonal relations and communal lives (Mazower 2000; Tai 2002; Yun 2003). The reconciliation of ideologically bifurcated genealogical backgrounds or ancestral heritages ('red' Communists versus anti-Communist patriots or, in other contexts, revolutionary patriots versus anti-Communist 'counter-revolutionaries') is a critical issue for individuals and for the political community (Kwon Heonik 2003; 2006: 154-64). In these societies, kinship identity is a significant site of memory of past political conflicts, and also can be a locus of creative moral practices.

The experience of the cold war as a violent civil conflict resulted in political crisis in the moral community of kinship. It resulted in a situation that Hegel characterises as the collision between 'the law of kinship', which obliges the living to remember their dead kinsmen,

---

[7] A full text of this poem in Korean is available online at www.jeju43.org/outlook/outlook-1_27.asp?area=bukjeju.

and 'the law of the state', which forbids citizens from commemorating those who died as enemies of the state. The political crisis was basically about a representational crisis in social memory, in which a large number of family-ancestral identities were relegated to the status that I have elsewhere called 'political ghosts', whose historical existence is felt in intimate social life, but is nevertheless traceless in public memory (Kwon Heonik 2007).

Hegel explored the philosophical foundation of the modern state partly with ethical questions involved in the remembrance of the war dead, drawing upon the legend of Antigone from the Theban plays of Sophocles (see Steiner 1984: 19-42; Stern 2002: 135-45). Antigone was torn between the obligation to bury her war-dead brothers according to 'the divine law' of kinship on one hand and, on the other, the reality of 'the human law' of the state, which prohibited her from giving burial to enemies of the city-state (Stern 2002: 140). She buried her brother, who died as the hero of the city, and then proceeded to do the same for another brother, who died as an enemy of the city. The latter act violated the edict of the city's ruler, and she was subsequently condemned to death as punishment. Invoking this powerful epic tragedy from ancient Greece, Hegel reasoned that the ethical foundation of the modern state is grounded in a dialectical resolution of the clashes between the law of the state and the law of kinship (Avineri 1972: 132-54; Williams 1997: 52-9). For Butler (2000: 5), the question is about the fate of human relatedness suspended between life and death and forced into the tortuous condition of having to choose between the norms of kinship and subjection to the state. Drawing upon these Hegelian ethical questions about kinship, law and the state, other contemporary normative political theorists have examined the relationship between the exclusion of 'bare life' from the polity and the modern form of political sovereignty (Agamben 1998).

The epic heroine Antigone met death by choosing family law instead of the state's ruling; survival, for many families in post-war South Korea, meant following the state's ruling in sacrifice of their rights to grieve and seek consolation for the death of their kinsmen. The state's repression of the right to grieve was conditioned by the wider politics of the cold war. Emerging from colonial occupation only to be divided into two hostile states, the new state of South Korea found its legitimacy partly in the performance of anti-Communist containment. Its militant anti-Communist policies included making a pure ideological breed and containing impure traditional ties, and engendered the concept of unlawful, non-normative kinship. Sharing blood relations with an individual believed to harbour sympathy for the opposite side of the bipolar world, in this context, meant being an enemy of the political community as an extension of the individual. Left or right in this political history was not merely about bodies of ideas in dispute, but also about determining the bodily existence of individuals and collectives. Likewise, the process 'beyond left and right' in this society has to deal with corporeal identity. If someone has become an outlawed person by sharing blood ties with the state's object of containment, that person's claim to the lawful status of a citizen involves legitimising this relatedness. This is how kinship emerges as a locus of the decomposing bipolar world in the world's outposts, and as a powerful force in the making of a tolerant, democratic society. Giddens (1998: 70-71) writes:

> If there is a crisis of liberal democracy today, it is not, as half a century ago, because it is threatened by hostile rivals, but on the contrary because it has no rivals. With the passing of the bipolar era, most states have no clear-cut enemies. States facing dangers rather than enemies have to look for sources of legitimacy different from those in the past.

He then proceeds to chart what he considers to be the new sources of state legitimacy, for which he highlights the political responsibility to foster an active civil society, that is, to further democratise democracy. In this light, Giddens paints the form of the democratic family as the backbone of active civil society after the cold war. As a new social form, the democratic family is meant to structurally reconcile individual choice and social solidarity, and to achieve a dialectical resolution between individual freedom and collective unity.

In Giddens' scheme, the social form of kinship has no direct association with the oppositions of left and right. Its role for societal development beyond the cold war is mediated by the state's changing identity and the related reconfiguration of its relationship to civil society. The end of the cold war, for Giddens, primarily affects the state, in the sense of losing the legitimacy of confronting external threats. The displacement of the state from the dualist geopolitical structure forces the state to build alternative legitimacy in an active, constructive engagement with civil society. The picture is essentially about substituting a constructive internal relationship with society for hostile external relationships with other states. The idea of the 'democratic family' enters this picture as a constitutive element of civil society, that is, as an important site of post-cold war state politics.

The composition of 'new kinship' presented by Giddens, however, allows little space for kinship practices that arise from the background of a violent modern history such as Cheju's. His account of right and left unfolds as if this political antithesis had principally been an issue of academic paradigms or parliamentary organisations, without mass human suffering and displacement. Giddens discusses social and political developments beyond left and right on the assumption that the end of the cold war is coeval with the advance of globalisation and that these two constitute what he sees as 'the emergence of a post-traditional social order' (Giddens 1994: 5). If the end of the cold war is at the same time an age of globalisation, as Giddens claims, and the third way vision speaks of the morality and politics of this age, it is puzzling why this vision, claiming to speak for the global age, draws narrowly on the particular history of the cold war manifested as a contest and balance of power, ignoring the war's radically diverse ramifications across different places.

Seen in a wider context, we cannot think of the history of right and left without the history of mass death. Right and left were both part of anti-colonial nationalism, signalling different routes toward the ideal of national liberation and self-determination. In the ensuing bipolar era, this dichotomy was transformed into the ideology of civil strife and war, in which achieving national unity became equivalent to annihilating one or the other side from the body politic. In this context the political history of right and left is not to be considered separately from the history of the human lives and social institutions torn by it, nor is the 'new kinship' after the cold war to be divorced from the memory of the dead ruins of this history. Family relations are important vectors in understanding the decomposition of the bipolar world. This is not merely because they are an elementary constituent of civil society, as Giddens believes, but rather because they have actually been a vital site of political control and ideological oppression during the cold war. Seen against this historical background, it is misleading to define the state in the post-cold war world merely as an entity without external enemies. Rather, we have to think of the state, as Hegel did, as an entity that has to deal with internal hostilities and reconciliation with society, a significant part of which the state condemned to an unlawful status.⁸ What has happened in Cheju since the early 1990s can be placed along this hopeful trajectory of reconciliation, and the recognition of the rights to remember and console the dead has been a central element in this important social progress beyond left and right.

---

⁸ Giddens (1994: 53-9, 252) blames Hegel for advancing a teleological concept of history, which he believes was sublimated in cold war modernity. From his history of left and right, it transpires that, for him, Hegelian historicism is one of the notable philosophic ills that nations and communities should be alert to in pursuing a progression away from the age of extremes toward a relationally cosmopolitan and structurally democratic political and social order. I argue in this article to the contrary—that Hegelian political ethical questions are crucial for social progression away from the age of violent bipolar politics.

REFERENCES

Agamben, Giorgio (trans. Daniel Heller-Roazen) (1998), *Homo Sacer: Sovereign Power and Bare Life*, Stanford CA: Stanford University Press

Appy, Christian G. (ed.) (2000), *Cold War Constructions: The Political Culture of United States Imperialism, 1945-1966*, Amherst MA: University of Massachusetts Press

Avineri, Shlomo (1972), *Hegel's Theory of the Modern State* (Cambridge Studies in the History and Theory of Politics), Cambridge: Cambridge University Press

Bettelheim, Bruno (1985), *Freud and Man's Soul: An Important Re-Interpretation of Freudian Theory*, London: Fontana

Bobbio, Norberto (trans. Allan Cameron) (1996), *Left and Right: The Significance of a Political Distinction*, Chicago: University of Chicago Press

Butler, Judith (2000), *Antigone's Claim: Kinship Between Life and Death*, New York: Columbia University Press

Cheju 4.3 Sakŏn Hŭisaengja Yujokhoe [The Association for the Families of the Cheju 4.3 Incident Victims] (2005), *4.3 Yujokhoeji* [Chronicle of the Association for the Families of the Cheju 4.3 Incident Victims], Cheju: Onnuri

Cheju 4.3 Yŏnguso [The Institute of the Cheju 4.3 Incident Studies] (2003), *4.3gwa Yŏksa*, [The 4.3 incident and history], vol. 3, Cheju: Kak

Cho-Han, Hyejong (2000), 'Tongil gongkangwa munhwa' [The spatiality of national unification and culture], in: Cho-Han Hyejong and Lee Woo-young (eds.), *Talbundan Sidaerŭl Yŏlmyŏ* [Opening a post-partition era], Seoul: Samin, pp. 315-33

Cumings, Bruce (1981), *The Origins of the Korean War: Liberation and the Emergence of Separate Regimes, 1945-1947*, Princeton NJ: Princeton University Press

Cumings, Bruce (1991), *Parallax Visions: Making Sense of American-East Asian Relations at the End of the Century*, Durham NC: Duke University Press

Giddens, Anthony (1994), *Beyond Left and Right: The Future of Radical Politics*, Cambridge: Polity Press

Giddens, Anthony (1998), *The Third Way: Renewal of Social Democracy*, Cambridge: Polity Press

Gwon, Gwi-sook (2006), *Giŏkŭi Jŏngch`i: Daeryanghaksalŭi Sahoejŏk Giŏkgwa Yŏksajŏk Jinsil* [The politics of memory: social memory of mass killings and historical truth], Seoul: Munhakgwa Jisŏng

Hyun, Kil-on (1990), *Uridŭlŭi jobunim* [Our grandfather], Seoul: Koryŏwŏn

Janelli, Roger L. and Dawnhee Yim Janelli (1982), *Ancestor Worship and Korean Society*, Stanford: Stanford University Press.

Kim, Dong-chun (2000), *Jŏnjaenggwa Sahoe* [War and society], Seoul: Dolbegae

Kim, Kwang-ok (1994), 'Rituals of Resistance: The Manipulation of Shamanism in Contemporary Korea', in: Charles F. Keys, Lauren Kendall, and Helen Hardacre (eds.), *Asian Visions of Authority: Religion of the Modern States of East and Southeast Asia*, Honolulu: University of Hawaii Press, pp. 195-221

Kim, Kwang-ok (2000), 'Jŏnt'ongjŏk 'gwankye'ŭi hyŏndaejŏk silch'ŏn' [The contemporary practice of 'traditional' relations], in: *Hankuk Munhwa Inlyuhak* [Journal of Korean cultural anthropology], 33 (2), pp. 7-48

Kim, Seong-nae (1989), 'Lamentations of the Dead: Historical Imagery of Violence', in: *Journal of Ritual Studies*, 3 (2), pp. 251-85

Kim, Seong-nae (1999), 'Gŭndaesŏnggwa p'oklyŏk: Cheju 4.3ŭi damlonjŏng ch'i' [Modernity and violence: the discursive politics of the Cheju 4.3 incident], in: Cheju 4.3 je 50junyŏn Ginyŏmsaŏp Ch`ujin Bŏmkukminwiwŏnhoe [The National Committee for the 50th Anniversary of the Cheju 4.3 Incident] (eds.), *Cheju 4.3 Yŏnku* [Cheju 4.3 studies], Seoul: Yŏksabipyŏngsa, pp. 238-67

Kwon, Heonik (2003), 'Jŏnjaenggwa mingansinang: talnaengjŏnsidaeŭi wŏlnam josangsingwa japsin' [War and popular religion: ancestors and ghosts in post-cold war Vietnam], in: *Minjokgwa Munhwa* [Nation and culture], 12, pp. 35-56.

Kwon, Heonik (2004), 'The Wealth of Han', in: Michel Demeuldre (ed.), *Sentiments doux-amers dans les musiques du monde*, Paris: L'Harmattan, pp. 47-55

Kwon, Heonik, (2006), *After the Massacre: Commemoration and Consolation in Ha My and My Lai*, Berkeley CA: University of California Press

Kwon, Heonik (2007), *The Ghosts of War in Vietnam*, Cambridge: Cambridge University Press

Kwon, Hyuk-bum (2000), 'Bangongjuŭiŭi hoeropan ilki' [Reading the cultural schema of anti-Communism], in: Cho-Han Hyejong and Lee Woo-young (eds.), *Talbundan Sidaerŭl Yŏlmyŏ* [Opening a post-partition era], Seoul: Samin, pp. 29-65

Laïdi, Zaki (1998), *A World Without Meaning: The Crisis of Meaning in International Politics*, New York: Routledge

Mazower, Mark (ed.) (2000), *After the War Was Over: Reconstructing the Family, Nation, and State in Greece, 1943-1960*, Princeton NJ: Princeton University Press

Park, Myong-lim (1999), 'Minjujuŭi, isŏng, gŭrigo yŏksayŏngu: Cheju 4.3gwa hankuk hyŏndaesa' [Democracy, rationality and historical research: the Cheju 4.3 incident and modern Korean history], in: Cheju 4.3 je 50junyŏn Ginyŏmsaŏp Ch`ujin Bŏmkukminwiwŏnhoe [The National Committee for the 50th Anniversary of the Cheju 4.3 Incident] (eds.), *Cheju 4.3 Yŏnku* [Cheju 4.3 studies] Seoul: Yŏksabipyŏngsa, pp. 425-60

Pyo, In-ju et al. (eds.) (2003), *Jŏnjaenggwa Saramdŭl* [War and peoples], Seoul: Hanul Academy

Steiner, George (1984), *Antigones: How the Antigone Legend Has Endured in Western Literature, Art, and Thought*, Oxford: Oxford University Press

Stern, Steve (2002), *Hegel and the Phenomenology of Spirit*, New York: Routledge

Suh, Joong-suk (1999), 'Cheju 4.3ŭi yŏksajŏk ŭimi' [The historical meanings of the Cheju 4.3 incident], in: Cheju 4.3 je 50junyŏn Ginyŏmsaŏp Ch`ujin Bŏmkukminwiwŏnhoe [The National Committee for the 50th Anniversary of the Cheju 4.3 Incident] (eds.), *Cheju 4.3 Yŏnku* [Cheju 4.3 studies], Seoul: Yŏksabipyŏngsa, pp. 97-146

Tai, Hue-Tam Ho (ed.) (2002), *The Country of Memory: Remaking the Past in Late Socialist Vietnam*, Berkeley CA: University of California Press

Westad, Odd Arne (2005), *The Global Cold War: Third World Interventions and the Making of Our Times*, Cambridge: Cambridge University Press

Williams, Robert R. (1997), *Hegel's Ethics of Recognition*, Berkeley CA: University of California Press

Whitfield, Stephen, J. (1996), *The Culture of the Cold War*, 2nd edition, Baltimore MD: Johns Hopkins University Press

Yun, Taik-Lim (2003), *Inlyuhakjaŭi gwagŏyŏhaeng: han ppalgaengi maŭlŭi yŏksarŭl ch'atasŏ* [An anthropologist's journey to the past: in search of history in a 'red' village], Seoul: Yŏksabipyŏngsa

THE POLITICAL ECONOMY OF PATRIOTISM: THE CASE OF *HANBANDO*

Mark Morris

Abstract

A blockbuster film with the title *Hanbando* ('The Korean Peninsula') opened in July of 2006. Preceded by a lavish advertising campaign, the film occupied one of every three cinema screens in South Korea during its initial run. Why this big-budget, patriotic film, featuring a number of well-known stars and evoking a wide range of topical issues of contention between South Korea and Japan, proved a financial failure and critical disaster is the story this article attempts to tell. A detailed examination of a section of *Hanbando* will consider the film-makers' choice of actors and choice of film style. Also taken into account will be the background of the production company, CJ Entertainment, and of the film's director Kang Woo-suk. Further matters looked at briefly include one other highly fictionalised film about Korean-Japanese conflict, *Phantom, the Submarine*, and the significance of the Japanese market for the products of South Korea's new cinema.

For Korea's confident and well-capitalized film industry, summer is a season to pull out the stops and offer the South Korean—and increasingly international—audience the most spectacular products it can produce. In the summer of 2006, one such blockbuster was the film *Hanbando* ('The Korean Peninsula'). It was produced by a syndicate of major companies headed by market leader CJ Entertainment and directed by Kang Woo-suk, well-known for genre action films like the *Two Cops* franchise and *Public Enemy* and the nationalistic action thriller *Silmido*. The film was backed by a huge advertising budget and saturation bookings: it occupied 550 screens during the opening week, roughly one out of every three in South Korea. The film seemed destined to be the phenomenon of the summer releases.

Hanbando is set in the near future. The two Koreas are moving swiftly towards reunification. TV-news footage shows families being reunited, sports teams combining members from North and South, road links opening. Now it is the turn of the railways. However, when the Japanese and other foreign representatives fail to appear at a grand ceremony to celebrate the re-opening of the rail link between Seoul and Pyongyang, signs are that reunification may be blocked. The villain behind the scenes proves to be Japan. On the basis of treaties signed, with highly questionable legality, during its take-over of the peninsula, at the beginning of the twentieth century, Japan now lays claim to 'its' railway system.

Below I will try to give some idea of what the film is like, unravelling a sample of the narrative—roughly, the first half-hour—and adding a few considerations considering cinematic style plus a brief introduction to three of the film's cast. Then, after some consideration of the makers of the film and of the critical reaction to *Hanbando*, the essay will return to look at several general aspects of film content and style. On the way to a conclusion, some observations will extend to recent Japanese films and to the Japanese media market for South Korean film. Rather than simply criticize the film, though criticize it I will, this essay will try to suggest how a an artistic and financial failure can teach us some interesting lessons about South Korea's contemporary film culture.

1   THE FILM: STORY, STYLE, STARS

An opening montage of news reports condenses the history of the recent past and blends it into images from a hypothetical near future. A rapid-fire collage of footage from conflicts in the Middle East is followed by an image of Kim Jong Il, the smoke pouring from the Twin Towers, and George W. Bush announcing the second Iraq invasion. Banner titles announce that 'Japan dispatches biggest overseas force to Iraq' below images of Japanese armoured units, then come scenes of Korea's Zaytun Division deploying in Iraq. In quick succession come clips of Chinese anti-Japanese protests and Korea ones directed at the disputed Tokdo islands—'Korean ships told to stay away'—and a number of scenes of protests over Japan's callous handling of 'the comfort women' issue. Cut to (now former) Japanese Prime Minister Koizumi in formal kimono at Yasukuni Shrine, then reports of heightened readiness of the Japanese Self-Defence Forces, including the possible deployment of nuclear missiles; that is rapidly followed by Chinese claims concerning historical documents proving that Korea was once a part of China. Next clips flash past presenting Bush's 'axis of evil' speech and reports of North Korea's development of nuclear weapons. And without allowing the spectator a moment to reflect—and having tweaked every raw nerve-ending concerning issues in dispute between Korea and Japan—the sequence shifts register. We learn that the Six Party Talks have taken a dramatic turn, then follow the optimistic, fictionalized scenes noted above. We see news footage edited to suggest roadways being unblocked, tearful family reunions, a joint Olympic Team, and more.

The on-rush of images and voice-over information doesn't allow for much critical distance. For instance, it is probably only well after experiencing this montage that you may have time to realize how, in juxtaposing the scenes of Japanese troops and Korean soldiers in Iraq, the editors manage to suggest that the two groups of soldiers might be rushing off, fully armed, to confront one another. This bit of manipulation ignores the peaceful nature of the work undertaken by the mainly medical staff and combat/civil engineers sent by both countries. The clips show Japanese troops on parade at home, hence the tanks rolling by; the Zaytun troops are in full battle gear for the TV cameras, not action. Much less dramatic would have been images of men repairing bridges or giving injections to Iraqi children. The montage sequence performs a work of simplification—reducing complex regional issues to bilateral conflict—and intensification—conflict and disagreement are to be interpreted as preliminaries to war. The images are throughout sustained by a welter of anxious voices-over and urgent titles, both shadowed by the kind of easy-listening martial music common to many blockbuster films in Korea and elsewhere. Welcome to *Hanbando*.

After all of the above, packed into a few minutes, comes finally the first real-time scene, an impending ceremony to re-open the Kyŏngŭi Railway Line, the main rail link between the Republic of Korea (ROK)'s capital Seoul and Pyongyang, that of Democratic People's Republic of Korea (DPRK). (It is staged to suggest the real ceremonies held in June of 2003 to open a ghostly rail line, one which still stands idle waiting for reconnection of two peoples and their socioeconomic and political structures.) The ROK president and a Kim Jong Il look-alike wait uneasily before a crowd of officials and military top brass from both nations, and young Koreans there to perform for them. An inserted graphic display has just shown the way in which this new line will link up to others in Korea and on across China towards Europe, and presumably a new future for the reunited nation.

Word finally comes that the Japanese are boycotting the event, claiming ownership of the railway system. The next scene takes place at the Japanese embassy in Seoul. The Japanese ambassador, played by a well-known Korean character actor, informs the president and his entourage that Japan has decided to enforce a claim to the railway system it built during the colonial period, based on a 1907 document bearing the official seal of the last Yi dynasty king, King Kojong. The ambassador and his scowling staff inform the president that Japan plans to use all its economic power and diplomatic leverage to reacquire the railways, and that it will withhold Japan's massive US$157 billion loan meant to support the reunification which this president has made his mission. Other scenes rapidly follow, such as a news conference at which a White House spokesman expresses US government criticism of Korea's failure to resolve this issue with Japan, or a Chinese newsreader expresses that country's straightforward disapproval of Korean reunification. This first ten-minute jumble of sequences ends with the president assembling his full cabinet and calling for a Presidential Truth Commission (an echo of current President Roh's proposals for truth commissions) to investigate the validity of the documents put forward by Japan. He notes that this day is the 17 November, the date on which in 1905 five Korean ministers signed the notorious Ŭlsa Treaty, making Korea in effect a protectorate of Japan. The president vows not to allow Japan to violate Korean sovereignty again.

The president is played by Ahn Seong-gi (b. 1952), the most respected male actor in the Korean film industry. He had recently played a very different sort of national leader in *The Romantic President* (2002), but his career goes back to childhood roles in the late 1950s, and extends through some very ordinary films made during the 1980s to work with the most significant directors of the past three decades.

Ahn is not the most expressive of actors, but he carries with him into any film a considerable gravity earned by earlier lead roles. Consider films he has appeared in by Im Kwon-taek, just one major director he has worked with: for example, *Mandara* (1981), *Taebaek Mountains* (1994) and *The Festival* (1996).

The script of *Hanbando* gives him very little to do other than deliver short speeches. It is a characteristic of the film's style to have main figures—here the president, later Queen Min or even King Kojong—deliver their lines framed squarely in the middle of a somewhat distanced close-up, looking just to the side of the camera lens. It is a strikingly un-cinematic technique, and as similar set pieces intervene in the narrative, a spectator may feel uneasy at this rather unrelenting speechifying, as when the president makes his first direct-to-camera address about the significance of 17 November. He seems to be lecturing us as well as speaking to others in the scene.

The next sequence of scenes opens with something of an actual history lecture. Maverick yet patriotic historian Choi Min-jae is filling a white-board with key names and events concerning an early Japanese assault on Korean sovereignty, such as the 1895 assassination of Queen Min, and the infamous 1905 Ŭlsa Treaty. No longer able, because of his unstintingly nationalist views, to find work in a regular university, Choi has been reduced to teaching a group of middle-class women about a history in which they manifestly have no interest. Choi challenges one of the women to tell him about the Empress Myŏngsŏng: the film always favours this more exalted, posthumous title for the queen. The reluctant student claims to recall her 'from the music video' version. This alludes to a TV drama about the 'Last Empress' and manages to suggest the superficial cultural competency of contemporary middle-class South Korea. And when Choi asks why this very day of 17 November is important, one of the women suggests their lecturer is being romantic, since everyone knows this is Diary Day, the day on which you share your intimate thoughts with your lover. Choi explodes, and chases the women from the room.

Choi Min-jae is played by Jo Jae-hyeon. He is small and wiry, with unusually large eyes which give the piercing glare regularly deployed by the character Choi extra impact. Jo began to appear on the screen in the early 1990s and is best known for roles in the films of controversial director Kim Ki-duk. From Kim's debut feature *Crocodile* (1996), through roles as a dog-butcher in *Address Unknown* (2001) or mute criminal-rapist in *Bad Guy* (2001), Jo has constructed a fairly scary screen persona. To cast him as the outsider-intellectual who will persevere in the pursuit of thwarting Japan's falsified claims certainly emphasizes the passionate nature of Choi's quest. It does not insist on history as a very balanced or objective academic enterprise.

We catch up with Choi later the same day as he stares into a large glass of *soju* at a street-side eatery. When he speaks aloud a toast to the spirit of the late King Kojong, the owner-cook echoes his words and shares the sentiment and a glass with him. Most scenes in *Han-*

bando involve middle-class men in suits and uniforms. This scene, where Korean scholar and Korean working-class bloke share the same patriotic nostalgia, is clearly meant to register the *vox populi*; that in turn can imply that the patriotism identified in the story most directly with the president and his supporters can be henceforth asserted as a natural expression of ordinary Koreans, and of ordinary Koreanness. When Choi learns of what has happened earlier that day to ruin the planned celebrations of the rail link, he resolves to act. That the *vox populi* should be called upon to get the committed historian up to speed concerning such a momentous occurrence is presented without irony.

The narrative next needs to bring the two foci of patriotism, the president and Choi, together, and it does so in the next few scenes. The president, with wife and entourage in tow, arrives at a concert to be given by visiting North Korean musicians.

Choi shouts out to him from a lobby balcony that the Japanese documents being talked about in the news are fake. We see security mean bundle him away, only for Choi to reappear in the next scene seated with the president and his most loyal advisor in a quiet briefing room. We learn more of Choi's background and his quarrels with authority and with mainstream, less patriotic historians. He is given a generous opportunity to spell out to the president his theory that it can be proved that the relevant Japanese treaties and other documents, supposedly approved by King Kojong, are fraudulent.

Choi claims that King Kojong, surrounded by more and more collaborators after the tragic murder of his queen, had hidden his genuine seal and replaced it with version bearing tell-tale flaws. It is this ersatz seal that the Japanese seized after Kojong's mysterious death—Choi calls it 'assassination'—in 1919 and used to validate their schemes. All this was foreseen by the wise old man, who trusted that his countrymen would in future detect the small discrepancies between the two seals. As the story moves on, one major subplot will be the search for the genuine seal and the effort to prove that the Japan government's claim to the rail system is not simply arbitrary and unjust, but illegal.

And here, only some twenty minutes into this long, convoluted tale, arrives the first of some five flashbacks set in the era between the 1895 assassination of Queen Min to the hypothetical poisoning of Kojong in 1919. The transition is dramatic: a street-level shot of marching feet cuts to a scene of Japanese soldiers surrounding the Kyŏngbok Palace; then from the distance marches forward a figure in a dinner jacket followed by a thuggish-looking mass of men in dark kimono. Most Korean viewers will understand the leader to represent a Japanese leader of the attack, such as Okamoto Ryūnosuke, the legation official who was directly involved on the day, or even the Japanese minister Miura Gorō, who planned it. This determined-looking man is headed to the palace with ultra-nationalist Japanese roughnecks, all pledged to put and end to Queen Min and her plotting to resist Japanese plans for the peninsula. That at any rate is one common version of the event. Inside the palace, Queen Min sits at a table leafing though a Western-language book; a stack of other books, a Russian one on top, awaits her studious attention. The image appeals to a widely held view of the queen as both patriotic and international-minded, a woman well ahead of her time whose loss to a Korea in peril was especially cruel.

Kang Su-yeon plays the queen. In recent years, she has become best known for her work in TV drama, notably playing the lead in the SBS 150-episode period drama *Ladies of the Palace* (2001-02) which located its intrigues in the Chosŏn court of the early sixteenth century. As a film actor she has appeared in some thirty films, a handful of them considered contemporary classics. Her starring role in Im Kwon-taek's *Surrogate Womb*, when she was only twenty, won her the Best Actress Award at the Venice Film Festival in 1987. While Korean films and Korean directors have won many international awards in recent years, no actor had matched Kang in winning such an accolade from one of the top three European film festivals until this May (2007) when Jeon Do-yeon was named best actress at Cannes. Audience familiarity with Kang in a popular period drama was probably more instrumental in her casting here than her roles in some memorable films.

With the attack on the queen, the film shifts into historical-action-movie mode. Once the palace is surrounded, collaborating Korean soldiers scale its walls to open the gates for the invading Japanese. When the Japanese regular troops enter, their first action is to gun down their Korean helpers; then they make way for the in-rushing sword-waving thugs. We are already rather far from historical accounts: it is known that Japanese troops dressed as Koreans prepared the way for the invaders; they were not shot down by their comrades. The spectator is being interpellated by a film genre, not offered docudrama.

Queen Min, despite the gunshots outside, refuses to hide. Meanwhile, Japanese minister Miura has confronted the king and promised, threateningly, that he will come to no harm, while in the corridors of the palace the dark-clad Japanese hack away at first the Imperial Guards, then every serving woman in sight. The climax takes place in an inner court. Kang Su-yeon's eyes brim with tears of rage and terror, as Queen Min gives her farewell to her king; she apologizes to Kojong, now captive inside his room close by, for having to abandon her royal duties and admonishes him to think not only of his title but also of the fate of his nation. On this occasion, the direct-to-camera staging is very melodramatic—the queen has been slashed and run through twice before the scene ends—but thanks to Kang's skill, it is hard to feel unmoved by the scene depicted. Now the waiting Japanese move in to finish off the queen and her entire entourage. Before we switch back to the present, a brief scene shows the king and his last loyal counsellor discussing the fate of the royal seal.

The film—still only 32 minutes into its 147-minute running time—returns to the present, in which Choi Min-jae is now explaining his theories about the royal seal to the full cabinet. The rather forced match between flashback and present scene established here via the seal subplot occurs in later portions of the film. I will note just one later example of such cross-cutting. One occurs soon after Korean radar has detected a fleet of the Japan's Maritime Self-Defence Force headed for Korean waters. The president and staff have gone to the Japanese embassy in Seoul, this time to meet with the Japanese foreign minister and his staff; they are urgently trying to avoid a military showdown with the large Japanese fleet. Here, the story jumps back a century, and seated in almost identical fashion to their twenty-first century avatars are Japanese officials decked out in Meiji-era uniforms, across the table from men in tall black hats and courtly Korean costume. We are most likely back at a particularly infamous moment in history, the negotiations leading up to the signing of the Ŭlsa Treaty in 1905; that treaty, making Korea a Japanese protectorate, would mean the beginning of the end for Korean national sovereignty. In both eras, Japanese officialdom declares its benevolent designs and its wish merely to protect Korea from hostile neighbours. Kojong sits at the head of the table in his time and place, so when we cut back to the present it is no surprise to see President Ahn Seong-gi seated in the equivalent spot at the tense embassy meeting.

It is the actor Moon Seung-gun's difficult task, playing a cold-eyed pragmatic, Japan-leaning prime minister, to provide a foil to Ahn's instinctively patriotic president. Moon is highly regarded for earlier roles in films by directors such as Park Kwang-su and Chang Sun-woo, two film-makers associated with the anti-authoritarian, left-humanist cultural movements of the politically repressive 1980s. He is particularly remembered for roles as a dissident intellectual in Park's *Black Republic* (1990) and *A Single Spark* (1995), or as a violent loner in Chang's *Petal* (1996), one of the most powerful Korean films ever made. Moon has been involved in a range of artistic and political activities. He has been a notable supporter of the Uri party, and helped organize (real) President Roh Moo-hyun's online election campaign. (See the koreanfilm.org website entry under his name for more.)

The prime minister is depicted in a far from sympathetic light. We see him, for example, try to bribe Choi to abandon the quest for Kojong's seal, or all but mock a young subordinate's appeals to patriotism and to the *minjok*—the racial/ethnic nation-people of Korea. His is a hard-edged, unromantic view of the world: it is far better to go along with Japan's outrageous claims than to risk economic disaster and political isolation. He even seems behind a plot to drug the president and put him into a coma; and he will seize the occasion to attempt to undo all the latter's plans, re-unification included. Yet the prime minister is the only complex, interesting character in the film. Where Ahn Seong-gi's role calls for straight-to-camera delivery of lines about the *minjok* or the need 'to show the world what Japan has done to our country' ('I am willing to sacrifice my life for this'), Moon's character is busy arguing, conniving and reasoning with people. He is not framed square-on, but in two-shots with others or shot from oblique angles in medium close-up. Moon is one of those actors whose secret seems partly to lie in never seeming to be acting; this gift makes him the exception in *Hanbando*.

After many plot twists and turns, the genuine seal is finally found, war is averted, the Japanese foreign minister ultimately forced not only to abandon the claim to the railways but to make a public apology for Japan's treatment of Korea in the past and offer compensation for the exploitation and injustices of the colonial era. At the very end of the saga comes at least one scene that seems to belong to a different, more sophisticated cinematic world. All the prime minister's plans to thwart the patriotic president have themselves been undone. He finds the president alone in his office and hands in his letter of resignation. There follows a bitter exchange between the two chief antagonists. The president maintains his patriotic posture; the prime minister holds his ground. The latter still insists that this president, in his patriotic idealism and plans for re-unification, is dangerously mistaken. What about the real 48 million citizens of the ROK, what good are these lofty ambitions to their lives in the here and now if reunification destroys thirty years of hard-won progress? With that, Moon Seung-gun turns about and marches towards the door. Freeze frame, roll credits.

2 THE COMPANY AND THE CRITICS

Hanbando, it is worth emphasizing, was neither financed nor directed by people new to the film business. CJ Entertainment is only one of many subsidiaries of CJ Corporation. The parent company was hived off from the Samsung group in the 1970s. While Samsung surged ahead into its extraordinarily successful future in electronics, CJ Corporation carried on mainly with the food processing business. In the mid-nineties, however, members of the CJ family involved the company in the start-up investment for a new Hollywood studio, DreamWorks (gobbled up since by Paramount); they set up CJ Entertainment to handle distribution of Hollywood product, and turned to the distribution and production of Korean films.[1] CJ Entertainment weathered the IMF crisis better than most competitors, and was able to move into exhibition as well. The first of a series of multiplexes opened in 1998; by 2000 CJ had produced and distributed Park Chan-Wook's hugely successful *Joint Security Area*. The box office records set by this film, and Kang Je-gyu's 1999 *Swiri*, primed the take-off of the new Korean cinema. (For an excellent overview of this period, see Paquet 2005). According to *Korean Cinema 2006*, the official report of the Korean Film Council, CJ Entertainment released 47 films in the single year, which sold over ten million tickets in Seoul alone—almost a quarter of the capital's total box office. CJ also managed to produce four of the top ten films in 2006: number 3, *Tazza: The High Rollers*, a gambling/crime thriller; number 6, *My Boss, My Teacher*, a gangster comedy; number 8, *Hanbando*; number 10, *Forbidden Quest*, a racy pe-

---

[1] For more about CJ Entertainment, see Russell 2005, English Wikipedia, and the company's website, available at http://www.cjent.co.kr/ccp/e_p_list.asp.

riod drama. A clear sign of the current financial success of the Korean film industry is the fact that during the past year, only two Hollywood films (*Pirates of the Caribbean: Dead Man's Chest* and *The Da Vinci Code*) ranked among the box office top ten.

Kang Woo-suk is regarded as one of the most influential men in film-making. Kang had 'been elected #1 in the "Top 50 Powerful" list chosen by *Cine 21* magazine for nine times in a row until 2005' (Kim 2007). He left the company he had founded in 1995, Cinema Service, right before making *Hanbando*, but remains influential in it still, and has close links to CJ as well.

Cinema Service, mainly a distributor, released 18 films in 2006, one of which was the surprise hit *King and the Clown*. Its domestic record of over 12 million admissions was only exceeded by the 13-million-plus box office of Bong Joon-ho's monster tragi-comedy *The Host*, the most successful film domestically and internationally in Korean film history. While *Hanbando* was still in pre-production, Kang Woo-suk, wearing his director's hat, said in an interview that he had in mind making a 'film that will make you feel all of the dignity of the people populating the Korea peninsula ... like in American films like 'Independence Day' or 'Air Force One' ... They're so proud of themselves, they think they can go around running the world, why are we Koreans shrivelling so much' (Kang 2005).

Posters and TV ads for *Hanbando* had begun again to appear from late June of 2006. The poster reproduced above was one of the most ubiquitous. It places 'President' Ahn Seong-gi in the centre, 'Prime Minister' Moon Seong-gun to the far left and Choi Jae-min/Jo Jae-hyeon far right. The top line of text declares: 'We have never once been true masters in this our land'. Below it, riding atop the main title 'HANBANDO' in massive white font, is a line saying: 'Search for the hidden genuine seal of the Great Han Empire!'

By August the film was holding onto the number five spot among the top ten, but it began to fade by September. Criticisms of the film appeared after the first press screenings, a few weeks before the general release in mid-July. Kang Woo-suk made an effort to deflect those aimed at what many saw as the film's crude nationalism. As the *Korea Times* reported on 27 June 2006:

> The film's director Kang Woo-suk doesn't cringe because of such negative criticism. He also does not hide his purpose and openly says that his film aims to criticize Japan. 'This is not a film that merely criticizes Japan without reason,' Kang told reporters earlier this month after the pre-screening of his film at Seoul Theater, downtown Seoul. 'Considering its thoughtless behavior, I really wanted to attack Japan through my film.'

Staff reporter/film reviewer Kim wrote, in a follow-up piece on 19 July, that 'such movies with nationalistic themes, however, didn't translate into automatic success at the box office. There are such commercial flops as "Phantom, the Submarine" (1999), "General of Heaven" (2005), "Fighter in the Wind" (2004) and "Rikidozan" (2004) and others.' Indeed, Kim was able to lay out the numbers to show that among the top ten box-office hits of Korean film coming into summer 2006, five did feature nationalism and patriotism—but all of these had focused on the North-South conflict, including Kang's own 2003 hit *Silmido*.[2] In his own review of the film on 13 July, Kim

---

[2] In January of 1968, a North Korean commando squad made an audacious attempt to assassinate Park Chung-hee. They were stopped before reaching the Blue House, and a bloody mêlée ensued until they were hunted down. Park wanted revenge, and had his KCIA work with air force personnel to train a commando squad that could be sent to kill Kim Il Song. When, after long brutal training which had cost the lives of seven of the 31-man commando their lives, a thaw in North-South relations made them surplus to a politics of entente, in August of 1971 they mutinied and headed to Seoul to press their case with Park. They in turn were gunned down, took their own lives or were executed.

Kang was himself pretty audacious in putting this long-covered-up incident on screen. A US$ 8 million investment allowed for the production of full-scale blockbuster which has recouped its costs many times over. In this 'faction' Kang glamorized the male roles with stars like Ahn Seong-gi and recast the narrative in the formulas of a South Korea *Dirty Dozen*. Yet the impact of the film did help force a newly

Tae-jong had grudgingly gave it 1½ out of 5 stars: 'Although the sensitive theme appeals to Korean audiences, who know the tragic history of Japan's rule, in the end it becomes a propaganda film full of radical nationalism. It lacks cinematic development, reality, and a balanced approach to historical events and the current situation'.

As another critic, Kim Kyu Hyun, more recently summed up: 'While it was by no means a commercial disaster, the film's final tally of box office tickets sold was around 3,880,000 tickets nationwide, falling short of the film's break-even point of approximately 4.5 million tickets and trampled flat by ... *The Host*' (Kim 2007).

3 POLITICS OF THE FLASHBACK

And so it seems makers of *Hanbando* had in mind making a blockbuster fiction-film along the lines of an *Air Force One*. At the same time, the film would be designed to take advantage of what many Koreans at present perceive in fact as Japan's 'thoughtless behaviour'. The opening montage catalogues what Kang had in mind as such behaviour. To quote director Kang Woo-suk from a pre-production interview once more:

> You could just see it as a Drama about the recurring past, present and near future, and the events that could happen. You know the word 'Faction (Fact+Fiction)'? 'Silmido' is one of those films, using reality as a foundation to create a fictional story. Instead, 'The Korean Peninsula' is the other way around: It uses fiction as its basis, but connections to reality keep emerging from the story. It'll be something that historians will be satisfied about (Kang 2005).

Presenting the film as a 'faction', however, assumes that it incorporates a reasonable degree of fact, of historical reality. I noted above just one minor rewriting of the assault on the Kyŏngbok Palace. Historians of the late-Chosŏn era are certainly unlikely to see much to be satisfied about in the film's handling of the assassination of Queen Min either. The details of the event are still hotly disputed, as a glance at the Wikipedia entry for 'Empress Myongsong' will attest. It is unlikely that this wily political realist presented herself for slaughter to the invaders for the sake of a final patriotic address to her husband.

---

democratized government to finally open up the files on the whole disaster. The Japanese *Wikipedia* has detailed entries on both the incident and the film; see as well the critical review by Darcy Paquet, http://koreanfilm.org/kfilm03.html#silmido.

She seems to have dressed as one of her own serving women, before being detected and killed by the Japanese. It is also probably a mistake, historically, to continue to describe or portray the actual killers as 'Japanese thugs' (Cumings 1997: 121). One Japanese historian has noted the sober fact that while the men involved in the killings at the palace did include some local Japanese roughnecks, many were journalists and correspondents—men such as Shiba Shirō, with a degree from an American university and budding career as political novelist. Intellectuals from samurai stock, equipped with modern educations but occupying careers on the margins of social and political influence, they represented just the kind of 'enlightenment' figures who would push the colonial project forward and not hesitate to advocate or use violence in its cause (Takasaki 2002: 61).

The historical flashback is one key cinematic and narrative device by which *Hanbando* works to construct a sense of patriotism based on a presumed collective Korean experience of Japanese infamy both in the past and in the film's projected near future. 'The flashback is a privileged moment in unfolding that juxtaposes different moments of temporal reference. A juncture is wrought between present and past and two concepts are implied in this juncture: memory and history' (Turim 1989: 1). It is hardly unusual for a feature film to simplify or to rewrite history for the sake of narrative effect or genre boundaries or in order to intensify rhetorical leverage, whether that leverage is exercised for commercial benefit or more clearly ideological ends. It is rather unusual, however, to find a cinematic 'faction' this single-mindedly determined to edit together events separated by a century without the least attention to the decades in between. *Hanbando* uses the flashback to exorcise among other things the long colonial period. This means the exorcism of the story of Korea's early modernization and, more specifically, of any accommodation to or collaboration with Japan's rule in Korea on the part of ordinary Koreans (Morris 2007).

Perhaps what makes the film's use of flashback particularly worth criticizing is the way it forces the issue of memory upon the spectator. The flashback is most familiar to film-viewers as a subjective device linking a character's past to events experienced in the present. The historical flashback as used in *Hanbando* depends upon the conjuring up of a collective subject—the Korean people, the *minjok*; the film unfolds in such a way that, through the rhetoric of cuts back and forth between the poles of its versions of then and now, the *minjok* is frog-marched through a lesson in righteous indignation—what in Korean is often summed up in the highly-charged term *han*. Such a commodification of *han* is what Kang Woo-suk and CJ Entertainment seem in fact to have sought to create. I think it is this simplistic, coercive visual rhetoric of pre-packaged *han* which has most assuredly turned the critics, and many ordinary viewers, against the film.

4 SCREEN WARS

As noted above, a little over an hour into the story, *Hanbando* weaves into its plot-lines of political thriller and quest for a missing seal, another set of genre conventions: a threat-of-war, looming-armed-conflict bundle of scenes and conventions. It asks the spectator to watch a sort of war film within the film.

The president receives an urgent phone call while visiting Choi. The maverick historian is by now leading a full-scale archaeological excavation in search of the genuine royal seal. The call claims that Japanese ships have been detected headed toward Korea. We cut to the interior of the Japanese ship leading the fleet and a tough-looking, chop-haired commander growling orders to subordinates in strongly accented Japanese. Up to this point, 'Japanese' characters, whether modern diplomats or their uniformed and be-medalled Meiji predecessors, have spoken in their normal Korean voices; sailors have that fictional license revoked. Later scenes shift to the war room at ROK defense headquarters. The president turns to an aide and asks, 'Who is chief of the Navy?' Patriotic credentials may excuse this lack of attention to detail; once again, no irony seems indicated in Ahn's straight-laced delivery. Considerable use of rapid cutting with ships steaming, helicopters taking off and jets scrambling, do give these portions of the film more momentum than the stagey scenes with the politicians. It is perhaps an unsurprising result of the production's political clout that they gained the participation of the Korean government and military to shoot crucial segments on secure military locations, although the Korean film industry is still some way from mobilizing whole fleets as Paramount could for major scenes in a Korea War film like *The Bridges at Toko-Ri* (1953). As for the Japanese forces, apart from ship interiors, they have to make do with computer generated images.

Tension builds, and soon an officer at the HQ decides to contact the Americans. He picks up a phone. The telephone call fails to get through to US forces, and we hear no more of the US. As for the

DPRK, their navy and their massive arsenal, they never appear. It is indicative of *Hanbando*'s lack of attention to verisimilitude and emphasis on bare-bones confrontation that its big naval scenes take place in an ocean cleared of all but the ships of the two protagonist nations. All that American weaponry and technology about to collide, and one failed telephone call leaves the super-power out of the loop.

Japanese film-makers have a long history of putting war on screen. The most recent variety of their war films, calculated to catch the current mood of neo-nationalism, have featured conflicts in a near future, such as *Aegis*, or a sci-fi inflected revision of the war with America, as in the submarine film *Lorelei*. Both of these films from 2005 show a highly contradictory sense of what is at stake in playing the patriot game, particularly given geo-political dependence on the US—the old enemy and, as some neo-national intellectuals might even suggest, potential future foe (Gerow 2006).

One obvious comparison for the South Korea-Japan confrontation embedded in *Hanbando* is that imagined by the 1999 Korean film *Phantom, the Submarine*, a film which was also released in Japan, in 2001. The film inherits and faithfully rehearses many of the clichés of the many submarine films set in the Second World War or cold war, but does so rather well and is, in terms of narrative coherence or cinematography, better crafted than the two Japanese films referred to above. The plot has it that South Korea has acquired a nuclear missile-equipped submarine from Russia in a near-future in which Japan, too, may be deploying nuclear missiles. The submarine, manned by a crew of men who have had their past identities expunged, has been sent on a mysterious mission. When is becomes clear that the mission is actually one to scuttle the boat with them still in it, the second-in-command has the captain killed and takes control of the boat. His plan is to attack Japan. The film's climax will occur as the seconds count down to missile launch. (Any resemblance to a Hollywood post-cold war thriller such as *Crimson Tide* [1995] is probably earned.)

What is striking is how, even within its genre limitations, *Phantom* presents the rogue commander's anti-Japanese patriotic zeal as pathological. Japanese submarines, once the intruder is located, act in a defensive, cautious manner; only when they are attacked by the Korean submarine do we encounter some old cinematic friends: silent running, depth-charge attacks, torpedoes whooshing on their sinister paths. And when the Phantom drags a Japanese submarine below its diving range, an intercom broadcasts the screams of the dying men around the ship. Hearing the agony of fellow submariners, the Korean crew begin to realize how dangerous their captain is. He turns off the intercom.

Phantom, the Submarine was released in Japan in 2001. It is no doubt the film's presentation of zealous patriotism as at best ambiguous which allowed it to find a Japanese audience. It may have even touched a chord among older spectators who could recall post-war films which portrayed the doomed heroism of the country's submariners in a way rather more akin to the great German TV production *Das Boot* than to Hollywood war films.

5 A KIND OF CONCLUSION

CJ Entertainment has usually done very well in the Japanese media market. Consider the case of the Alzheimer-themed melodrama *A Moment to Remember*. As the Japanese Wikipedia tells the story, this CJ product premiered in Korea in November 2004, and was at the top of the box office for three weeks. It was an adaptation of a Japanese television drama. For the Japanese premiere, both lead actor and director went to Japan in October 2005, to be greeted at a press conference by the Japanese star of the original program. Under the Japanese title 'An Eraser Inside my Head', and thanks to a carefully planned ad campaign, the film became the first Korean film to top the box office charts in Japan, earning some 3-billion yen, roughly US$ 25 million. That makes it more profitable than the blockbusters which launched the new Korean cinema in Japan, such as *Joint Security Area* (Japan release 2001) and *Swiri* (Japan release 2000). Director Kang Woo-suk's own action-'faction' film *Silmido*, produced by his Cinema Service, did fairly well in Japan when released there in 2004. CJ has more recently launched in Japan the CJ Series, a collection of multi-disk DVDs of its more popular films with Japanese subtitles.

Other production companies have involved Japanese actors in their productions, used Japanese theme songs, made entire films (*Rikidō-zan, Fighter in the Wind*) concerning Koreans who became famous in Japan while hiding their origins. It has even been reported that the first big hit of the new Korean cinema, *Joint Security Area*, is to be remade as a Japanese 20-part TV drama (see Japanese Wikipedia, 'JSA'/ *Kyōdō keibi kuiki*'). While some media figures claim the enthusiasm for the 'Korean Wave' may be waning in Japan, there is still a lucrative market in Japan for romantic comedy, melodrama and action films.

Hanbando has been largely ignored in Japan. There appear to be no plans for a release there, and neither is there as yet a DVD version of the film available with Japanese subtitles.

So why make the film in the first place? The decision by CJ Entertainment and director Kang to make such a stridently nationalistic film may be based on elements of genuine patriotism. It more plausibly seems based on the financial calculation that 2006 was ripe for a film exploiting political tensions and ill-feelings filling TV screens and newspaper pages. This time, the Japanese market could be sacrificed, and the all-important domestic market[3] relied upon to buy tickets for a story evoking as many as possible issues of dispute between South Korea and Japan.

Consider the contrasting case of the biggest success of 2006, Bong Joon-ho's *The Host*. The overall budget of US$11 million was shored up by pre-sales to Japan, accounting for some 40% of the funds needed. This meant not only that Boon could make the film he wanted to make—and be free to wager over a third of the budget on CGI and animatronics—but by the time he took *The Host* off to the Cannes Film Festival that summer, he felt confident that he would be able to recoup investment from Korean and Japanese exhibition even before launching the film on the international market. 'In Cannes .. it caused a bidding frenzy' (Roddick 2006: 33).

The Korean Film Council has, in its last official report *Korean Cinema 2006*, noted that films currently in pre-production, with possible release dates in 2007-08, include a number of examples of 'faction films about modern history that stimulate nationalism and intellectual curiosity'. The fascination with the late-Chosŏn dynasty and the rehabilitation of the royal family seems likely to continue, with films in development about 'Empress Myŏngsŏng',[4] about the tragic legend of

---

[3] As Darcy Paquet reported in 2005, 'Korea's TV, cable and video/DVD markets remain miniscule. Online piracy and high prices have stunted the DVD sector, which is dominated by rentals rather than sell-through. Surveys indicate that only 29% of the two million households that own a DVD player have ever bought a DVD. Whereas US or European releases can double their revenues on DVD sales alone, Korea more resembles the US in the 1970s, when films had to earn two and a half times their budget in theaters just in order to break even': see Paquet 2005a.

[4] In addition to being the star of a 2001 KBS television 2001, the romanticised empress is celebrated in a full-scale musical. *The Last Empress* premiered in 1995 and is still in business. See the detailed English and Korean website on this 'spare no ex-

'Lee Shim', wife of a French diplomat and one of Kojong's romantic entanglements, even about the American wife of the last Korean prince, Julia Mullock. On the other hand, the *Hanbando* tactic of big-budget anti-Japanese patriotism may be tried yet again if the film 'Tokdo Defense Force' gets the go-ahead.

Korean films will continue to plunder and re-write the Korean past and to intervene in contemporary political and ideological debates. Not all the films will be good, some will be awful, others will win awards at film festivals around the world, and a few may even earn profits on the monster scale of *The Host*.[5] Some production companies will be outward-looking and seek to cultivate the Japanese and wider international audience, others may focus on the domestic box office; a big company such as CJ Entertainment will no doubt try both routes. But no one should under-estimate the financial or cultural presence of the new Korean cinema.

---

penses spectacle executed with exquisite taste', available at http://www.thelastempress.com/.

[5] On the way to its success, *The Host* has illustrated one of the extrinsic factors by which cinematic achievement on the domestic commercial level continues to worry observers concerned about the overall artistic health of the industry. In a country with a total of some 1500 screens in cinemas nation-wide, companies promoting large-scale productions pour increasingly huge amounts into advertising campaigns and have also, so far at least, managed to organize saturation bookings on proportions perhaps only possible in a moderate-sized country with a resurgent, highly competitive entertainment sector. As *The Korea Times* film specialist Kim Tae-jong observed on 4 September 2006: 'Many people believe that the film has opened a new era for the film industry, but there are also concerns over shadows that the film casts on the industry as a whole. As the film opened on 620 screens and the domination continued for several weeks, were unable to find available theatres'. *Hanbando* certainly owed its early earnings to the fact of occupying some 550 screens during the first week of its release. Whether seriously complex films about anything as challenging as the past or present relationship of Korea and Japan can succeed, or survive, in this climate remains to be seen.

REFERENCES

Cumings, Bruce (1997), *Korea's Place in the Sun: A Modern History*, New York and London: WW Norton & Company

Gerow, Aaron (2006), 'Fantasies of War and Nation in Recent Japanese Cinema', *Japan Focus* (20 February). Online: www.japanfocus.org/products/toppdf/1707

Kang, Woo-suk (2005), 'Kang Woo-suk talks about Hanbando', originally in: Film2.0 (26 October); English version, www.twitchfilm.net. Online: http://www.twitchfilm.net/archives/006309.html

Kim, Kyu Hyun (2007), 'Hanbando' review. Online: http://koreanfilm.org/kfilm06.html#hanbando

Korean Cinema 2006, Korean Film Council. Online: http://www.koreanfilm.or.kr/

Morris, Mark (2007), 'Melodrama, Exorcism, Mimicry: Japan and the Colonial Past in the New Korean Cinema', in: Darren Aoki, Chris Berry and Nicola Liscutin (eds.), *What a Difference a Region Makes* [provisional title], Hong Kong: University of Hong Kong Press (forthcoming)

Paquet, Darcy (2005), 'The Korean Film Industry: 1992 to the Present', in: Chi-yun Shin and Julian Stringer (eds.), *The New Korean Cinema*, Edinburgh: University of Edinburgh Press, pp. 32-50

Paquet, Darcy (2005a), 'Essays from the Far East Film Festival'. Online: http://koreanfilm.org/feff.html

Roddick, Nick (2006), 'Red River', *Sight & Sound* (December), pp. 32-4

Russell, Mark (2005), 'CJ Entertainment at 10', *The Hollywood Reporter* (3 October). Online: http://www.hollywoodreporter.com/hr/search/article_display.jsp?vnu_content_id=1001220250

Takasaki, Sōji (2002), *Shokuminchi Chōsen no Nihonjin* [Colonial Korea and the Japanese], Tokyo: Iwanami Shoten

Turim, Maureen (1989), *Flashbacks in Film*, London: Routledge

NEGOTIATING WITH NORTH KOREA: LESSONS LEARNED AND FORGOTTEN

Robert Carlin[1]

ABSTRACT

The experience gained from dealing with North Korea from 1993-2000 is largely forgotten. During those years, the US and the DPRK logged thousands of hours of contact. The inability of most observers to remember the legacy of these contacts is a central reason for the sterile nature of the diplomacy since 2001. Conventional wisdom remains the same: It is impossible to deal with the North Koreans. Yet, from 1993-2000, the US Government had more than twenty issues under discussion with the North. A large percentage of those talks ended in agreements, almost all of which went beyond the declaratory stage to concrete implementation. The range of subjects expanded, moving past the 1994 Agreed Framework and finally culminating in the October 2000 US-DPRK Joint Communiqué, which laid a foundation for new progress. The path was bumpy, with numerous mistakes. Nevertheless, lessons were learned and put to good use. These lessons the new administration discarded in favor of its own mythology when it took office in January 2001.

In diplomacy, beginning from scratch is not unprecedented, nor by itself necessarily a bad thing. In early June 1993, a United States negotiating team assembled in New York to deal with a crisis caused by a Democratic People's Republic of Korea (DPRK—North Korea) announcement of its withdrawal from the Nuclear Non-proliferation Treaty (NPT). The principal members of the US team had never met a North Korean before and knew virtually nothing about North Korean history, culture, economy, or political system. When talks began, the crisis seemed to be about to go over the edge. Instead, after nine tense days, the US and North Korea agreed on 11 June on their first-ever

---

[1] My deep appreciation to Professor John Lewis of The Centre for International Security and Cooperation at Stanford University for his help and encouragement in writing this article.

joint statement, beginning eight years of intense negotiations and diplomatic accomplishments.

The experience gained from dealing with North Korea over that period (1993-2000) has now largely vanished into a thicket of misapprehension and myth. Even where there has been some attention to the detail of events during those years, most of the focus has been on the Agreed Framework, signed the following year. But the negotiating experience gained is broader—and the lessons much deeper—than simply the 1993-94 talks that culminated in the Agreed Framework of 21 October 1994.

From 1993-2000, the US and North Korea logged thousands of hours of face-to-face contact in formal and informal settings. The inability of most observers to remember, much less utilize, the legacy of these contacts is perhaps one of the central reasons for the sterile nature of the diplomatic process and the shallowness of the public discussions on the Korean issue during much of the Bush Administration. By contrast, the inability of the North Koreans to forget that legacy compounds their disdain for the current US approach, which explicitly rejects the achievements of the past, even as a basis for forging new agreements. The most recent efforts by current US officials to distance their accomplishments from those of the past would be comical if they were not so painful to watch.

1 THEMES AND TOPICS

1.1 *You can't deal with them*

The conventional wisdom, at least in the US, is much what it has always been: It is not possible—or at best, nearly impossible—to deal with North Korea. Forgotten is the reality that from 1993-2000, the US Government had twenty or more different issues under discussion with the DPRK in a wide variety of settings.[2] A large percentage of those talks ended in agreements or made substantial progress. Almost all of those agreements went beyond the declaratory stage and entailed concrete and complex implementation. In the first years after the Agreed Framework was signed in October 1994, most of the talks were linked to implementing that document. The range of subjects

---

[2] A list of these discussions and negotiations will be found at the end of this article.

expanded over time, however, and eventually culminated in the US-DPRK Joint Communiqué (12 October 2000) laying a foundation for new progress in many areas. This was not necessarily a smooth and steady ascent. Certainly, mistakes were made. Nevertheless, lessons were also learned and experience garnered that was put to good use.

1.2 *Empty words*

Talks with the North are usually characterized as painful, lengthy, and arduous. The talks that took place from 1993-2000 were never simple, but, in fact, most of the negotiations that ended in agreements were concluded quickly. The most time-consuming part of the negotiating process often involved getting to the talks themselves. The Agreed Framework negotiations stretched from June 1993 to October 1994, but the largest chunk of that period (August 1993-June 1994) was spent in discussions about how to get back to talks, which were suspended by Washington after the second round in July 1993.

It was never entirely clear to US negotiators what considerations weighed most heavily in a North Korean decision to move into serious discussions on any given subject. What was clear, or at least became clearer over time, was that once such a decision had been made, the general pattern was for the talks to proceed steadily towards resolution. Underlying the specific calculations for each set of talks, apparently, was a basic, 'strategic decision' made by Kim Il Sung in the early 1990s to press for engagement with the United States and even accept a continuing US military presence on the peninsula as a hedge against expanded, potentially hostile, Chinese or Russian influence. The North Koreans somewhat clumsily signalled this new position as early as January 1992 in high-level talks in New York between Under Secretary of State Arnold Kanter and Korean Worker's Party Secretary Kim Yong Sun. It was repeated numerous times thereafter to those willing to pay attention. Certainly it was a point made at the highest level during Secretary of State Albright's visit to Pyongyang in October 2000.

Kim Il Sung's new policy line did not, of course, prevent the North from threatening to withdraw from the NPT in March 1993, but it did serve to bring it back to the negotiating track only a few months later. The full import of Kim's decision to seek engagement with the US as a hedge against his continental neighbours was only dimly perceived in Washington for many years and has now been almost totally forgotten. This lapse in understanding probably prevented the US from moving more quickly to resolve the nuclear problem and then to broaden the discussions to a wider range of issues. It was much the same sort of mistake the US made decades earlier in Vietnam, in not fully recognizing the antipathy between the Chinese and Vietnamese.

1.3 *Overall pace*

Altogether, the Agreed Framework negotiations took only five sessions. The most productive phase occurred in the final three sessions, over the space of less than 90 days (August-October 1994). Other critical negotiations, though they often felt complicated and difficult to the negotiators on the scene, were equally rapid. For example, the agreement on the Kŭmchang-ri underground inspections took just five months (November 1998-April 1999). Talks leading to the October 2000 statement on terrorism were concluded successfully after three relatively short sessions spread out over about a year. The missile moratorium took from July to September 1999 to work out. Talks on the three main Korea Peninsula Energy Development Organization (KEDO) protocols—very detailed documents—took about a year.[3]

Working-level talks—such as those concerning the canning of spent fuel, monitoring of heavy fuel oil, and the recovery of the remains of US military personnel from the Korean War—were generally barometers of the broader state of play in relations. Canning took longer than expected, partly due to technical problems and partly because the North was determined to use the pace of progress on canning as negotiating leverage over the US elsewhere. Tactical considerations aside, overall, in each of these working-level talks, the trend was towards rather than away from agreement.

2 ROLE OF THE AGREED FRAMEWORK

The Agreed Framework talks, it must be remembered, started near the beginning of the Clinton Administration. This was a learning period

---

[3] KEDO was formed in 1995 to carry out the US obligations to provide North Korea with light-water reactors and heavy fuel oil.

for both sides, following the collapsed effort at rapprochement between the two Koreas and the yearlong tensions between Pyongyang and the International Atomic Energy Authority (IAEA). Just weeks after the Clinton Administration took office, the North announced its intention to withdraw from the NPT in accordance with the treaty's withdrawal provision calling for 90-day notification. The US reacted swiftly. By June a lead negotiator, Assistant Secretary Robert Gallucci, had been appointed, and a regular, if still somewhat informal, channel had been opened between Washington and North Korea's UN mission. Barely a week before North Korea was scheduled to complete its withdrawal from the NPT, the first meeting took place in what turned out to be a journey to completion of the Agreed Framework. The early talks have received scant attention from observers, who have focused mostly on the dangerous episode that came close to war in June 1994. Few 'experts' remember that in the second round of talks in July 1993, at a meeting that took place in the DPRK's mission in Geneva, the North's chief negotiator put on the table what he termed Pyongyang's 'bold, new instructions' to trade the existing, gas-graphite nuclear program for new light-water reactors.[4] Despite the ups and downs of the next fifteen months, that proposal became the basis of the core bargain in the Agreed Framework.

One of the most serious, pernicious misunderstandings about the Agreed Framework is that it was, at heart, a non-proliferation agreement. It was not. The engine of the framework was always its political provisions (section II). The Framework required both sides to 'move toward full normalization of political and economic relations', including:

- Within three months [of the 21 October 1994 Agreed Framework] to reduce barriers to trade and investment;
- To open a liaison office in the other's capital;
- To upgrade bilateral relations to the Ambassadorial level;
- For the US to provide formal assurances to the DPRK, against the threat or use of nuclear weapons;
- To provide alternative energy in the form of heavy oil for heating and electricity production; and

---

[4] Joel S. Wit, Daniel B. Poneman, and Robert Gallucci, *Going Critical: The First North Korean Nuclear Crisis* (Washington, DC: Brookings Institution Press, 2004), p. 71.

- To provide the DPRK a light-water reactor (LWR) project with a total generating capability of approximately 2,000 MWe by a target date of 2003.

For its part in the bargain, North Korea agreed to freeze its graphite-moderated reactors in operation or under construction and other related facilities, and to cooperate to 'store safely the spent fuel' from their 5MWe experimental reactor, remain a party to the NPT, and accept IAEA monitoring. Added on, a little like the tail of a dog, was the provision for the North to 'take steps to implement the [January 1992] North-South Joint Declaration on the Denuclearization of the Korean Peninsula'.

Early on, the Agreed Framework negotiations were stuck until the US recognized the agreement would have to go beyond non-proliferation. After the agreement was reached, implementation of the Framework became progressively hobbled as Washington fell back into treating it largely as a non-proliferation tool. The North, by contrast, saw the entire agreement in political terms. For Pyongyang, even the US obligation to supply light-water reactors had a political—rather than strictly an economic—rationale. The North Koreans saw the LWR construction as a means of ensuring US involvement with the DPRK over a long period, thus improving—so they hoped—the chances of normalizing political relations.

In broadest terms, the Agreed Framework provided a floor, structure, and cohesiveness to all of the US-DPRK talks that followed. Any negotiations that did not fit that structure (whether or not they were specifically prescribed in the document itself) did not move forward. Part of that may have been for reasons having to do with internal North Korean dynamics, on which more below. Beyond words on a piece of paper, the Agreed Framework began a process of interaction in Northeast Asia, which helped the parties establish new norms for cooperation.

3 Implementation

3.1 *Falling short*

The Four-Party Talks (1997-99) and bilateral US-DPRK missile talks (1996-2000) were the notable exceptions to the overall trend toward reaching agreement. Pyongyang did not want to have either of these negotiations. It eventually took part in them, after much US cajoling, not because it sought progress in these particular areas but because of a calculation that refusal to accept Washington's proposals to talk risked souring the atmosphere for progress in political relations with the US, a key DPRK goal throughout this period.

In particular, the Four-Party Talks[5], announced by President Clinton in April 1996, struck the North Koreans as a distraction from the Agreed Framework just as that agreement was beginning to get traction. In effect, it appeared to be a dilution of US focus on its framework obligations. Moreover, Pyongyang opposed the four-party setting because, by involving the Chinese, it went counter to a basic Pyongyang policy goal; that is, to limit Chinese influence by improving US-DPRK relations. The Four-Party Talks proved difficult to organize, awkward to run, and ultimately, impossible to sustain.

The effort was not wasted, however. It did put North and South Korean diplomats together at a time when inter-Korean relations were at a low point. The meetings provided an opportunity to pursue US-North Korean talks on other issues. And, they proved to be a training ground for the Chinese Foreign Ministry's later efforts, in 2003, to avoid a crisis over the North Korean nuclear issue by organizing first three-way and then six-party talks.

3.2 *Missile talks*

These went nowhere until 2000, and then only produced the most tender shoots of progress before the ground froze. Whether or not the talks could have made progress from 1996-99 is an open question, but the fact is the US never effectively tested the proposition because it was unable to force the North to concentrate seriously on the issue. By the end of the first meeting in Berlin in April 1996—and probably even as soon as the US delegate had finished his opening remarks—the North had little doubt that the US had come to the table with little more than declaratory positions.

Washington's failure to press for missile talks on anything more than a leisurely schedule (about once a year) also convinced the North Koreans that this was not an issue that demanded priority attention, let

---

[5] The Four Parties were the US, North Korea, South Korea, and China.

alone serious negotiations. Certainly, it undercut any efforts the North Korean Foreign Ministry might make to its own leadership that this was a significant foreign policy issue and thus something for the ministry's involvement, rather than purely (or mostly) a subject that rightly belonged with those elements in the Workers Party and the military dealing with the production and sale of missiles. The result was that the talks never had a chance to develop a momentum of their own or move much beyond mere repetition of each side's position.

The weight of the Agreed Framework in the North's calculations on the missile issue is illustrated by two events, barely two years apart. In the autumn of 1996, it seems likely that Washington successfully prevented a North Korean missile test, at a time when the Agreed Framework still appeared to hold promise and Pyongyang was reluctant to risk damaging the agreement's prospects. By contrast, in the summer of 1998, the Agreed Framework appeared moribund, a factor that apparently figured in Pyongyang's decision to go ahead with the Taepodong missile launch despite US warnings.

The missile talks finally appeared to be getting traction in July 2000, when Kim Jong Il signalled that Pyongyang had reformulated the issue: Progress on each side's concerns was the key to improving US-DPRK relations, and improvement in relations would lead to a breakthrough on the missile issue. The argument sounded somewhat circular, but it appeared designed to open the door to more productive discussions. July 2000 was late in the game, however, with only four months before US presidential elections. That was not enough time. A last ditch US attempt to achieve a breakthrough in a meeting in Kuala Lumpur in November failed, a victim of insufficient preparation and overly high expectations.

3.3 *Mechanics*

Apart from substantive concerns, there were always moving parts to consider in negotiating with the North. The particulars included: the level of the talks, the context, the sequence, and what might be termed the operational plateau. Sometimes talks bogged down because of the need for North Korea to make tactical decisions, over which the US had only minimal influence. One such set of decisions frequently involved pacing. Pacing is an important psychological tool for the North Koreans, something they frequently use well and to excruciating effect. At other times, however, the question of whether or not to meet revolved around other—seemingly more central—concerns in the North Korean leadership. These were not immediately apparent to outsiders and needed concerted probing before the problem could be understood, much less addressed.

Attempts to deal with key North Korean leadership concerns became a bone of contention in Washington and eventually led to the mythology about 'bribery' that has by now become gospel in some circles. From 1995-99, obtaining food was a priority for Pyongyang, and North Korean negotiators devoted considerable effort to meeting that imperative. In fact, for much of that period, carrying out negotiations was especially difficult because DPRK diplomats had such a short time horizon. Fixing problems with long-term solutions did not interest them—they were under pressure for short-term action, i.e., establishing when the next shipment of food would arrive in the North. Given that overwhelming focus on food, it made sense to ensure that food shipments (already planned on humanitarian grounds) be used to best advantage in the negotiations.

3.4 Getting to the talks

Except in one instance (the Four-Party Talks), the US and the DPRK were not hampered by so-called 'shape of the table' problems. The US negotiators rarely had procedural issues to worry over, especially once they had established the patterns and standard logistical arrangements for meetings. The two sides developed a routine for calling and agreeing to meeting times and places. As the broader process of engagement developed, moreover, it started to generate its own momentum. Instead of having only a single basis for progress on a specific set of talks, there were multiple talks underway, each of which could feed into the others. Taken together, the range of talks continuously elevated the 'operational plateau', an increasing level of confidence and familiarity between the two sides—especially between the negotiators—that allowed them to put operational questions to one side and focus on substance.

In some cases, when the US negotiators did face difficult-to-understand operational problems, these were apparently connected to internal demarcation disputes within the DPRK. For issues on which the DPRK Foreign Ministry had the lead—and that meant virtually anything directly connected with the Agreed Framework—the Americans could usually arrange meetings with minimal difficulty. Issues outside the clear purview of the Agreed Framework, by contrast, raised problems, because they engaged competing organs within the DPRK hierarchy.

3.5 At the talks

No two sets of talks were exactly alike, but once meetings became routine, most tended to follow similar patterns. There would be an initial period for stating 'principled' or highly general opening positions. These would be followed by sessions devoted to defining the problem; then an exploration of the mechanics for solving the problem; and finally, bargaining on the details and sequence of the resolution.

Defining the problem had to go beyond simply a statement of what the US side was concerned about, objected to, or demanding of a particular series of steps from the North Koreans. Instead, before Pyongyang would move on, there had to be an agreement, if only implicit, that this was a shared problem, one whose solution needed joint efforts and whose positive outcome would meet the interests of both sides. Over time during the late 1990s, the growing understanding between the two sides and their principal negotiators would attune them to possible ways to formulate and refine the shared problem.

In many cases, different sets of talks were conducted by the same delegations on both sides, sometimes even at the same venue. For example, in 1999, the US delegation to the Four-Party Talks met separately with the DPRK delegation to discuss the US concerns that the North Koreans had built a clandestine nuclear facility at Kŭmchang-ri. At other times, meetings on separate issues took place in different venues but as part of a sequence of talks—as when broader US-DPRK negotiations took place in Berlin, then the two delegations flew to Geneva to take part in Four-Party Talks.

The North Korean Foreign Ministry had a core group of officials who were involved in virtually all negotiations. They were almost always led by Vice-Foreign Minister Kim Gye Gwan. Sometimes in more technical talks, additional DPRK officials took part. The US, by contrast, tended to have separate teams with little overlap. Thus, the

North Korean delegations had a good sense of the overall process, while each US team tended to be more narrowly focused.

3.6 *Multilateral aspects*

Although the negotiations themselves were, for the most part, carried out bilaterally—between US and DPRK negotiating teams—they were actually the operational tip of a long and sometimes complicated process of multilateral coordination. Both Japan and the ROK sent teams of diplomats to Geneva during the Agreed Framework talks for the purpose of coordinating with the US negotiators. Later, the Perry process (1999-2000)[6] established a high-level US-ROK-Japan trilateral coordination group (TCOG) to try to ensure that the three capitals understood and were following an agreed strategy toward Pyongyang.

KEDO represented a plunge into the multilateral diplomacy in the most complete sense. The organization (1995-2007) was funded and staffed by the US, the ROK, and Japan and later the European Union. Decisions on KEDO's policies and operations were reached by consensus among the four parties; likewise, KEDO negotiating teams dealing with the North Koreans were composed of personnel from all four. At first, the North insisted that every negotiating team be 'led' by an American—if only nominally—but that requirement eventually fell away.

4 PROBLEMS

The most difficult, and in some ways least successful, part of the negotiating process was the follow-up. Negotiators on both sides at some point had to hand over control for implementation to parts of their bureaucracies or official institutions (such as the Congress in the US case) that were less familiar with, and in some cases less well disposed towards, the process and outcome of the talks.

At that point, a new dynamic emerged. For one thing, performance in implementing established agreements became important to support progress in other ongoing negotiations. Mechanisms (not already es-

---

[6] This followed on from the 1999 review of US policy towards North Korea by former US Secretary of State for Defence William Perry.

tablished) had to evolve for dealing with complaints from both sides. Slowly, it became obvious that prior planning and preparations on implementation would be crucial not only for carrying out agreements but also for reaching agreements in the first place.

Performance-related issues, moreover, defined the battleground internally in each capital. Some wanted to treat every performance failure as fatal and a matter of principle, with no sense of perspective. On the North's part, problems in implementation were used to highlight the two sides' mutual—and often reciprocal—obligations, as well as a way of testing Washington's commitment to full compliance. Gradually, US negotiators came to an important realization—that failure by the North Koreans to implement fully or promptly a particular set of obligations was not necessarily a sign of irresponsible behaviour; rather, it was often a function of DPRK perceptions of and response to US performance. To the North, which viewed itself as weak and disadvantaged, implementation was not simply an obligation but necessary leverage to ensure better US compliance.

4.1 *Obsession with 'cheating'*

The complex and largely successful eight-year effort to engage the North is now forgotten, a victim of the notion that the North 'cheated' on the Agreed Framework. As noted in the earlier summary of its terms, the Agreed Framework was designed as a political document, setting down on paper mutually reinforcing obligations by the two sides, some tied to specific timetables, some set out as eventual goals. The understanding was that no side was compelled to follow through on any or all of its obligations, but if it did not, the other would be equally free to stop its own performance. In addition, the North Koreans were warned that although some things were left vague in the document, they should clearly understand that certain types of activity on their part would cause 'political' problems in Washington that would sink the deal. For the US, verification was a key ingredient in making the deal work, and Washington therefore decided that nothing would be included (such as uranium enrichment) that could not be verified.

The argument is sometimes made that the reference in the Agreed Framework to the January 1992 North-South Joint Declaration on Denuclearization was meant to reaffirm the North's pledge not to 'possess uranium enrichment facilities' and thus an obligation not to pursue enrichment even though that was not explicitly forbidden in the framework. Such an indirect reference would, at best, have been a weak reed on which to rest so crucial an obligation. In any case, the negotiating record would not support even that interpretation. The two sides did not focus on references to the inter-Korean agreements until virtually the end of the negotiations, and then very much as an afterthought at the insistence of the South Koreans, who were not concerned so much with the details as with the symbolic imperative of having a reference to their own role. The North Koreans strongly objected to bringing North-South agreements into the Agreed Framework (this was obviously a difficult subject for the Foreign Ministry to touch for internal reasons). The last weeks of the talks bogged down as numerous attempts were made to find the language that would satisfy both Seoul and Pyongyang; no one really intended that the reference to the North-South agreement would constitute one of the core DPRK obligations under the Agreed Framework or believed that it was a good way to cover uranium enrichment or any other similar technology or material not specifically mentioned in the Agreed Framework.

Thus, while developing a uranium enrichment program (UEP) can be seen as truly bad political judgement on Pyongyang's part, whether or not it is 'cheating' is at best an open (and probably feckless) question. In 1999 and 2000, it did not come as a surprise to learn that the North Koreans might be exploring the enrichment option, and there were discussions in Washington about how to confront Pyongyang diplomatically at the proper time, in the proper way, to get them to stop. In talks in June 2000, US negotiators obliquely raised with the North the potential need for additional Kŭmchang-ri-like inspections in the future. The 12 October 2000 US-DPRK Joint Communiqué explicitly endorsed 'the desirability of greater transparency in carrying out [the] respective obligations under the Agreed Framework'. In this regard, it continued, the two sides 'noted the value of the access which removed US concerns about the underground site at Kŭmchang-ri'. This language had no purpose but to look ahead to negotiations on inspections that would address additional US concerns about the North's nuclear program—a point that Pyongyang could not have missed. Together, the visits of Vice-Marshal Jo Myong Rok to Washington, and Secretary of State Madeleine Albright to Pyongyang, in October 2000 probably transformed the atmosphere sufficiently to provide the basis for dealing with the uranium enrichment issue much as the Kŭmchang-ri issue had been dealt with successfully in 1999.

We still do not know today the factors that went into the DPRK decision to begin exploring a UEP. Neither do we know what would have happened if the US had dealt with the enrichment issue within the context of the Agreed Framework, rather than arguing—as it did in 2002—that the program was a fatal blow to the Agreed Framework. In the good versus evil constructs that governed US approaches to North Korea after 2001, the accusation that the DPRK had cheated needed no proof and brooked no response other than an admission of guilt and total capitulation.

The Agreed Framework did not, as is sometimes asserted, 'fail', It was purposefully destroyed, and that destruction did not begin in October 2002. The Bush Administration came to office already intent on killing the agreement. That intent was specific and public. The administration deemed the Agreed Framework fatally flawed and said so repeatedly. If there were any at senior policy levels who thought otherwise, none of them was prepared seriously either to defend the agreement in public or even to argue for ways to improve it. The existence of the UEP was already being used by early 2002—that is, before the issue surfaced in the Pyongyang meeting that October—as an excuse to withhold and/or undermine funding for promised heavy fuel oil shipments under the Agreed Framework, as a step toward dismantling the Agreed Framework. The argument for 'presumptive breach', made by some officials in the administration, was also a sign of the times. A legal concept that had nothing to do with the negotiating record for the Agreed Framework, presumptive breach was applied in a rather tortured way: the Agreed Framework had called for the North to be in compliance with its NPT obligations by the time key components for the promised LWRs were shipped. The IAEA claimed it would take several years to answer crucial questions about the history of the North's nuclear program. Putting the two schedules (for LWR construction and IAEA verification) side by side, it was apparent the former would occur considerably in advance of the latter. Thus, it was asserted, the North could already been seen to be in breach of its obligations.

The problem was real—getting the delivery of critical LWR components in line with full IAEA verification of the history of the North's nuclear program. If one wanted the North Koreans to accept inspections earlier than laid out in the Agreed Framework, there were ways to try to achieve that. Indeed, American negotiators had already begun thinking along those lines in 2000. Instead, the Bush Administration thought up a new obligation for the North and then declared it in violation. One can argue whether this was calculated duplicity or just a result of wilful unfamiliarity with the terms of the Agreed Framework itself.

Many issues were still on the table in January 2001, when the new administration took office. Yet, there was a strong feeling in both capitals that the elements were definitely in place for positive developments. Pyongyang had already made clear, in an important article[7] published in the party newspaper *Rodong Shinmun* just before the November 2000 US presidential elections that it would continue to abide by both the Agreed Framework and the Joint Communiqué no matter who became the next US president. Thus, the incoming administration was handed the best possible situation and on a number of issues was made fully aware of the extraordinary opportunity for continued progress.

Certainly, the new administration could have started negotiations to modify the Agreed Framework, something that needed to happen in any event and which Pyongyang was probably prepared to accept. Washington could have explored how far the North was prepared to go on a missile deal. It could have pressed ahead with cooperation to support and encourage international efforts against terrorism as laid out in the 6 October 2000 Joint Statement. It did none of these things. Worst of all, it forgot (or rather, never tried to learn) the real lessons of the preceding eight years. Once the knowledge and experience was thrown away, the foundation for productive negotiations was also lost.

5 Looking to the Future

Diplomatic agreements are not easy to reach. The pain often comes not so much in dealing with the other side but in dealing with your own. Unless you are dictating terms to a defeated enemy, you are going to have to compromise on something, probably several somethings, that will make many people unhappy.

Even if the diplomats can get their capitals to stomach the compromises, greater difficulties loom. Absolutely essential to keeping

---

[7] *Rodong Shinmun*, 12 October 2000.

any agreement viable is understanding that implementation is not a simple act of translating words into action. Implementation is a complicated choreography transitioning from theory to reality. The process is perilous, yet when done correctly, it also creates opportunities to build momentum and trust—two essential ingredients that transcend the literal terms of the agreement. Diplomacy can often change reality as it moves ahead; the momentum of implementation, in turn, can often provide the speed necessary to propel events over the barriers that exist in minds of nations. When they want to, the North Koreans certainly know how to move quickly in order to generate this sort of momentum.

The hard fact is that implementation of any agreement designed to grapple with the nuclear question on the Korean peninsula will necessarily be uneven and much less precise than the words on the paper would suggest. If the agreement contains provisions for supplying electricity—or electrical generating capacity—unanticipated technical realities will challenge the uninitiated diplomat. Forces will impinge that are unforeseen, schedules will slip, small mistakes will be made and cascade, signals will get crossed. Especially in the early days, when eagle eyed critics are watching for problems, there will be a tendency to imagine molehills are mountains. The word 'cheating' will be whispered around. But there is a body of experience on which to draw in dealing with these problems.

List of Major Negotiations 1993-2000

Negotiation	Outcome
Agreed Framework 1993-94	agreement
LWR model 1994-95	agreement
Helicopter incident 1994	agreement
Liaison offices 1994-98	no agreement
KEDO supply agreement 1995	agreement
Canning 1995-96	agreement
KEDO protocols 1995-2000	agreement
HFO monitoring 1995-96	agreement
Missile talks 1996-2000	no agreement
Submarine apology 1996	agreement
Terrorism talks 1996-2000	agreement
Korean War remains 1996-2005	agreement
Four-Party Talks 1997-99	no agreement
Food monitoring 1995-2000	some progress
Kŭmchang-ri accusations 1998-99	agreement
Perry visit 1999	agreement
Missile moratorium 1999	agreement
US persons held in North Korea (consular)	agreement
Preparations for expanded nuclear inspections	preliminary stages
General Officer's talks	under discussion
Joint communiqué 2000	agreement
Secretary of State 2000 (visit preparations)	agreement

PERILOUS JOURNEYS:
THE PLIGHT OF NORTH KOREANS IN CHINA[1]

Peter Beck, Gail Kim and Donald Macintyre

ABSTRACT

This article examines the factors leading to cross-border migrations in North Korea and then describes the politically charged but fragile and increasingly mercenary networks through which North Koreans seek refuge. Some 10,000 North Koreans have safely resettled in South Korea and elsewhere, but many more suffer exploitation while in hiding or on the run. China's repatriation policy and South Korea's ambivalent postures have resulted in the networks to explore various other alternatives, testing the limits of Beijing and Pyongyang's tolerance. Although indifference and fears of mass migration have kept relevant governments from pressing for a halt to all forced repatriation or pursuing the quiet cooperation necessary to protect the asylum seekers, this article identifies practicable strategies to access, relocate and resettle the most exposed while relieving some of the pressures to escape.

1 INTRODUCTION

The economic collapse of the Democratic People's Republic of Korea (DPRK)—North Korea—and the famine in that country in the 1990s and subsequent food shortages have prompted scores of thousands to escape their country's hardships and seek refuge in the People's Republic of China (PRC)—China—and beyond, contributing to a humanitarian challenge that is playing out almost invisibly as the world focuses on North Korea's nuclear programme. The international community has failed to find an effective means of dealing with this situation. Despite billions of dollars in humanitarian assistance over the past decade and increasing awareness of human rights violations, conditions for the vast majority of citizens in North Korea remain dire,

---

[1] This article is a revised version of Crisis Group Asia Report no. 122, *Perilous Journeys: The Plight of North Koreans in China and Beyond,* 26 October 2006.

while conditions for those who reach the PRC are only marginally better. In China, the border crossers live in hiding from crackdowns and forcible repatriations by China and neighbouring countries, vulnerable to abuse and exploitation. If repatriated to the North, they face harsh punishment, possibly execution. That North Koreans in China are virtually invisible makes it impossible to give an accurate assessment of their numbers. Only a little over 10,000 have made the journey to safety in the Republic of Korea (ROK)—South Korea, or in a small number of cases, to Japan, Europe or the United States. However, on the basis of the assessments of several non-governmental organisations (NGOs) and first-hand interviews with border crossers and Korean-Chinese in the border area, the total is likely to reach up to 100,000.

The plight of these North Koreans has emerged as a source of tensions, not only between the two Koreas, but also between China and its neighbours, South Korea and the US, and has even become a sticking point between the US and China. China and South Korea have held back, even during the United Nations Security Council debate in October 2006 over post-test sanctions, from applying as much pressure as they might to persuade Pyongyang to reverse its nuclear policy, in part because they fear that the steady stream of North Koreans flowing into China and beyond would become a torrent if the North's economy were to collapse under the weight of tough measures. While there is marginally more hope Beijing will change its ways than Pyongyang, concerned governments can and must do far more to improve the situation of the border crossers as events could get much worse if famine looms again.

Hunger and the lack of economic opportunity, rather than political oppression, are the most important factors in shaping a North Korean's decision to leave the country. A lack of information, the fear of being caught by Chinese or North Korean security agents and financial limitations are more significant barriers than any actual wall or tight security at the border. China compensates for the virtual absence of border guards with a relentless search for North Koreans in hiding. In October 2006, Chinese authorities began to build a fence along the frontier and conducted neighbourhood sweeps to find and arrest border crossers (Caryl 2006). Despite these obstacles, the willingness among North Koreans to risk their lives to escape is growing stronger, and arrivals in the South hit a record in 2006. The most important pull factor shaping the decision to leave is the presence of family members in China and, increasingly, South Korea. The nearly 10,000 defectors in the South are able to send cash and information to help others to escape. To a lesser but significant extent, information is beginning to spread in the North through smuggled South Korean videos, American and South Korean radio broadcasts, and word of mouth—all exposing North Koreans to new ideas and aspirations. Most North Koreans do not arrive in China with the intention of seeking official asylum, but because Beijing is making it ever more difficult for them to stay, a growing number are forced to travel thousands of kilometres and undertake risky border crossings in search of refuge in Mongolia or Southeast Asia.

A handful of North Koreans have legal, documented permission to visit China, but the vast majority are there illegally. The lack of protection of North Koreans in China has forced them into hiding, leading to smuggling, trafficking and *ad hoc* diplomacy, with the weakest falling through the cracks. China, which has bilateral agreements with the North concerning 'escaped criminals' and 'border affairs', views the border crossers as economic migrants subject to repatriation.[2] The classification of North Korean border crossers as illegal economic migrants subjects them to repatriation under these bilateral agreements and denies them international protection or access by the Office of the United Nations High Commissioner for Refugees (UNHCR). The UNHCR considers them 'persons of concern',[3] while international human rights and humanitarian groups and the media commonly refer to North Koreans as 'refugees'.

There are legal debates over the interpretation of the 1951 Convention on Refugees but we believe many if not most North Koreans in China have compelling cases to be recognised as refugees or 'refugees *sur place*', because the North's usually harsh treatment of border crossers amounts to persecution.[4] However, they often do not have the

---

[2] The DPRK and the PRC signed an 'Escaped Criminals Reciprocal Extradition Treaty' in 1960, and a 'Border Area Affairs Agreement' in 1986.

[3] For definition of the term, see UNHCR/Inter-Parliamentary Union Handbook for Parliamentarians no. 2 (2001), *Refugee Protection: A Guide to International Refugee Law*, Annex 2, Glossary of Key Protection-related Terms, p. 131. Online: http://www.unhcr.org/publ/ PUBL/3d4aba564.pdf.

[4] For discussion of the legal issues, including the concept of 'refugee *sur place*', see Appendix C, 'Refugee Law and the Office of the UN High Commissioner for Refugees' in Crisis Group Asia Report no. 122, October 2006. The text of the 1951 Convention on Refugees and its 1967 Protocol is available on the web site of the UN High Commission for Refugees. Online: http://www.unhcr.org/protect/3c0762ea4.html.

opportunity to avail themselves of international protection. Regardless of their official status, all North Koreans in China and other transit states deserve such protection from forcible repatriation and subsequent persecution. China does not yet have a domestic legal framework that addresses the needs of asylum seekers, but it and other transit countries can and should, nonetheless, follow through on their international legal obligations to respect the principle of non-refoulement, which prohibits such returns.[5]

This article is believed to be the first to look comprehensively at the hidden, often shifting networks through which North Koreans seek safety. Some life-saving and others violent and exploitive, these networks largely determine whom North Koreans meet, where they live, how much danger they are exposed to and what options they have. Examining the formation and development of these networks and the policies of related countries provides the basis for understanding the situation that North Koreans face today. This in turn helps identify specific areas in which new policies of protection can be advanced.

Building on more than 50 interviews with North Koreans in China and Southeast Asia in 2006 and over 50 more in South Korea, this article examines the factors leading to cross-border migrations and why the networks have been forced underground. It focuses on the activities of network operators and North Koreans in China and concludes with discussion of ways to improve the situation for refugees and asylum seekers. To protect individuals and the 'underground railway', many details, particularly about escape routes and particular governments and groups, have not been included.

2 Leaving the 'Workers' Paradise'

The denial of political and economic rights in North Korea is entrenched in the country's social architecture. A three-tiered caste sys-

---

[5] The principle of non-refoulement is set out in Article 33 of the 1951 Convention on Refugee: 'Prohibition of Expulsion or Return ("Refoulement")', ('Non-Refoulement', Executive Committee of the UNHCR, no. 6 (xxviii), 1977). For a comprehensive definition see 'UNHCR and International Protection: A Protection Induction Programme' (2006). Online: http://www.unhcr.org/cgi-bin/texis/vtx/publ/opendoc.htm?tbl=PUBL&id=44b4bbcd2. For further discussion of the principle of non-refoulement and China's related international law obligations, see Appendix C, 'Refugee Law and the Office of the UN High Commissioner for Refugees' in Crisis Group Asia Report no. 122, October 2006.

tem structures society, effectively suppressing rights for those of the lower 'wavering' and 'hostile' classes. Those who leave the country, even if only for food or to earn money, can face forced labour if caught. Eye-witness accounts and satellite images leave no doubt that prison camps and public executions are realities (Hawk 2001).

North Korea's social controls and indoctrination have proved amazingly effective. Before 1990, there were only a handful of defections to South Korea and some clandestine cross-border remittances or trade with relatives in China. Little information flowed in or out of the country. It was not until the economic collapse and ensuing famine of the 1990s that a wave of North Koreans moved into China. That economic collapse and persistent difficulties are directly linked to the policy decisions of the regime in Pyongyang. Nevertheless, the vast majority of North Koreans who cross into China appear to be driven by economic necessity rather than direct political oppression.

2.1 *The border region*

The border between China and North Korea is 1,416 km, marked primarily by the Amnok (Yalu) and Tuman (Tumen) rivers.[6] The 790-km Amnok portion is wide and deep, essentially impassable without a boat. In some areas, however, it becomes both narrow and shallow enough to wade across with ease. The Tuman, which runs north of the Amnok for 546 km, is no more than knee deep at certain points and can be crossed on foot. North Korea's border with Russia is only 17 km, dominated by the strong currents of the Tuman river delta. Most of the region's rain falls in the summer months, with floods accompanying the rainy season. In the winter, the rivers freeze over for three to four months, and temperatures drop well below freezing.

Fourteen official border crossings at twelve points connect China and North Korea. North Korea reinforced border guards on its side with troops in 2004.[7] A North Korean who lived near the border claimed the number of guards increased from two every 500 metres to four.[8] On the Chinese side, press reports suggested that a greater number of soldiers replaced border guards in 2003 (Kahn 2003). However,

---

[6] For more on the border, see Crisis Group Asia Report no.112, *China and North Korea: Comrades Forever?*, 1 February 2006.

[7] Crisis Group interview, defector and NGO worker, Seoul, January 2005.

[8] Crisis Group interview, defector from Onsong, northeast China, 27 April 2006.

on several visits we observed little or no visible military presence on either side of the border.[9] Traffic is fairly light on the bridges that link to the PRC's Yanbian Korean Autonomous Prefecture, where the large concentration of ethnic Korean-Chinese nationals live.[10] Occasionally, trucks loaded with rice or fertiliser can be seen crossing (Suh 2006). Furthermore, the border region has been home to both large- and small-scale efforts at economic development in recent years.[11]

Despite the seemingly light security at the border, Chinese authorities take the flow of North Koreans very seriously. Beijing does not want a steady stream of border crossers to become a flood, causing economic havoc in the region and possibly stoking latent Korean nationalism there.[12] In addition to crackdowns, a new barbed-wire fence was seen being built along the Amnok in Dandong after summer floods damaged crops and infrastructure in North Korea (Lee Myŏngjin 2006a). Signs posted on the Chinese side read: 'It is forbidden to financially help, harbour, or aid in the settlement of people from the neighbouring country who have crossed the border illegally' (Delaunay 2002).

A significant consequence of this Sino-North Korean contact has been the increased flow of information, not least via pre-paid Chinese cell phones. The phones, which sell in China for US$50-US$100,[13] are necessary for doing business along the border, but also give separated families and guides on the underground railroad a way to keep in touch and pass along information. Despite the black-market status of these phones, an estimated 20,000 North Koreans had access to them in early 2005 (MacKinnon 2005). Owners allow others to use their phones for a modest fee. One asylum seeker who borrowed a cell phone from a border town resident said, however, that ownership or use can be punished by long sentences to labour camps (*kyohwaso*).[14]

---

[9] Crisis Group observations, November 2005, April and July 2006.
[10] ibid.
[11] For more details, see Crisis Group Asia Report no. 112, *China and North Korea*, p. 26.
[12] Crisis Group email interview, Roberta Cohen, Brookings Institution, 1 October 2006. For more on rising nationalism and regional tensions, see Crisis Group Asia Report no. 108, *North East Asia's Undercurrents of Conflict*, 15 December 2005.
[13] Figures denoted in dollars (US$) in this article refer to US dollars.
[14] Crisis Group interview, northern Thailand, 8 June 2006.

2.2 Crossing over

From 1997 to 1999, during the worst of the famine and the height of the 'first wave' of relief activity, the border was fairly porous, and sympathy on the Chinese side of the border was high. Chinese officials were largely unconcerned, and it became almost a common practice to bribe North Korean border guards. The going rate was about US$13, although some parts of the border were more expensive. North Koreans could cross the border on their own and did so mostly with the intention of acquiring provisions or perhaps working for cash, then returning to their families in the North. Some border crossers did not have any particular contacts or plans and relied on the generosity of strangers. One who entered China with three other women in the late 1990s simply 'approached one of the houses ... and told [the owner] about [their] situation' (Lankov 2005).

Christian churches in China were particularly active in supporting the early cross-border survival strategy. An organisation based in Yanji, the capital of the Yanbian Korean Autonomous Prefecture, supported 'house churches' along the border, providing food, clothes and basic medical kits. Hundreds of border crossers passed through each of fifteen to twenty house churches in this one network alone. Many would come in the middle of the night, pick up provisions and return to North Korea before daybreak. Others would stay in the border area for a few days, while still others would move further into China towards Yanji.[15] Another pastor remembers supplying several shelters along the border with thousands of dollars' worth of winter clothes in the late 1990s. The situation was 'loose back then', allowing aid workers and North Koreans in border areas to move around with relative ease. Some donated goods were even diverted to the marketplace.[16]

Surveys conducted along the border in 1998 found the North Koreans in China to be 'a diverse, highly mobile, and largely hidden population' (Robinson et al. 1999). Most were in their twenties and thirties and had entered China in search of food or work. Aid workers estimate that over two-thirds eventually returned home (Robinson et al. 1999). Residents from North Hamgyŏng province formed almost 80

---

[15] Crisis Group interview, South Korean pastor and aid worker, Seoul, 12 April 2006.
[16] Crisis Group interview, US pastor and activist, Seoul, 22 March 2006.

percent of those surveyed (Robinson et al. 2001: 286-92). Not only is this province closest to the border, across the Tuman river from Chinese cities with large ethnic Korean populations, but it used to have considerable heavy industry. As state-owned enterprises closed, unemployment grew, and food shortages prevented the distribution of daily rations. With little arable land for cultivation or foraging, residents of North Hamgyŏng had few alternatives for coping (Smith 2005; Robinson et al. 1999). In the past few years, North Koreans as far from the border as Pyongyang and beyond have made their way to China, an indication of continuing hardship as well as of more established escape routes.

Since 1999, more women and children and more single individuals with no stable family unit to return to in North Korea have made the crossing. Surveys along the border in 1999 found roughly equal numbers of men and women, but women now outnumber men three to one (Robinson et al. 1999).[17] Men, who are more likely to be married or divorced, tend to go home with provisions for their families, while single women can access the 'bride trade' in the border region (Robinson et al. 1999: 291-5). Women who are married but not employed are also more likely to leave their homes, since they will not be missed at work and have no direct access to the public distribution system. These women sometimes work as cross-border traders, selling cigarettes and other goods from China on North Korea's black market to help provide for their families. Women are also given more lenient punishments if caught and repatriated, so long as they seem to have been in China only to find food or work (Lee Keum-soon 2006).

Official Chinese figure for summer 1998 estimate that the number of North Koreans in China during the peak famine years ranged from 10,000 to 300,000 (Seymour 2005). At least half of those included in the higher-end figure stayed for less than three months, and over 70 percent stayed for less than six months. When viewed in context, this estimate does not indicate an exodus of hundreds of thousands, but rather underscores the fluidity of the early cross-border network.

---

[17] Crisis Group interview, bureau chief of NGO helping defectors in South Korea, Seoul.

3 GOING UNDERGROUND

3.1 *Crackdowns*

There is a consensus among missionaries, aid workers and NGOs that Beijing has steadily increased the pressure on North Korean asylum seekers and those helping them.[18] It implemented a system of rewards for turning in North Koreans and fines for supporting them. Aid workers quoted rewards as high as US$400 and fines as high as US$3600, but recent reports cite rewards of US$630 (Amnesty International 2000; Marquand 2000; Research Institute for the North Korean Society 2006b). According to the US Committee for Refugees and Immigrants, at least 6,000 North Koreans were repatriated in 2000, a marked rise from earlier years (US Committee for Refugees and Immigrants 2001). A 100-day campaign of raids and repatriation was begun in December 2002, resulting in the repatriation of 3,200 North Koreans and the detention of 1,300 others in the Chinese border towns of Tumen and Longjing (Médecins Sans Frontières 2003; Yonhap News, 21 January 2003). In October 2003, the Chinese government was running half a dozen detention facilities inside military bases along the border with North Korea and repatriating up to 200 to 300 North Koreans every week (Macintyre 2005). Since 2000, China has increasingly targeted the NGOs and aid workers who help North Koreans.[19]

3.2 *Changes in the Chinese border area*

In the midst of the crackdowns, China's main area for receiving border crossers has undergone several important changes. The Yanbian Korean Autonomous Prefecture was a major source of support and a staging area for many NGOs. There is sympathy towards North Koreans that can be attributed to ethnic solidarity (many North Koreans, especially from northern areas, have at least one relative in China) as well as memories of North Korean aid during the famine that accompanied the Great Leap Forward (1958-60) in China. Since the early 2000s, however, Yanbian has played a reduced role for

---

[18] Crisis Group interviews, March-June 2006.
[19] Crisis Group interview, NGO worker, Seoul, 19 September 2006.

North Koreans. Chinese crackdowns have been effective. Fearing fines or arrest, some employers and lodgers abruptly began turning out North Koreans. The increased presence of police has forced asylum seekers to retreat to rural areas or to change apartments constantly in urban centres.[20]

Prior to the crackdowns, homeless North Korean children (*kkotjebi*) could be seen on street corners and sometimes in tourist centres begging for money and food (Chung 2003). The *kkotjebi* and other North Korean asylum seekers no longer have a visible presence in China. Also, despite their rising economic status, the Korean-Chinese (*Chosŏnjŏk*) are not wealthy, and the provincial economy is generally sluggish. North Koreans still receive direct help from more financially stable relatives or find employment in Korean small businesses. However, there have been several testimonies of exploitive working conditions, especially for North Korean women, and donor fatigue has set in (Charny 2005). Border crossers have also been associated in the Chinese media with assaults and robberies (Liu 2001). In September 2006, reports emerged that Chinese authorities had undertaken a new crackdown on North Koreans residing illegally in China, sweeping through neighbourhoods at sunrise unannounced to check the residency papers of each household (Lee Myŏng-jin 2006b; Caryl 2006).

Changing economic opportunities for ethnic Korean-Chinese nationals present another twist for border crossers seeking aid from the Korean community in China. In pursuit of a higher standard of living, Korean-Chinese are moving out of Yanbian to urban centres such as Beijing, Shanghai and Shenzhen, where South Korean companies have taken root. Low birth rates and migration to South Korea have also contributed to the fall in Yanbian's Korean population (Kim 2003). In 2000, ethnic Koreans in Jilin province, where Yanbian is located, numbered 842,000, 39 percent of the population (Zhonghua Renmin Gongheguo Guojia Fazhan he Gaige Weiyuanhui 2001). By the end of 2005, the percentage had dropped to 33 percent (*Chosun Ilbo*, 10 March 2006). If it drops below 30 percent, Yanbian could be in danger of losing its status as an autonomous prefecture. Anticipating this, the government there has drafted legislation that would dismantle the prefecture's county lines and regroup Tumen, Yanji and Longjing cities into one region. The smaller region would have an

---

[20] Crisis Group interviews, northeast China, April-May 2006.

ethnic Korean majority and could be eligible to form an autonomous government (*Boxun Xinwen Wang* 2006).

Losing autonomous prefectural status could result in tighter social controls for churches, one of the bases of support for North Koreans in need of shelter or provisions. Indeed, churches seem to have already downsized activities, although there is no straightforward correlation here. One missionary estimates that there are 200-300 ethnic Korean churches in Yanbian, but few are still involved in supporting Northerners (*Mirae Hanguk*, 3 May 2006). Some missionaries do not want the risks of giving support to compromise their programmes for Chinese nationals. Others are accountable to donors who are indifferent to the refugee issue.

3.3 Changing push-pull factors

The network's move underground has also resulted in new pull factors. North Koreans, particularly those in border areas, have had more exposure to China and contact with relatives in China and South Korea. South Korean television programmes and films have also penetrated the North as smuggled videos and DVDs, inspiring dreams of moving south.[21] Recent defectors estimate that more than half of all North Koreans have watched banned South Korean entertainment.[22] Several defectors also report having listened to shortwave radio broadcasts by Voice of America and Radio Free Asia, which air for only a few hours per day.[23] Still others report being impressed by propaganda leaflets, not so much because of the usually over-the-top messages, but because of the quality of the paper.[24] People talk secretly of South Korea, and most know that its standard of living is much higher. A woman had heard from a friend in South Korea that work there is hard and people unfriendly, but that conditions are better than in China.[25] North Koreans who have already reached South Korea

---

[21] Crisis Group interview, woman from Pyongyang, northeast China, 29 April 2006.
[22] Crisis Group interviews, Seoul, May and August 2006.
[23] Crisis Group interviews, defector from Pyongyang, Seoul, August 2006. Crisis Group interview, Yoon Gook-han, Korean Service, Voice of America, Washington DC, 24 August 2006.
[24] Crisis Group interviews, Seoul, September 2006.
[25] Crisis Group interview, woman from Ch'ŏngjin, 23 April 2006.

may also be in a financial position to support the escape of their relatives.

The role of relatives in South Korea is critical because they inject money into the network, funding a 'niche market' of relatively safe but expensive defections. This means that some North Koreans, many of whom have relatives already in China or in South Korea or have themselves crossed the border before, go to China not as a last-resort survival strategy, but in search of a higher standard of living. Indeed, as Sino-North Korean contacts increase, economic difficulties persist and more information about the outside world filters in, relatively better off and better educated North Koreans are taking advantage of the underground railroad's growing sophistication and its connections to South Korea and the West. Such paid defections have driven the price of bribes up, presenting new barriers to crossing for those who cannot afford the payments.

The underlying push factor, however, is still hunger and poverty. Living standards have slightly improved only for those who have access to foreign currency, but many more are still desperate to meet basic needs. While North Korea's economy has improved slightly, the benefits reach only a small minority. Economic reforms were introduced in 2002 in the context of a growing network of black markets and cross-border traffic.[26] The introduction of market mechanisms, especially through monetisation, was first met with some optimism abroad but has stalled from a serious lack of infrastructure and resources and has yet to be matched by necessary structural reforms. Meanwhile, prices have skyrocketed, alongside unemployment and lagging wages, so that an ordinary worker's purchasing power for rice has dropped thirty-fold (Frank 2005). The re-imposition of the public distribution system in late 2005, combined with the curtailment in international humanitarian relief efforts and the July 2006 floods, could be the perfect storm presaging return to famine and a new exodus to China (Charny 2006). Given the already chronic shortage of food, North Korea's nuclear test on 9 October 2006 will have an adverse impact on international humanitarian assistance to its population, with countries holding back their aid. Jean-Pierre de Margerie, North Korea country representative for the World Food Programme (WFP), announced on 9 October 2006 that they have already seen a fall in inter-

---

[26] For more on North Korea's economic reforms, see Crisis Group Asia Report no. 96, *North Korea: Can the Iron Fist Accept the Invisible Hand?*, 25 April 2005.

national aid, including a drop from China of 60 percent (Beck and Blanchard 2006). With food shortages threatening to return to famine levels, migrating to different cities or to China will be one of the coping strategies used by hungry North Koreans with the means to undertake such journeys.

Political motivations for leaving the North are still unusual but a growing trend. People who, through time spent in China or contacts abroad, realise that a higher standard of living could be achieved outside the country, come to resent not only their economic situation but also the restrictions and punishments they face when trying to better their lives, and the government officials they see as responsible. Leaving the country is seen not as a criminal or treasonous move, but as an act of survival and even courage.[27] In China, defectors express increasingly frank criticism of and hostility towards the regime.[28] Over the past several years, there has been a growing realisation that the cause of North Koreans' hardships is not the US or the weather.

4 NEW PATTERNS, NEW NETWORKS

Forced underground and faced with changing circumstances, networks for asylum seekers have become more sophisticated and diverse even as the number of individuals involved has declined. Rather than indicating a notable improvement in circumstances inside North Korea, this fall in participants is likely to be a result of the networks' move underground. Some continue to cross into China on their own, but increasingly, North Koreans seek to secure money and contacts before leaving. Financial constraints and fear keep the number of border crossers in check.

In 2003, the UNHCR estimated that 100,000 North Koreans remained in China (*Chosun Ilbo*, 19 June 2003). Private NGOs conducting surveys the following year concurred (US Committee for Refugees and Immigrants 2004). More conservative estimates for the same period are around 30,000-50,000 (Suh 2006). Figures have generally fallen over the past three years. Good Friends, a Seoul-based organisation working with North Korean refugees, whose 1999 survey set the high-end estimate of 300,000 North Koreans in China, now puts the

---

[27] Crisis Group interview, refugee from Namp'o, northern Thailand, 7 June 2006.
[28] Crisis Group interviews, April-May 2006.

figure at 150,000, a third of whom are children of North Korean women and Chinese men (Noh 2006). The NGO US Committee for Refugees and Immigrants has also lowered its estimates from 100,000 refugees in 2003-04 to 50,000 in 2005 (US Committee for Refugees and Immigrants 2006). The US Department of State estimates that 10,000-30,000 asylum seekers remain hidden in northeastern China (Congressional-Executive Commission on China 2005). In the spring of 2006, Antonio Guterres, UNHCR High Commissioner, said 300,000 North Koreans were living in China, but that 'the number of North Koreans in China in need of international protection is limited, maybe reaching 50,000' (*Lusa News*, 23 March 2006).[29] Of the several North Koreans he met during his March 2006 visit to Beijing, 'only one was in the category of refugee *sur place*' (*Lusa News*, 23 March 2006).

Given the combination of crackdowns, slightly improved conditions in North Korea and the high cost of departing, it is likely that fewer North Koreans are leaving today than during the peak famine years. Simultaneously, more and more are reaching third countries, with a record number for 2006. The constant threat of exploitation, arrest and/or repatriation forces North Koreans in China to be invisible, precluding a reliable estimate. However, based on extensive interviews with asylum seekers and ethnic Korean Chinese, lower estimates in the tens of thousands seem most plausible.

4.1 *Temporary border crossers*

A sizable number of North Koreans still cross into China for temporary stays, hoping to meet relatives, earn money, find food or medical treatment or acquire goods to sell at home. Their main goal is to amass cash and provisions to take back to family members in the North. North Koreans can receive official permission to visit relatives in China, but the process is riddled with corruption and difficult to negotiate.[30] An invitation from the relatives is taken to a contact in the State Security Agency, along with US$125.[31] Applicants may wait for

---

[29] For more on the UNHCR position regarding the protection needs of North Koreans in China, see Appendix C, 'Refugee Law and the Office of the UN High Commissioner for Refugees' in Crisis Group Asia Report no. 122, 2006.

[30] Crisis Group interview, NGO worker, Seoul, March 2006.

[31] Crisis Group interview, northeast China, April-May 2006.

months before receiving a travel permit that grants them a one-month stay in China. Although many have relatives there, few can afford to pay the fees and bribes demanded by the State Security Agency. Those who can secure permission are sometimes allowed to extend their stay and usually return to North Korea with food, medicine, clothing and some cash. Although the number of families helped by such supplies is limited by the number of travel permits granted and how much security agents confiscate for themselves, this form of assistance is significant for two reasons. First, it takes much-needed goods as well as information into North Korea; secondly, it gives North Koreans legal protection throughout their journey.

Many more make the crossing without permission, risking arrest and imprisonment. Brokers who arrange for passage from inside North Korea to China charge up to US$1,250 and either escort their clients across the border or simply relay information about where and when it is safe to cross.[32] Some asylum seekers find their own way through North Korea's barely-functioning transportation system.[33] At the border, they sometimes avoid detection, relying on luck, their knowledge of the area, or tips and favours from family members associated with the border guards. In 2005, North Korean border guards collected bribes of US$25-US$38 per head for crossing the Tuman river.[34] A South Korean missionary cites the current rate as closer to US$50, as do several defectors.[35] By comparison, the rate was US$13 in the late 1990s.[36] Women may offer sexual favours in lieu of money (Research Institute for the North Korean Society 2006d). North Koreans trying to cross into China without money will sometimes promise to pay a guard upon their return. Because the Chinese guards patrol by car, it is easier to avoid detection there, and there are few accounts of 'entry bribes'.

However, moving from different parts of the border to a safe place further inside China can be difficult and dangerous. One elderly woman walked for ten days to reach a town where she could hide.[37]

---

[32] Crisis Group interview, defector, Seoul, September 2006.
[33] Crisis Group interview, defector, Seoul, September 2006.
[34] Crisis Group interview, pastor and aid worker, Seoul, May 2006.
[35] Crisis Group interviews, north east China, April-May 2006, and northern Thailand, June 2006.
[36] Crisis Group interview, aid worker who used to work in China, Seoul, 12 April 2006.
[37] Crisis Group interview, refugee from Musan, China-North Korean border, 23 April 2006.

Those who meet brokers at the border and travel under their guidance are still vulnerable to the border guards who patrol the area. In some cases, brokers turn out to be traffickers.[38] Even during short stays, North Koreans in China live in constant fear of deportation. Most women enter into some kind of relationship with a Chinese or ethnic Korean man to gain a measure of protection. A minority survive on their own, working as waitresses in restaurants. Long-time observers in northeast China say a majority of North Korean women in China have suffered some form of abuse, the most egregious cases involving systematic rape and prostitution. Men sometimes work on farms or factories but are in greater danger of arrest and repatriation. On days when he could find a job, one man living in Yanji would work all day for US$2.50.[39]

Information about surviving in China and trying to reach third countries circulates through word of mouth and media outlets. Young North Koreans who venture into Chinese Internet cafes armed with a few keywords can quickly access a wealth of information about NGOs that support North Korean human rights and asylum seekers, sometimes making contacts to arrange for passage to South Korea.[40] But, ever vulnerable to repatriation and exploitation, North Koreans are wary of doing anything that could lead to arrest or trafficking.

Moreover, since NGOs have scaled back their activities, there is very little help for North Koreans living in China. Two active NGOs currently handle about 40 border crossers each. One group tries to blend North Koreans into urban areas, placing them in rented apartments and moving them periodically. NGOs may also arrange for Korean-Chinese in rural areas to house North Koreans in groups of two or three. Medical care seems to be available to those who can afford it, but not many North Koreans or NGOs can.[41] Forged documents can be important for getting around China. The crudest forged identification cards cost as little as US$10-US$25 but are easily spotted. Prices rise dramatically for cards with identification numbers actually included in the Chinese household registration system (*hukou*). Depending on quality, they start at around US$1,260.

---

[38] Crisis Group interview, woman from Pyongyang, China-North Korean border, 29 April 2006.
[39] Crisis Group interview, refugee from Onsong, China-North Korean border, 27 April 2006.
[40] Crisis Group interview, South Korean NGO worker, Seoul, 24 March 2006.
[41] Crisis Group interview, Médecins Sans Frontières worker, Seoul, 6 April 2006.

4.2 Traffickers and rural brides

Marriage between Chinese or Korean-Chinese men and North Korean women as a method of survival has evolved from isolated cases of introduction or referral to outright trafficking in persons. The demand for trafficked brides—a consequence of the one-child policy and preference for sons, combined with uneven development that has pulled young women into the industrial work force—is highest among older or disabled men in rural areas. In 2002, reports linked North Korean runners to Korean-Chinese operating as traffickers. Runners kept in touch with traffickers across the border via Chinese cell phones and received US$63 for each woman they led to the border. The women, regardless of their marital status, were sold for US$380-US$1,260 (*Chosun Ilbo*, 22 July 2002). Other reports corroborate this sum, citing broker fees from US$120-US$1,200 per woman, with brides in their late twenties typically costing US$380-US$630 (Lankov 2004). More recently, Chinese men have secured 'introductions' to North Korean women, most of whom entered China since 2004, for US$880-US$1,890. Chinese brides, by comparison, are sold for US$3,780-US$6,300 (Research Institute for the North Korean Society 2006a). In some cases, a woman knows she is being sold into marriage, although she may not realise how harsh the conditions in China are. In other cases, women are lured across the border by marriage brokers posing as merchants. They are persuaded to pursue cross-border trade, and once on the Chinese side, they are completely vulnerable to extortion (Suh 2006). Traffickers have also posed as brokers, accepting payment to guide a woman out of China only to sell her as a bride.

With this so-called bride trade dating back to the early years of crossings, there is now a sizable group of North Korean women who have been married to Chinese nationals for nearly ten years. Despite the long-term, settled nature of their circumstances, these women face considerable barriers to securing legal Chinese residency. The state does not recognise their marriages, and the children they have are ineligible for registration on the *hukou* despite their father's Chinese nationality. These stateless children have no legal protections and will not be able to pursue their education beyond middle school. Local officials sometimes accept bribes of US$125-US$378 to place these children on family registers. North Korean mothers can also be registered, but most families can barely afford to register the children. Moreover, even if a woman or child is listed in the register, neighbours and local officials who know of the mother's background are a threat to her security. Rural locations provide relative safety from raids, but the authorities do appear in response to crime or reports of illegal immigrants. Sometimes, residents receive advance notice of 'raids', giving them a huge amount of leverage over their North Korean neighbours (Suh 2006). Being in favour with the authorities, or at least being able to afford bribes, can be crucial to the safety of North Korean women and their families.

Because the families that these women marry into are concentrated in farming, economic opportunities are limited. For those who are still in touch with home, sending money back to their families can be a source of strain on their relationships with husbands and in-laws. Runners who deliver cash collect either a flat fee of US$63 or 20-30 percent of the remittance (Suh 2006).[42] Another reported source of strain is the fear that wives will relocate to South Korea, abandoning their Chinese husbands and children (Suh 2006).

All North Koreans in China are at risk of extortion, but women are especially vulnerable. Husbands may be abusive and many keep their purchased brides under virtual house arrest lest they run away or are discovered by authorities. A broker may sell a woman into marriage and instruct her to run away once he has received payment, only to catch and sell her again, sometimes repeating the scheme several times (Human Rights Watch 2002: 13-14). Many women fall prey to prostitution or are forced to work in places of entertainment.

For all their hardships, women who enter into 'stable' marriages are better off than the many who are drawn into prostitution or trafficking rings. Three women who recently left China even had Han Chinese husbands who arranged for their passage to South Korea. Each paid only US$250—about a tenth of the average cost—and was linked to the smuggling network by a long chain of her husband's relatives and friends. They spoke fluent Chinese and said their husbands sent them away to escape crackdowns triggered by the approach of the 2008 Olympics. All three have children who are still in China, speak Chinese and attend Chinese schools. One has been officially registered as his father's son at a cost of US$125. A broker, who has been part of the network for nearly ten years, noted that men who send their wives out of China do so not out of sentiment or morality, but in order to

---

[42]Crisis Group interviews, refugee from Chungjin, northern Thailand, 8 June 2006, and South Korean aid worker, Bangkok, 10 June 2006.

secure Korean citizenship through official international marriages. The scheme, he says, is not new and is most effective when children are involved.[43]

4.3 *The underground railway*

Some North Koreans in China enjoy relative safety, but all are open to sudden arrest and possible repatriation. Many say that if they had some measure of legal protection, they would opt to stay. Given the harsh policies of the Chinese government, however, most have no choice but seek refuge elsewhere. The majority quickly learn that it is possible to reach South Korea, and an increasing number are also aware of possibilities to settle in the US or other Western countries. However, many lack concrete information and reliable contacts. The vast majority simply do not have the money to pay a broker or network operators for fake passports and plane tickets, which can cost up to US$10,000 per head. They are essentially stuck in China. Such high barriers have encouraged North Koreans and activists to pursue other routes to safety, including foreign mission sit-ins and requests for asylum or transfer in third countries. The most hopeful either have the support of NGOs or relatives in South Korea. Some NGOs ask North Koreans to repay them once they are in the South, but with low wages and unstable working conditions, it is nearly impossible for a North Korean to save enough to hire a broker on his or her own.

Currently, a small number of NGOs with diverse backgrounds and agendas continue to move people on the underground railway. NGOs started to drop out of the smuggling network as China began to crack down on asylum seekers and arrest their helpers in the late 1990s. Financial constraints also squeezed them out, as church groups who initially provided funds apparently grew wary of South Korean government audits.[44] Some NGOs have reduced their scope to operations within China, shying away from transfers to South Korea or third countries. Others have turned to promoting change inside North Korea through aid, economic development and information-sharing. Furthermore, it is not uncommon for NGOs to hire brokers when moving

---
[43] Crisis Group interview, Bangkok, 10 June 2006.
[44] Crisis Group interview, NGO worker, Seoul, May 2005.

people out of North Korea or China (Powell 2006).[45] Most of these NGOs have only a handful of paid staff and operate on a shoestring budget, but often have North Korean defectors on their payrolls.

Around 2002, North Korean defectors already in Seoul started to fill the gap. For those short of job skills and struggling to find and keep work in South Korea, brokering was profitable, though dangerous. Many had access to contacts inside North Korea and China. Moreover, they had taken the underground railway themselves and could communicate effectively with North Koreans trying to leave home or get out of China. Most of the North Korean 'brokers' do a few operations on an *ad hoc* basis, usually to help family members or friends; only a handful are full-time professionals.[46] Since Seoul cut cash subsidies by two-thirds at the end of 2004, defector-brokers have also been dropping out of the network.

Organisations differ in their access and attitudes toward the media. Some shy away from the public eye and insist North Koreans are safest when operations are kept as quiet as possible. Others welcome the attention and use it as a tool to increase awareness, support and legitimacy, not least for influencing government policies. One activist credits media coverage with forcing China and South Korea to engage on the issue of North Korean asylum seekers.[47] Press coverage and international attention may or may not have been the driving force behind China's and South Korea's efforts at quiet diplomacy, but when this channel is operating, it offers the safest and most desirable route. While there is value in increasing public awareness about the plight of vulnerable populations, there is almost always a backlash to such campaigns. Concerned about stability and order, China tends to crack down after major events on North Koreans in hiding, sending warning signals lest others be encouraged to follow their example (Lee Keum-soon 2006).[48] When strains cause quiet diplomacy to go public, countries scale down drastically their role in the network, partly to preserve relationships with North Korea, China and South Korea, but also because they do not want to be known as a target country for illegal migrants or floods of asylum seekers.

---

[45] Crisis Group interviews, South Korean pastor and activist, 12 April 2006, and broker, 12 May 2006.
[46] Crisis Group interview, defector and NGO worker, Seoul, January 2005.
[47] Crisis Group interview, NGO worker, Seoul, May 2005.
[48] Crisis Group interview, former network operator, Seoul, 31 May 2006.

4.3.1 Shortcut: over the wall or through the front door

A significant number of North Koreans reach freedom directly from China, either through scaling the wall of a diplomatic mission or, as the barbed wire has become thicker, by walking through the front door using forged documents. Journalist Jasper Becker alleges the Chinese have punished embassies in Beijing that have given refuge by not allowing the asylum seekers to leave for five or six months.[49] He says in the first years of the North Korean famine, Beijing did not have a fixed policy on the issue, and ties with North Korea were strained. Only in 1999 and 2000 did it organise police action against North Koreans on a large scale. It was a top-down policy before it became a local police effort, which is what impelled NGOs to attract international attention and apply pressure by encouraging incursions. In response, Becker says, China started arresting the people behind the actions and made it more difficult for them to work along the border. The incursions have been criticised by some observers as exploitive and counter-productive. Detractors decry the fees paid and profits made by opportunistic broadcasting stations, saying the victims are the North Koreans remaining in China, whose hiding places are often disclosed during exit interviews (*Shiminŭi shinmun*, 14 March 2005). While it is difficult to attribute specific crackdowns to the incursions, North Korea has certainly taken notice. In March 2006, it issued warrants for the arrest of four Japanese NGO workers suspected of participating in planned defections (Lee Young-in 2006).

Many more embassy incursions go unreported in China and Southeast Asia, with the governments involved quietly working out a mutually acceptable solution.[50] Foreign missions are usually willing to cooperate with Chinese authorities to improve embassy security to avoid future 'invasions', so network operators use illegal documents to get North Koreans through the front door, at which point they can declare their purpose (Choe 2006). In virtually all such cases, Chinese authorities eventually allow the North Koreans to leave the country, usually for South Korea.

---

[49] Press conference, Seoul, June 2005.
[50] Crisis Group interviews, various Asian capitals, March-September 2006.

4.3.2 *Expensive passage*

According to NGOs and guides, getting someone from the border area in the northeast to Southeast Asia costs at least US$2,000-US$3,000. Some defector groups based in South Korea have charged as much as US$5,000-US$6,000, offering better security for the higher cost.[51] A South Korean NGO claims that for US$10,000, a potential defector can receive fake documents that are so good the individual can go from his home in the North to Seoul in as few as five days.[52] Brokers with higher fees and supposedly 'strong connections' say that a weak network will lead to clients in China getting caught and sent back to North Korea in seven out of ten cases.[53] Around 2005, brokers started asking for money upfront, possibly in response to Seoul's new policies regarding resettlement funds, which reduced lump sum cash payments.[54]

5 FORCED REPATRIATION

According to reports from NGOs and network operators, North Korea has tightened the border, targeting brokers and defectors. Smuggled video footage of public executions in 2005 involved charges of trafficking in people and illegal border crossing (Amnesty International 2006). In February 2006, 300 people were arrested in the northern border town of Hoeryŏng for planning to defect or having connections in South Korea or China.[55] In May 2006, 217 North Korean agents posing as asylum seekers were rumoured to have been deployed to China as part of a broad information-gathering operation (*Mirae Hanguk*, 3 May 2006). China continues to arrest and repatriate North Koreans without referral to the UNHCR, despite international scrutiny and direct pleas from the US State Department urging compliance with UN conventions (White House press release 2006). It also targets the missionaries, aid workers and brokers involved in sheltering or transporting North Koreans. Observers in China and South Korea at-

---

[51] Crisis Group interview, NGO worker, Seoul, January 2005.
[52] Crisis Group interview, NGO worker, Seoul, 14 March 2006.
[53] For insight into the brokers' operations, see Crisis Group Asia Report no. 122, *Perilous Journeys: The Plight of North Koreans in China and Beyond*, October 2006: 17.
[54] Crisis Group interviewe, NGO worker, Seoul, May 2005.
[55] Crisis Group interview, defector, May 2005.

tribute current crackdowns near Shenyang to a 'clean-up' campaign in preparation for the 2008 Olympics (Research Institute for the North Korean Society 2006c). North Koreans who had lived in China for several years cited pre-Olympic measures as a motivating factor for their recent flight to South Korea.[56]

On the basis of our interviews with aid workers, an estimated 150-300 North Koreans are repatriated from China every week.[57] The large numbers of unauthorised border crossers have caused the North Korean government to ease sentences and change the penal code. The 1999 code distinguished between 'unlawful border crossing' and crossing 'with the intent to overturn the Republic' (Lee Keum-soon 2006). The 2004 revision further distinguishes between 'crossing' and 'frequent crossings', with the latter subject to punishment of up to two years in labour camps (by comparison with three years in the 1999 code). Acts of treason, such as 'surrendering, changing allegiance, [and] handing over confidential information', are punishable by five to ten years of hard labour, or ten years to life in more serious cases (Lee Keum-soon 2006). Despite some changes in the law, however, the political and sometimes arbitrary use of imprisonment, torture and capital punishment continues, and summary executions and long sentences of hard labour are still enforced,.

Punishments tend to depend on the age, gender and experiences of repatriated North Koreans (Lee Keum-soon 2006). Women and children have received sentences as light as two weeks in a detention centre, but longer sentences of several months in labour camps are also common. The consequences of repatriation are most severe for pregnant women, who suffer forced abortions under poor medical conditions, and for those who confess to meeting with South Koreans or missionaries (Hawk 2001). Authorities are wary of prisoners falling ill and dying on their watch (Charny 2005). Those who seem close to death are released, often only to die the following week. Many prisoners take advantage of the opportunity to escape when transferring from labour training camps to provincial detention centres or go back to China after they are released. As many as 40 percent of those repatriated to North Korea re-enter China (*Donga Ilbo*, 27 February 2002).

---

[56] Crisis Group interview, 6 June 2006.
[57] Crisis Group interview, Tim Peters, 31 January 2006.

6 RECOMMENDATIONS

The primary responsibility for the humanitarian issues discussed in this article lies, of course, with North Korea. It could resolve those problems and many others by respecting fully the human rights and fundamental freedoms of its citizens. Given the nature of the regime and its concern for internal security, it is unrealistic to expect such a dramatic change, and we confine our recommendations to Pyongyang to urging it to explore at least small steps of travel liberalisation, including some increase in the numbers of those permitted to travel legally to China, more family visits and special provisions for those living near the border, as well as relaxation of the harsh punishments that are meted out to those who make unauthorised attempts to cross the border.

The PRC is otherwise the key to improving the human rights of North Korean refugees and asylum seekers. However, given its own widely criticised human rights record and the high priority it places on maintaining stability (internally and externally), as well as its close ties with North Korea, it is difficult to be optimistic about a more enlightened Chinese policy in the foreseeable future. Beijing has increasingly not only targeted and forcibly repatriated asylum seekers but also arrested their helpers. It allows other states a fair degree of latitude in dealing with North Koreans who manage to enter diplomatic missions, only to take measures to discourage future incursions.

Some modest steps can perhaps be suggested, particularly in light of the approach of the 2008 Olympics, when all eyes will be on China's behaviour.[58] Allowing North Korean women who have married Chinese nationals and their children to remain and granting them provisional residency would be in the interests of its own citizens, given the shortage of wives for Chinese farmers. Cracking down on the most exploitative venues where North Korean women work, such as karaoke bars, is another action that would increase the security of the most vulnerable while boosting China's image. The PRC has signed the Convention on the Elimination of Violence against Women and the Optional Protocol to the Convention on the Rights of the Child on the sale of children and child prostitution and now needs to devote greater resources to preventing human trafficking. The basic rights of children—including to education—should be honoured as outlined in

---

[58] Crisis Group interview, David Hawk, Seoul, 10 October 2006.

the Convention on the Rights of the Child, which China signed in 1990. China and its neighbours should make medical care more accessible and stop arresting NGO workers for trying to help North Koreans. In all such measures, the PRC and receiving countries would benefit from coordination and support by international agencies such as UNICEF, the United Nations Fund for Population Activities (UNFPA) and the UN Office on Drugs and Crime.

6.1 Seeking asylum

All North Koreans in China and other transit countries must be protected from forcible repatriation and subsequent persecution in the North. As a signatory to the 1951 Convention on Refugees and its 1967 Protocol, China has an obligation under international law to respect the principle of non-refoulement and to protect asylum seekers in its territory, even though a domestic legal framework to address such cases is not yet in place.[59] Further, China should abide by its 1995 Agreement with the UNHCR, which aims to ensure cooperation and reiterates the Refugee Convention's injunction and authorisation for any party to the Convention to invoke binding arbitration before the International Court of Justice in disputes over its interpretation and application (Article 38).[60] Despite this agreement, the UNHCR, which ultimately relies on the goodwill of host governments, officially has been denied access to North Koreans in China. The UNHCR has taken a cautious stance on this group of people, acknowledging them only as 'persons of concern' and seeking engagement with Chinese officials. The High Commissioner for the UNHCR was optimistic about future progress after 'open and frank' discussions on 'everything' during his March 2006 visit to Beijing. China is said to be working with the

---

[59] See 'Refugee Law and the Office of the UN High Commissioner for Refugees' in Crisis Group Asia Report no. 122, 2006. China is also a member of the UNHCR executive committee and has ratified a number of international human rights treaties, including the International Covenant on Economic, Social and Cultural Rights, the Convention against Torture, and the Convention on the Rights of the Child.

[60] Crisis Group email interview, UN official, 16 October 2006; 'Agreement on the Upgrading of the UNHCR Mission in the People's Republic of China to UNHCR Branch Office in the People's Republic of China', signed in Geneva, 1 December 1995, contained in UN Treaty Series, vol. 1898/1899, I-32371, pp. 61-71; 1951 Convention on Refugees.

UNHCR to build legal institutions for a national asylum system, but action on the issue is required (*Lusa News* 2006).

Even if China does not allow North Koreans to seek official asylum on its territory, it should at least stop all forcible repatriation. The UNHCR should press China to fulfill its obligations regarding this matter. At least until Beijing accepts these obligations, neighbouring countries should not turn North Koreans crossing from China back to Chinese authorities, but instead contact either South Korea or the UNHCR. Other governments willing to accept North Korean asylum seekers should demand greater access in order to play a more active role and renew their commitment to this group.

7 Conclusion

The plight of North Koreans seeking refuge in China from the deprivations they face back home is likely to get much worse until greater pressure is placed on China to adjust its practices. Without a more sustained effort on the part of those who have been the loudest on North Korean human rights, namely the US, the European Union and Japan, to persuade Beijing to do the right thing, North Koreans will continue to suffer. Concerned governments must back up their words and resolutions with a greater commitment to recognise and accept North Korean refugees. It is time for the international community to put its money where its mouth is.

References

Amnesty International (2000), 'Persecuting the starving: the plight of North Koreans fleeing to China', press release, 15 December 2000
Amnesty International (2006), *Report 2006*. Online: http://web.amnesty.org/report 2006/prk-summary-eng.
Beck, Lindsay and Ben Blanchard (2006), 'N. Korea Provocations Leave Aid Situations Precarious', Reuters, 9 October 2006
Boxun Xinwen Wang [Boxun News], 'Dismantlement of Yanbian Autonomous Region, Korean-Chinese in Danger of Disappearing', 13 March 2006 [in Chinese]
Caryl, Christian (2006), 'Fed up with Kim? Everybody is exasperated with the capricious leader, including his allies in Beijing', in: *Newsweek International*, 9 October 2006
Charny, Joel R. (2005), *Acts of Betrayal: The Challenge of Protecting North Koreans in China*, Washington DC: Refugees International. Online: http://www.refugees international.org/files/5631_file_ActsofBetrayal.pdf
Charny, Joel R. (2006), *North Korea: Nuclear Brinkmanship Likely to Result in Greater Displacement*, Washington DC: Refugees International. Online: http://www. refugeesinternational.org/content/article/detail/9539
Choe Sang-Hun (2006), '"Traitors" of North Korea plead desperately for Asylum', in: *International Herald Tribune*, 26 September 2006
Chosun Ilbo, 'Never-ending Escape of North Korean Refugee', 22 July 2002 [in Korean]
Chosun Ilbo, 'UN Official Decries Starvation in North', 19 June 2003 [in Korean]
Chosun Ilbo, 'End for China's Autonomous Korean Region?', 10 March 2006 [in Korean]
Chung Byung-Ho (2003), 'Living Dangerously in Two Worlds: The Risks and Tactics of North Korean Refugee Children in China', in: *Korea Journal*, 43 (3), pp. 191-211
Congressional-Executive Commission on China (2005), *2005 Annual Report*, Section VII, North Korean refugees in China. Online: http://www.cecc.gov/pages/ annualRpt/annualRpt05/2005_7_refugees.php.
Delaunay, Sophie (2002), *Médecins Sans Frontières, testimony to the House Committee on International Relations, Subcommittee on East Asia and the Pacific*, Washington DC
Donga Ilbo, '100, 000 Refugees: Grim Life in China', 27 February 2002 [in Korean]
Frank, Ruediger (2005), 'Economic Reforms in North Korea (1998-2004): Systemic Restrictions, Quantitative Analysis, Ideological Background', in: *Journal of the Asia Pacific Economy*, 10 (3), pp. 278-311
Hawk, David (2001), *The Hidden Gulag: Exposing North Korea's Prison Camps*, Washington DC: US Committee for Human Rights in North Korea
Human Rights Watch (2002), 'Invisible Exodus: North Koreans in the People's Republic of China', *Human Rights Watch*, 14 (8) (C), November 2002. Online: http://www.hrw.org/reports/2002/northkorea/norkor1102.pdf
Kahn, Joseph (2003), 'China Moves Troops to Area Bordering North Korea', in: *New York Times*, 16 September 2003
Kim, Si Joong (2003), 'The Economic Status and Role of Ethnic Koreans in China', in: C. Fred Bergsten and Inbom Choi (eds.), *The Korean Diaspora in the World Economy*, Special Report 15, Institute for International Economics, pp. 101-130
Lankov, Andrei (2004), 'North Korean Refugees in Northeast China', in: *Asian Survey*, 4 (6), pp. 856-73

Lankov, Andrei (2005), 'Rejecting North Korean Refugees Part 2: A Long, Winding and Dangerous Road', in: *Asia Times Online*, 8 January 2005
Lee, Keum-soon, (2006), 'The Border-Crossing North Koreans: Current Situations and Future Prospects', Studies Series, Korea Institute for National Unification
Lee, Myŏng-jin (2006a), 'A Visit to the Border Reveals Intensified Searches for North Koreans', in: *Chosun Ilbo*, 30 September 2006 [in Korean]
Lee, Myŏng-jin (2006b), 'At Border Town, Some Chinese View North Korea Warily', Reuters, 11 October 2006
Lee, Young-in (2006), 'North Korea and Planned Defections: Warrants for Arrests of Japanese Suspects', in: *Hankyoreh Shinmun*, 3 March 2006 [in Korean]
Liu, Xiaoyan (2001), 'Blood in Corn Field', in: *China Youth Daily*, 25 December 2001 [in Chinese]
Lusa News, '50,000 North Koreans in China Need International Protection: Guterres'; 'China: Guterres Meets with North Korean Refugees on Visit to China', 23 March 2006 [in Portuguese]
MacKinnon, Rebecca (2005), 'Chinese Cell Phone Breaches North Korean Hermit Kingdom', in: *YaleGlobal Online*, 17 January 2005
Macintyre, Donald (2005), 'The North's Bitter Harvest', in: *Time Asia*, 13 June 2005
Marquand, Robert (2002), 'A Refugee's Perilous Odyssey from N. Korea', in: *Christian Science Monitor*, 16 August 2002
Médecins Sans Frontières, 'Urgent appeal for protection of North Korean refugees in China', press release, 19 January 2003
Mirae Hanguk, '217 North Korean Agents Deployed to China', 3 May 2006 [in Korean]
Noh, Ok-jae (2006), 'Assessments and Prospects on Actions to Improve the North Korean Human Rights Condition', 2nd Peace Foundation Symposium, Seoul, 11 July 2006
Powell, Bill (2006), 'Long Walk to Freedom', in: *Time* (Asia), 23 April 2006
Research Institute for the North Korean Society (2006a), 'North Korea Today', Seoul: Good Friends: Centre for Peace, Human Rights and Refugees, issue 12
Research Institute for the North Korean Society (2006b), 'North Korea Today', Seoul: Good Friends: Centre for Peace, Human Rights and Refugees, issue 23
Research Institute for the North Korean Society (2006c), 'North Korea Today', Seoul: Good Friends: Centre for Peace, Human Rights and Refugees, issue 29
Research Institute for the North Korean Society (2006d), 'Report on daily life', in: 'North Korea Today', Seoul: Good Friends: Centre for Peace, Human Rights and Refugees
Robinson, W. Courtland, Myung Ken Lee, Kenneth Hill and Gilbert Burnham (1999), 'Mortality in North Korean Migrant Households: A Retrospective Study', in: *The Lancet*, 354, no.9175 (24 July 1999). Online: http://www.thelancet.com/journals/lancet/article/PIIS0140673699022667/fulltext
Robinson, W. Courtland, Myung Ken Lee, Kenneth Hill, Edbert Hsu and Gilbert Burnham (2001), 'Demographic Methods to Assess Food Insecurity: A North Korean Case Study', in: *Prehospital and Disaster Medicine*, 16 (4), pp. 286-92
Seymour, James (2005), 'China: Background Paper on the Situation of North Koreans in China', *Writenet*, January 2005 [commissioned by UNCHR, Protection Information Section]
Shiminŭi shinmun [Corean NGO Times] 'Japanese Broadcasting: Cash Flows for Embassy Incursions', 14 March 2005 [in Korean]
Smith, Hazel (2005), 'North Koreans in China: Defining the Problems and Offering Some Solutions', in: Tsuneo Akaha and Anna Vassilieva (eds.), *Crossing Na-*

tional Borders: International Migration Issues in Northeast Asia, Tokyo: United Nations Press

Suh, Hae-yong (2.2006), 'Sorrows and Pains of North Korean Refugee Women in China's Northeastern Provinces', *FreeOpinion*, February 2006 [in Korean]

United Nations High Commissioner for Refugees (UNHCR), High Commissioner's statements, press release, 23 March 2006

US Committee for Refugees and Immigrants (2001, 2004, 2006), World Refugee Survey: Country Report China [for years 2001, 2004, 2006]

White House, Statement on China's treatment of Kim Chun-hee, press release, 30 March 2006

Yonhap News, 'China: Crackdown on North Koreans, 3,200 Forcibly Repatriated to the North', 21 January 2003 [in Korean]

Zhonghua Renmin Gongheguo Guojia Fazhan he Gaige Weiyuanhui [National Commission for Development and Change of the PRC] (2001), 'Report on Survey Regarding Decline of Ethnic Korean Population in Yanbian', 17 December 2001 [in Chinese]

A BRIEF HISTORY OF THE SINO-KOREAN BORDER FROM THE 18TH TO THE 20TH CENTURY

Larisa Zabrovskaya

ABSTRACT

This article studies the long history of formation of the Sino-Korean border. The Amnok and Tuman rivers were considered the frontier between Qing China and Korea. The establishment of a neutral zone at the beginning of the 18th century further strengthened the border. Disagreements between Qing China and Korea arose from the 1870s when the Qing authorities became aware of Korean settlements on the left side of the Tuman river. Russian interest in the region sharpened Chinese anxiety. Two treaties signed in the early 20th century, between China and Korea and China and Japan, recognised these settlements, known as Jiandao (Kor.: Kando), as a part of Qing Chinese territory. After 1949 the exact demarcation of the frontier became an issue of dispute between the People's Republic of China (PRC) and the Democratic People's Republic of Korea (DPRK), in which the North Korean view appears to have prevailed. Freedom of passage across the border itself since the 1950s has reflected the varying political and economic conditions within both states. The frontier dispute between the PRC and the DPRK seems to have been settled, but issues arising from this dispute, such as the Korean population residing in the Chinese northeast, that have led to tensions in the past, have not yet been solved.

1 THE EARLY FRONTIER

In the 17th century, before the Manzhou conquest of China, the frontier between Korea and Manchuria marked on Chinese maps followed a line along the Changbaishan ridge to the northeast of the peninsula, embracing Mt Paektu (Ch.: Baitoushan) to the north, and at its westerly end following the line of fortification known as the Willow Palisade, which was somewhat to the north of the eastern end of the Great Wall of China.

After the establishment of the Manzhou Qing dynasty in 1644, the area of Mt Paektu was declared a restricted zone both for it residents and for those making a temporary stay, because it was considered to be an abode of the spirits of the Manzhou ancestors (Pozdneev 1897: 68). In practice, the restriction was not observed, first of all by Korean peasants, who crossed the Tuman river (Ch.: Tumenjiang) in search of new virgin lands and settled to the north of the river in territory considered to belong to the Manzhou. In the opinion of modern Korean historians (*Hanguksa* 1968, vol. 4: 117), the murder of five Qing subjects who were searching for ginseng near Mt Paektu in 1710 served as grounds for the Sino-Korean frontier control expedition of 1712. The Qing Office of Ceremonies (Libu) informed the Korean government about the joint border inspection beforehand.

In order to elucidate the causes of the various territorial claims in this region, it is necessary to trace the evolution of Sino-Korean border relations during the several past centuries.

A Chinese review of relations between China and Korea, published in 1951, wrote that, since the Ming dynasty (1368-1644), for 'over 400-500 years there were no frontier misunderstandings with Korea; it was only in 1712 that the Sino-Korean border near Mt Paektu was given consideration' (*5000 nian lai-de Zhong-Chao youhao guanxi* 1951: 109).

The expedition sent to Manchuria in 1712 by the Qing government to inspect Mt Paektu was headed by Mukedeng, chief commander of Ula (now Harbin city). Accompanied by Manzhou and Korean officials, Mukedeng examined the area around the mountain and the lake at its summit, and drew a map of the Sino-Korean border near Mt Paektu. The expedition started their ascent from the frontier town of Musan (Ch.: Maoshan) situated on the right bank of the middle reaches of the Tuman river. The Korean senior officials were unable to ascend to the top of the mountain peak because of their age and accordingly had to limit themselves to sending their map of Mt Paektu and its vicinity to the Qing delegation (*Hanguksa* 1968, vol. 4: 117; James 1888: 452-4). However, the Qing officials accompanied by guides and several Korean officials of lower rank reached the summit of Mt Paektu.

In the saddle of the two rivers, the Amnok (Ch.: Yalujiang) and the Tuman, more than ten *li* (five km) to the southwest of the top of the mountain, there was installed a stone bearing an inscription. Not far from the stone, an *abatis* (a type of fence made from felled trees) was raised, 'lest anybody should cross the frontier illegally' (*Hanguksa* 1968, vol. 4: 118). The inscription on the stone read as follows: 'Mukedeng, chief commander of Ula, obeying orders from Mukden, has inspected the frontier, arrived at the place mentioned and established that, from olden times, Yalu has been a frontier in the west and Tuman in the east, and this inscription about it is made' (Lee 1932: 93). Thus, in the course of the first Sino-Korean demarcation, it was not determined to whom Mt Paektu belonged. However, on the basis of the correlation of the geographical locations of the heads of the Amnok and Tuman rivers and also of the site of the frontier stone installation, it should follow that the whole of the mountain is on the Chinese side. The stone with its inscription was carefully preserved till the early 1940s, and pictures of it appeared in Korean and Japanese books (see Lee 1932).[1]

The inscription on the frontier stone contained the names of the members of the expedition who ascended to the top; the names of the Korean officials followed those of the Chinese. According to the inscription, three Qing and six Korean officials participated in the frontier inspection, but because the Chinese outranked the Koreans, it is unlikely that the opinion of the Korean side was taken into account. The whole of the inscription, made on behalf of the chief commander of Ula, testifies to this. The Korean officials were involved as witnesses only, who had no voice in it. The 1712 demarcation was virtually left to the discretion of the representatives of Qing China, who ignored the dual character of the expedition. As a result, the lands lying to the north of the Tuman river passed to Jilin province of Qing China. Evidently, at the time, the governments of both nations did not attach great importance to the exact position of the frontier line.

After the 1712 demarcation, the Qing government took measures to strengthen the protection of the frontier, erecting fortifications and founding military settlements. Thus, in Hunchun, 'the walls were reconstructed in 1714 and the *zuolin* [a military company] was quartered there to govern the country' (Vasiliev n.d.: 25). However, military settlements were insufficient to guard the frontier. To eliminate con-

---

[1] Japanese scholars also wrote on the subject. Murayama Jiojo produced a description of Mt Paektu, published in Dairen [Dalian] in 1942, which contains an old Manchurian map of Mt Paektu; and Tanaka Hidesaka published a geographical description of the new state of Manzhouguo (1932, Mukden [Shenyang]). (*Ed.* Russian translations were consulted and consequently the original Japanese titles of these works and the correct forms of the authors' names have not been identified.)

tacts between people living on both sides of the frontier, the Qing and Korean governments concluded an agreement that prohibited anybody from building houses and ploughing up land 'in the strip 70 kilometres wide' to the north of the Amnok and Tuman rivers (Choe 1972: 85). The neutral zone was limited to the north by a fence that probably was not an extension of the Willow Palisade but a local fortification.

When, in 1731, a problem arose over the establishment of a Qing military settlement in the zone near the Amnok river, the Korean king appealed to the Beijing court 'not to break the order established earlier' (Rockhill 1970 reprint: 29). The issue arose again in 1748, when the Qing government informed the Korean king that it intended to establish a military settlement in the neutral zone. The Korean government had to ask again that this should not be done and that the neutrality of the zone should be maintained. In its pleas, the Korean government insisted that a concentration of suspicious people at the frontier would lead to various disorders (Rockhill 1970 reprint: 29). The Qing emperor consented to leave the former agreement in force.

For more than one hundred years after the 1712 joint frontier inspection there were no border disagreements between China and Korea. At that period, Qing China maintained the frontier with Korea within the limits of the Willow Palisade.

2 Transformation of the Neutral Zone into Jiandao

The neutral zone between China and Korea existed till 1875, when, at the proposal of the Chinese statesman Li Hongzhang, it was joined to China 'as a territory originally belonging to it' (Rockhill 1970 reprint: 29). The reason that prompted the Qing government to absorb the neutral zone was the consolidation of Russia in the Far East. Korea, whose feudal society was experiencing crisis and decline, took no action to counter this claim.

In fact, despite the strictness of Korean laws imposing the death penalty for any unauthorised crossing of the frontier, illegal penetration by Korean peasants into northeastern Manchuria persisted on a large scale. Meanwhile, the Qing government did not even suspect that their own subjects were settling in that restricted area of the Qing empire. In 1878, they repealed the law forbidding settlement there but, against expectations, that did not result in the accelerated colonisation of Manchuria. The Chinese peasants were not accustomed to swampy soils and mountains covered with impenetrable forests or to conditions unfavorable to their traditional irrigated farming. This was also a seismic zone: Mt Paektu was an active volcano as late as 1904.

In 1881, the governor-general of Jilin province found that Koreans had been settling in the vicinity of Hunchun city. It was the Korean authorities of Hamgyŏng province who had issued permits to till the lands there, as the king of Korea and his government considered the territory to be their own. The Jilin governor-general submitted a report to the Chinese emperor, proposing that the Korean peasants who had settled there should be granted Chinese citizenship. The Qing authorities accepted the situation in 1881 and opened up these lands to Korean settlers. However, the Korean king, in his turn, demanded that his subjects should be sent back to Korea. The Chinese 'imperial' response was to permit this within a year. As it turned out, in the course of that year the Koreans not only did not move, but, on the contrary, continued to arrive there with permission of the Korean government (Kuner 1912, vol. 1: 12).

The king of Korea wrote to the Beijing court (see Zabrovskaya 1993b: 352-3):

> It is generally known that the vicinity of the Tuman river should be considered a frontier between Korea and Jilin province of China ... Earlier, in that locality, nobody could settle, but, since settling, the Koreans have been penetrating and acquiring arable lands. The Korean authorities cannot keep them under control and, in proper time, stop their migration there.
>
> At present, many migrants live quietly in that locality and, moreover, they are within the Korean boundaries, so, it would be inhuman to drive them out one day. It is obvious that one should reconcile oneself to the situation and leave those migrants in peace, strictly prohibiting them from inciting riots. That would be an act of high humanism shown by the Great [Chinese] Nation to its vassal.

It should noted that, in the Ming and Qing periods, Korea still was a vassal of China and the latter always protected its vassal ('Papers from Seoul: Letters of the Ambassador in Tokyo', 1886, AFARI). Korean authorities accordingly used their vassal relations with Qing China to settle Korean subjects on the territory that was north of the Tuman river and which Chinese authorities conceded was Chinese.

The frontier conflicts were not limited to disputes concerning the rights of the Koreans to settle on the left, i.e. north, side of the Tuman. In 1882, China brought troops to the areas adjacent to the frontier with Korea to order to seize a strip of earth along the left side of the river to give northern Manchuria access to the Sea of Japan (East Sea). The Qing government also pursued international objectives: if China had obtained access to Posiet bay, Korea would have been cut off from Russia. In September 1883, three thousand Chinese soldiers were concentrated along the Chinese side of the Tuman river.

At the same time, the Qing government unilaterally made a demarcation in the lower reaches of the Amnok (Yalu) river, fixed in 'Twenty-four rules of frontier trade between the people of Mukden and Shandong provinces and Korea', laid down by Li Hongzhang in 1883. Article 3 of the rules reads that 'everywhere in the vicinity of the mouth of the Amnok river and P'yŏng'an province of Korea, commoners, especially Korean ones, are forbidden to fish in secret' (*Zhongwai jiu yuezhang huibian* 1957, vol. 1: 418). Qing China thereby extended its jurisdiction over that area.

However, the upper areas of the Tuman river were the most disputed. The presence of Russia in the Far East impeded China from establishing an exact frontier in this area at its own discretion, as it had with the Amnok, and impelled it to begin consultations with Korea. In 1885, in the vicinity of the head of the Tuman river, a joint frontier inspection was conducted by representatives of China and Korea. 'From the very beginning disagreements arose. The Koreans insisted that the frontier established in ancient times should pass along the "northern head" of the Tuman river near Mt Paektu. However, the Chinese officials demanded that the frontier should pass along the southern head of the river; in that case a considerable area would have been cut off in favour of Jilin province. An agreement was not reached ...' ('Papers from Seoul: Letters of the Ambassador in Tokyo', 1886, AFARI). Contesting the upper reaches of the Tuman, China did not give up its attempts to reach the Sea of Japan at the lower reaches of the river.

Russia could not allow China to obtain access to the sea in northern Manchuria. So, on Russian initiative, Sino-Russian negotiations were conducted for re-demarcation of the frontier in the area of the Tuman river. In 1886, in the settlement of Novokievsky, a protocol was signed of the inspection of boundary marks at the state frontier between Russia and China.

This step by Russia enabled Korea again to raise a claim to the Manchurian lands inhabited by Korean peasants. The next meeting between Chinese and Korean representatives took place in 1887. Having conducted an inspection of the frontier stone near Mt Paektu, both sides agreed to recognise the Tuman river as the state frontier. The upper reaches of the river caused disagreements: the Korean representatives considered the northern tributary of the river to be its source and the Chinese representatives considered the southern tributary as such. However, the middle reaches of the Tuman, from the town of Musan to the river mouth, were recognised as the undisputed frontier between the two states. That meant that the waste plots of land colonised by Korean peasants were recognised as Chinese territory (Kuner 1912, vol. 1: 16), while the question of demarcation in the upper reaches of the Tuman river was left open.

The recognition of Qing China's jurisdiction over the territory colonised by Korean peasants to the north of the Tuman brought up the problem of Korean subjects. As the Chinese population was very scarce in the Russian-Chinese frontier area, the Qing government, in 1887, adopted a law which said that all the Korean peasants living to the north of the sources of the Amnok and the Tuman had became Chinese subjects. According to this law, the tilled lands belonging to the Koreans should have been measured and had a tax put on them (*Narodu vostochnoy Asii* 1965: 651). The area of eastern Manchuria where the Korean migrants lived was later named as Jiandao (Kor.: Kando), meaning 'intermediate island'.

Qing state documents assert that by 1890, the majority of Korean migrants had already adopted Chinese customs and obeyed the Qing empire's laws. However, the Koreans continued migrating to Jiandao. They did not automatically become subjects of Qing China. Qing officials repeatedly addressed appeals to Yuan Shikai, the Qing Resident-General and Commissioner of Commerce in Seoul from 1885 to 1894, asking him to solve the problem and to stop Korean migration to the area. Especial stress was put on the Qing government's intention to order the Jiandao Koreans 'to change their hair style and clothes and to live like the Chinese' (*Ku Hanguk oegyo munsŏ* 1973, vol. 8: 723). By 1890, according to data of the Qing administration, tens of thousands of Koreans lived in the Jiandao territory (*Ku Hanguk oegyo munsŏ* 1973, vol. 8: 729). In 1891, a report from the Zongliyamen (Chinese Foreign Office) to the Emperor (see Rudakov 1903: 119) stated:

> At present, one cannot expect a quick solution of the problem of the frontier definition at the source of the Tuman river. It would therefore be reasonable to make improvements to the Korean settlements in order to set them at rest in their yearnings to become Chinese subjects ... In

view of their distress resulting from the oppressions of Korean officials, subjecting the settlers to our milder taxation system would be a happy issue to them ...

Similar Chinese actions naturally displeased both the Koreans in Jiandao and the Korean government, which continued to give permits to till Manchurian virgin lands (Kuner 1912, vol. 1: 247) and sent officials to collect taxes from the Korean peasants, the more so as not all of them had become subjects of Qing China.

In their new place, the Korean migrants to Manchuria were busy not only with their traditional occupations of hunting and gathering of ginseng. They also felled trees and floated timber along the rivers, ploughed free land, drained marshes and cultivated rice, gaoliang, beans, and other crops. The products were exported to the northern provinces of Korea, which often suffered from poor harvests and natural disasters.

3 THE BORDER ISSUE AND KOREAN MIGRANTS

At the beginning of the 20th century, two frontier treaties were signed: the secret Sino-Korean Jilin treaty of 1904 and the Sino-Japanese treaty of 1909. Under the terms of these treaties, Qing China, Korea and Japan recognised Jiandao as part of Chinese territory and the Tuman river as a Sino-Korean state frontier. The articles of both treaties granted the Korean residents of Jiandao the same rights of property that the Chinese had (Zabrovskaya 1993a: 71, 73-4). However, the status of the Korean immigrants in Jiandao was not really defined by the treaty of 1909. The Qing court, in exchange for unconditional recognition of Chinese jurisdiction over Jiandao, permitted the Japanese intervention in Korea. This enabled China to settle certain problems with Korean immigration into that district. Later, these problems and the Japanese expansion in Korea aggravated Sino-Japanese contradictions.

Japan's annexation of Korea in 1910 and the naming of the country as the Chōsen government-general had aroused alarm in China. The 1911 revolution in China prompted regulation of the Sino-Korean frontier dispute. The Chinese republican government considered the Korean immigrants living in Jiandao as potential supporters of Japanese policy in Manchuria. Therefore, in order to neutralise their actions and establish control, it was decided, after the Korean Declaration of Independence of 1 March 1919, to reorganise Jiandao into an autonomous region with its centre in the town of Yanji and to form a legislative body known as the Jiandao National Assembly (Yi 1968: 13). It lasted till 1920. The object of the National Assembly was to rally the Korean immigrants and direct their activities against Japanese expansion in Manchuria. When, in 1932, the Manzhouguo state was established, the area of Jiandao was reorganised into Jiandao province. By that time, 400, 000 Koreans were living in the territory, outnumbering by three times other national minorities in the province (*Manchoukuo* 1933: 96).

Japan gave special attention to the exploitation of mineral resources in the vicinity of Mt Paektu, extracting coal, gold, copper lead and zinc. In addition, there were prospected deposits of silver, iron, antimony, phosphate and oil-bearing shales (Ye and Zhun 1957: 5).

It is not known if any border treaties were concluded between Japan and Manzhouguo. However, a map of the Manzhouguo territory inserted in a dictionary of the history and geography of Manchuria compiled by the French missionary Lucien Gibert, shows that so-called Eastern Jiandao, centred on Hunchun city and the most economically developed region with a railway junction and rich minerals, was included in the governorship-general of Chōsen (Gibert 1934). Later, this fact gave Kim Il Sung a reason to tell the Chinese Communists that Eastern Jiandao should be included in the territory of the Democratic People's Republic of Korea (DPRK), but his argument did not make a good impression on the Chinese authorities.[2]

4 Sino-Korean Border Line After the Second World War

After the liberation of Manchuria and northern Korea by the Soviet army in 1945, the matter of the status of Jiandao arose again. After the establishment of the People's Republic of China (PRC) in 1949, the Chinese Communist Party did not consider allowing minority peoples the right of self-determination, but it did establish autonomous governments at various levels from county to province in areas where a minority group was either predominant or well established. According to data in Ye's and Zhun's work (1957: 12) on China's Korean Na-

---

[2] The source of this information is a conversation the author had with Professor Evgeniy D. Stepanov in 1976.

tional Autonomous Prefecture, part of the Korean population of Jiandao demanded independence under the slogan 'Autonomy is bad while independence is good'.

In August 1952, the Chinese government adopted 'Regulations on autonomy of Minority Areas', which led to the establishment of Yanbian Korean Autonomous Region on 3 September 1952 in the territory of former Jiandao, with the administrative centre in the town of Yanji. In 1953, when the Autonomous Region became an Autonomous Prefecture, Korean residents numbered 538,243; according to the 1955 census, there were 543,800 Koreans, who formed 70.1 percent of the total population of the prefecture.

In the first years after the establishment of the PRC and the DPRK, the frontier was not closed for the migration of population. However, after 1956, when repressions began in the DPRK, the migration of Koreans to northeastern China was noted, and soon after that the frontier on both sides was closed. At that time, frontier control was restricted in accordance with the terms of the 'Agreement on floating structural timber over the Amnok and Tuman rivers' concluded between the PRC and the DPRK in Beijing in 1956, to be valid till 1976 (*Zhonghua renmin gongheguo wai yuezhang huibian* 1958, vol. 5: 24-9). This stipulated, among other things, that floating should be restricted to daytime and halted under unfavourable weather conditions. The agreement gave the Chinese frontier authorities greater scope to control the Sino-Korean border than it did the Korean side. The intensified frontier control on the Chinese side obstructed passage over the border for those Koreans who had relatives in the Yanbian Korean Autonomous Prefecture.

The following year in China, Ye's and Zhun's book (1957) showed the lake at the summit of Mt Paektu marked as part of Chinese territory. In its turn, in the detailed geographical atlas of the DPRK published in Pyongyang in 1958 (*Chosŏn chidoch'aek*: 58), the frontier is indicated as a line passing along the upper reaches of the Tuman river at its very north, including a middle section of the lake at the summit of Mt Paektu.[3]

At that point, the 'cartographic war' stopped and the dispute itself continued in the form of publishing the texts of older treaties. In 1959, the PRC published the text of the secret Sino-Korean Jilin treaty of 1904. It revealed that both nations had agreed to provide free passage

---

[3] For an alternative source, see volume 19 of *Chosŏn chŏnsa* 1981: 185-6, 297-8.

over the border for their subjects. The same volume (*Zhongwai jiu yuezhang huibian* 1959, vol. 2: 281-2) gave the text of the Sino-Japanese Treaty of 1909. After that, no counter-arguments followed from the Korean side. It is thus generally considered that the DPRK government tacitly accepted all the Chinese arguments on the Sino-Korean border line.

At the beginning of the Chinese cultural revolution (1966-76), a migration of Chinese Koreans took place from northeastern China to the DPRK and bilateral control of the frontier was strengthened. During these years, the Chinese authorities are said to have resettled more than forty thousand Chinese Koreans from the Sino-Korean border to the Chinese west, to Shanxi, Hebei and other provinces. It is not clear if they have returned. During that same time, Chinese *hongweibing* (red guards) were reportedly settled along the Sino-Korean and Sino-Soviet border lines.

5 Territorial compromise by China

During the years of the Chinese cultural revolution, the PRC brought to a head its disagreements with other socialist countries. However, it did take certain steps to improve its relations with the DPRK, and in April 1970, Sino-Korean relations entered a new stage, when the Chinese prime minister, Zhou Enlai, visited the DPRK, making the first top-level contact since 1964. Although the joint communiqué which resulted was markedly cautious, it signalled that China and the DPRK had again found some common ground (Jo and Marshall 1983: 117). What actually motivated the renewed friendship was uncertain, but mutual fear of Japanese militarism, Soviet ideological revisionism and American aggressiveness seemed to be one likely reason. Indirect data (see following sentence) enable us to suppose that during Zhou Enlai's visit a new border agreement was concluded between the two states, whereby the frontier line would pass over the middle part of the lake at the summit of Mt Paektu. A coloured photograph showing the late president Kim Il Sung standing on the top of Mt Paektu and viewing Ch'ŏnji (Celestial lake) might offer some support for this supposition and would suggest that the Korean view of the problem had won. Certainly, in geographical maps issued in the PRC in recent years, the frontier with the DPRK is indicated across the lake at the summit of

Mt Paektu. These maps show that the northern part of the lake is Chinese territory.

The 1970s and 1980s in China were marked by an economic boom, and many North Koreans tried to get to the Chinese northeast to make a better living. Frontier control weakened, and the North Koreans could again freely pass over the Tuman, to visit their relatives in China and seek marriage with Chinese Koreans, with Chinese Koreans coming in the opposite direction. The Sino-Korean frontier regime took on a character which had been envisaged by the frontier agreements between Qing China and Korea in 1904 and between Qing China and Japan in 1909.

Since the beginning of the 1990s, the economic situation of the DPRK has worsened, and many North Koreans looking for a better life have crossed over the Tuman to escape to China. This situation has led the authorities on both sides to strengthen border control. At the end of the 1990s, there were reports that more than two or even three hundred thousand North Koreans were working illegally in the Chinese northeast (see, for instance, Welsh 1999). The Chinese government, worried by the situation, wanted to deport not only illegal workers, but North Koreans married to Chinese citizens as well. The Chinese Korean population in the Chinese northeastern provinces has grown many times in comparison with 1890 (see Table 1). In 2000-05, this group formed 2 percent of the total population of this region of the PRC and continues to be the biggest national minority in the region.

Table 1   Growth and decline of the Chinese Korean population of the Chinese northeastern provinces, 1890-2005 (thousands of persons)

Year	1890	1896	1900	1910	1935	1955	1964	1982	2000	2005
Number	10	21	50	110	850	963	1,340	1,771	920	850

Sources: *Chaoxian yanjiu luncun* [Collected research papers on Korea] (1989), part 2, Yanji: Yanbian renmin chubanshe [Yanbian People's Press], pp. 115, 252, 263.

However, since 2000 the total size of the Korean population of the Chinese northeast has been falling. Some Koreans have been assimilated, others have moved to different regions of China, yet more (around 100,000 persons a year) are said to have moved to South Korea to work as 'gastarbeiters', as Jilin province, where the main body of Chinese Koreans is located, is a very poor district in the Chinese northeast.

During the period 1993-8, three states—Russia, China and the DPRK—seeking to realise the Tuman River Project and make the area an attractive place for foreign investment, inspected the mouth of the Tuman river six times before, in Pyongyang on 3 November 1998, concluding an agreement between the governments of Russia, China and the DPRK on the 'definition of a line of demarcation in the border water space of the Tuman river'. The agreement, consisting of three articles, came into force on 20 June 1999 (*Sbornik Rossiysko-Kitaiskih dogovorov 1949-1999* 1999: 318-19). It pointed out a place on the Tuman river where the borders of the three states met and constituted the Tuman as an international water artery.

6 Conclusion

The history of the Sino-Korean frontier is a component part of the state relations between the two countries. The permanent cause of the Sino-Korean border problems has been the Korean population residing in the Chinese northeast. Although the frontier dispute between the PRC and the DPRK has been settled, the factors that, in the past, caused frontier conflicts have not yet been resolved.

Over a long period, the reason prompting Korean people living near both sides of the Sino-Korean border has been and continues to be an economic one. Recently the issue has arisen of North Korean economic refugees who have illegally crossed the Tuman river and caused many problems for border authorities not only in China and the DPRK, but in Russia as well.

Since the North Korean nuclear test on 9 October 2006 (which was carried out not far from China's Jilin province), the Chinese authorities have reportedly begun to build border fortifications of concrete and wooden walls with the addition of barbed wire. They have thereby decided to close down free passage across the border line, and Korean relatives from the both sides of the Tuman river cannot visit each other freely as they could before. A new stage in Sino-Korean border relations has been reached.

Ed. All translations from languages other than English have been made by the author and have been edited where necessary.

References

Choe, Ching Young (1972), *The Rule of the Taewŏngun, 1864-1873: Restoration in Yi Korea*, Harvard East Asian Monographs, Cambridge MA: Harvard University Press

Chosŏn chidoch'aek [Geographical atlas of Korea] (1958), Pyongyang

Chosŏn chŏnsa [Complete history of Korea] (1981), vol. 19, Pyongyang: Kwahak paekkwa sachon chulpansa

Gibert, Lucien (1934), *Dictionnaire historique et géographique de la Mandchourie*, Hong Kong: Imprimerie de la Société des Missions-Etrangères

Hanguksa [History of Korea] (1968), Seoul

James, H.E.M. (1888), *The Long White Mountain: or, A Journey in Manchuria, with some account of the history, people, administration, and religion of that country*, London and New York: Longmans, Green and Co.

Jo, Yung-hwan and Ralph Marshall (1983), 'Linkage Sources of North Korean Foreign Policy', in: Park Jae Kye and Kim Jung-Gun (eds.), *The Politics of North Korea*, IFES Research Series No. 12, Seoul: The Institute for Far Eastern Studies, Kyungnam University, pp. 163-82

Ku Hanguk oegyo munsŏ [Documents of Korea's earlier international relations] (1973), Seoul: Korea University East Asia Research Centre

Kuner, Nicolay V. (1912), *Statistiko-geographicheskiy i economicheskiy ocherk Korei, Yaponskogo general-gubernatorstva Chiosen* [Statistical, geographical and economic essay on Korea, Japanese Government-General of Chosen], vol. 1, Vladivostok: Vostochnuy Instityt [Institute of Oriental Studies]

Lee, Hung-gu (1932), *Manchuwa Chosŏnin* [Manchuria and the Koreans], Kyongsŏng [Pyongyang]: Hansŏngdosŏ chusikhoesa

Manchoukuo (1933), Hsingking (Xinjing) [Changchun]: no publisher listed

Narodu vostochnoy Asii [The far eastern nations] (1965), Moscow: Nauka

'Papers from Seoul: Letters of the Ambassador in Tokyo', in: Arhiv Vneshney Politiki Rossiyskoy Imperii (AVPRI) [Archive of the Foreign Affairs of the Russian Empire (AFARI)], Fond 'Yaponskiy stol', Opic' 493, Delo 1, List 79 [Japanese Table, Inventory No. 493, Dossier 1, Sheet 79], 26 May 1886

Pozdneev, D. (ed.), Kantseliarii Ministra Financov [Office of the Ministry of Finance] (compilers) (1897), *Opisaniye Manchyrii* [A description of Manchuria], St Petersburg: Ministra Financov [Ministry of Finance]

Rockhill, William W. (1905), *China's Intercourse with Korea from the XVth Century to 1895*, London: Luzac; reprinted 1970, New York: Paragon

Rudakov, Nicolay V. (1903), *Materialu po istorii kitayskoy kyltyru v Girin'skoy provintsii* [Materials on Chinese culture in Jilin province], Vladivostok: Vostochnuy Instityt [Institute of Oriental Studies]

Sbornik Rossiysko-Kitaiskih dogovorov 1949-1999 [Collected agreements between Russia and China 1949-1999] (1999), 'Soglashenie mezhdy Pravitelstvom RF, Pravitelstvom KNR I Pravitelstvom KNDR ob opredelenii linii razgranicheniya pogranichnuh vodnuh prostranstv trioh gosudarstv na reke Tumannaya' ['Agreement between the governments of Russia, China and the DPRK on the definition of a line of demarcation in the border water space of the Tuman river'], Moscow: ROSPEN Press, 1999, pp. 318-19

Vasiliev, Vasiliy P. (n.d.), *Opisaniye Manchyrii* [A description of Manchuria], n.p.

Welsh, T. (1999), 'Few Signs of Life: A US Missionary's Trip to the NK Border Bolsters his Relief Efforts', in: *Korea Newsreview*, 28 (11), pp. 10-11

Ye, Shangzhi and Zhun Li (1957), *Women weida-de zuguo Yanbian Chaoxian minzu zizhizhou* [Yanbian, the Korean National Autonomous Prefecture of our great motherland], Beijing: Renmin chubanshe [People's Publishing House]

Yi, Hong-jik (1968), *Kuksa taesajŏn* [Large dictionary of national history], Seoul: Paengmansa

Zabrovskaya, Larisa V. (1993a), 'Consequences of Korean Emigration to Jiandao', in: *Korea Journal,* 33 (1), pp. 69-78

Zabrovskaya, Larisa V. (1993b), 'The Traditional Foreign Policy of the Qing Empire: how the Chinese reacted to the efforts of Europeans to bring the Chinese into the Western system of international relations', in: *Journal of Historical Sociology,* 6 (3), pp. 351-58

Zhonghua renmin gongheguo wai yuezhang huibian [Collected international treaties of the People's Republic of China] (1958), vol. 5, Beijing: Renmin chubanshe [People's Publishing House]

Zhongwai jiu yuezhang huibian [Collection of China's former international treaties], vol. 1 (1957); vol. 2 (1959), Beijing: Renmin chubanshe [People's Publishing House]

Zhou, Yiliang (ed.) (1951), *5000 nian lai-de Zhong-Chao youhao guanxi* [5000 years of friendly relations between China and Korea], Beijing: Renmin chubanshe [People's Publishing House]

ABOUT THE AUTHORS AND EDITORS

Peter M. Beck
directs the International Crisis Group's Northeast Asia Project in Seoul. He is also an adjunct professor at Ewha University, a columnist for *Weekly Chosun*, and a member of the Ministry of Unification's Policy Advisory Committee. Peter M. Beck received his B.A. from the University of California at Berkeley, completed the Korean language program at Seoul National University, and conducted his graduate studies at U.C. San Diego's Graduate School of International Relations and Pacific Studies.
Email: pbeck@crisisgroup.org

Robert Carlin
was chief of the Northeast Asia Division in the U.S. State Department's Bureau of Intelligence and Research between 1989 and 2002. Between 1993 and 2002, he served concurrently as Senior Advisor to the US Ambassador for talks with North Korea. In that capacity, he took part in all significant negotiations with the DPRK, including Four-Party Talks and meetings on the nuclear issue, normalization of relations, terrorism, and missiles.
Email: chertovod@yahoo.com

Judith Cherry
Ph.D., is Lecturer in Korean Business and Management in the School of East Asian Studies at the University of Sheffield. Her research interests include European foreign direct investment in South Korea, Korean investment in Europe, state-business relations and post-crisis reform in Korea. Her first book *Korean Multinationals in Europe* was published in 2001 and her most recent book *Post-Crisis Investment in Korea: European investors and 'Mismatched Globalization'* was published by Routledge in the autumn of 2007.
Email: j.a.cherry@sheffield.ac.uk

Rüdiger Frank
is Professor of East Asian Economy and Society at the University of Vienna. He holds a M.A. in Korean Studies, Economics and International Relations from Humboldt University of Berlin and a Ph.D. in Economics from Mercator University Duisburg. He held Visiting Professorships at Columbia University, New York, and Korea University, Seoul. He is a Council member of the Association for Korean Studies in Europe, Vice-Speaker of the Vienna School of Governance, founding member of the Europe-Asia Working Group of the European Association of Development Research and Training Institutes. His first five-month visit to North Korea took place in 1991. His major research fields are socialist transformation in Asia and Europe (with a focus on North Korea) and state-business relations (with a focus on South Korea). See www.koreanstudies.de/frank.
Email: ruediger.frank@univie.ac.at

Valérie Gelézeau
Ph.D. in Geography, is Associate Professor in Korean Studies at the EHESS (Ecole des Hautes Etudes en Sciences Sociales), Paris, France, and is attached to the Centre de recherches sur la Chine, la Corée, le Japon, UMR 8173 CNRS-EHESS, in Paris. She is also a member of the University Institute of France. She is the author of *Séoul, ville géante, cités radieuses* (Paris: CNRS Editions 2003) which analyses the rise of apartments in South Korea. The book was awarded the Francis Garnier Prize by the French Geographical Society in 2003, and its Korean-language version was recently published in Seoul (*Ap'at'ŭ konghwaguk*, Seoul: Humanitas 2007).
Email: vgelezeau@yahoo.com

Ronda Hauben
is a researcher, writer, journalist and netizen. She has pioneered research and writing about the history and impact of the Internet for the past 15 years, and is co-author with Michael Hauben of the book *Netizens: On the History and Impact of Usenet and the Internet* (1997). She has been undertaking research and writing about the democratic processes being developed by netizens in South Korea for the past four years. Active in exploring the potential of online journalism to provide a new more socially oriented form of journalism, she has been writing for Telepolis (Germany) since 1998 and for OhmyNews since 2004.
Email: rh120@columbia.edu

James E. Hoare
Ph.D., retired from the British Diplomatic Service in 2003. His last appointment was as British Chargé d'Affaires and Consul General in Pyongyang. He now writes and broadcasts about East Asia. Among his recent publications are *A Political and Economic Dictionary of East Asia* (Routledge 2005) and *North Korea in the 21st Century: An Interpretative Guide* (Global Oriental 2005), both written with his wife, Susan Pares. He is a Research Associate of the School of Oriental and African Studies, London, and Consultant on Security in East Asia, David Davies Memorial Institute of International Studies, Aberystwyth. He lives in London.
Email: jim@jhoare10.fsnet.co.uk

Gail Kim
is a research intern for the Future of Peace Operations Program at the Henry L. Stimson Center in Washington, D.C. She previously served as a Research Associate with International Crisis Group, focusing on North Korean refugee networks in China and Southeast Asia. She received her B.A. in International Relations from the Johns Hopkins University in Baltimore, Maryland.
Email: gailkim@gmail.com

Joon-Kyung Kim
is Senior Fellow at the Korea Development Institute (KDI). He was an assistant professor at Virginia Tech before joining KDI. He served as a World Bank consultant and on the Advisory Council for the Presidential Commission on Policy Planning in Korea. His recent research has focused on Sino-Korean economic integration, and on restructuring and institutional reforms in Korea's financial and corporate sectors. His work on the Korean economy includes recent articles in the *Asian Economic Journal, Journal of the Asia Pacific Economy, Journal of Restructuring Finance* and *Journal of the Korean Economy*. He holds a Ph.D. in Economics from the University of California at San Diego and a B.S. in Computer Science and Statistics from Seoul National University.
Email: joon@kdi.re.kr

Patrick Köllner
is Acting Director of the Institute of Asian Studies, GIGA German Institute of Global and Area Studies. He holds a Ph.D. and a *venia*

legendi in Political Science. Between 1996 and 2006 he was sole editor of the German-language Korea Yearbook. His research focuses on Japanese and Korean politics and political parties more generally. Recent publications include a country study on South and North Korea (*Südkorea und Nordkorea*, co-edited with Thomas Kern, Campus 2005), a comparative volume on factionalism in political parties (*Innerparteiliche Machtgruppen*, co-edited with Matthias Basedau and Gero Erdmann, Campus 2006), and a monograph on the organisation of Japanese political parties (*Die Organisation japanischer Parteien*, GIGA Institute of Asian Studies 2006).
Email: koellner@giga-hamburg.de

Heonik Kwon
Ph.D., is Reader in Social Anthropology at the University of Edinburgh and held a research fellowship at the Economic and Social Research Council, UK. He did fieldwork in Siberia (Sakhalin Island), Vietnam and, most recently, in South Korea. Among his recent publications are *After the Massacre: Commemoration and Consolation in Ha My and My Lai* (2006) and *The Ghosts of War in Vietnam* (2007). He is now completing a book on the legacy of the Korean War.
Email: H.Kwon@ed.ac.uk

Chung H. Lee
Ph.D., is Professor of Economics and Associate Dean of the College of Social Sciences at the University of Hawai'i at Mānoa. His recent publications relating to Korea include 'Financial Reform, Institutional Interdependency and Supervisory Failure in the Post-Crisis Korea', *Journal of East Asian Studies*, 6 (3), 2006; 'Institutional Reform in Japan and Korea: Why the Difference?', in Magnus Blomström and Sumner La Croix (eds.), *Institutional Reforms in Japan*, Routledge 2006; 'The Political Economy of Institutional Reform in Korea', *Journal of the Asia Pacific Economy*, 10 (3), 2005; and 'Korea's Direct Investment in China and Its Implications for Economic Integration in Northeast Asia', in Michael Plummer (ed.), *Empirical Methods in International Trade*, Edward Elgar 2004.
Email: lchung@hawaii.edu

Donald A.L. Macintyre
was senior advisor to the International Crisis Group, Seoul. He is currently a Pantech Fellow at the Asia-Pacific Research Center, Stanford

University. He received his B.A. from the University of British Columbia, Vancouver, and his Maitrise in Political Science and Philosophy from the Nanterre University, Paris.
Email: donald.macintyre@mac.com

Mark Morris
Ph.D., is University Lecturer in Japanese Cultural History at the University of Cambridge and a Fellow of Trinity College. His main teaching and research interests concern Japanese modern fiction and film, and Korean film. Work in progress includes a study of South and North Korean film which locates films and film genres in their social and historical contexts and also in a more general, comparative film-historical context.
Email: mrm1000@cam.ac.uk

Susan Pares
has worked in Research Department of the Foreign and Commonwealth Office and, since 1987, as an editor and writer in East Asian subjects. She edited *Asian Affairs*, 1997-2001, and between 2000 and 2007 the *Papers of the British Association for Korean Studies*. She served in the British Embassy in Beijing, 1975-76 and accompanied her husband, James Hoare, on postings to Seoul (1981-85), Beijing (1988-91) and Pyongyang (2001-02). They are co-authors of several books dealing with East Asian and specifically Korean affairs. The most recent is *North Korea in the 21st Century: An Interpretative Guide* (Global Oriental 2005).
Email: spares@myway.com

James C. Schopf
received his Ph.D. in Political Science from the University of California, San Diego, and has taught as a Post-doctoral Fellow of Korean Studies and Political Economy at Washington University in St. Louis, and as Assistant Professor of Political Science and International Relations at Korea University in Seoul (2005 to present). His work examines the effects of democratization on government policy, and includes studies of industrial restructuring and corruption, as well as foreign aid provision.
Email: jcschopf@hotmail.com

Larisa V. Zabrovskaya
Ph.D., is Senior Researcher at the Institute of History, Archaeology and Ethnography of the Peoples of the Far East, Far Eastern Division of the Russian Academy of Sciences. She was a Visiting Research Fellow at the Sejong Institute, and received grants from the Korea Foundation in 1995 and 2001. Her major academic interests include international politics and economic relations in East Asia. She has published numerous academic articles and books on history, politics and foreign affairs in East Asia. They include *Rossiya I KNDR: oput proshlogo i perspective bydyzhshego* [Russia and the DPRK: the former experience and future prospects] (1998), *Kitaiyskiy miroporiadok v Vostochnoy Asii i formirovanie mezhgosudarstvennuh granits* [China's world order in East Asia and state boundaries] (2000) and *KNDR v epohu globalizatsii: ot zatvornichestva k otkritosti* [The DPRK in the age of globalization: from a hermit life to open-mindedness] (2006).
Email: larisa51@hotmail.com

MAP OF THE KOREAN PENINSULA

Design and Imaging Unit, Durham University.